God
Inside
Out

God Inside Out

ŚIVA'S GAME OF DICE

Don Handelman and David Shulman

Photographs by Carmel Berkson

New York Oxford • Oxford University Press 1997

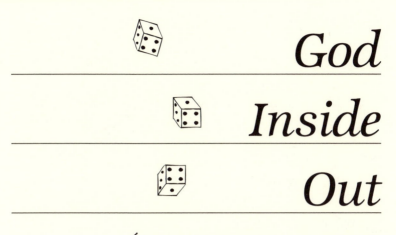

Oxford University Press

Oxford New York
Athens Auckland Bangkok Bogota Bombay Buenos Aires
Calcutta Cape Town Dar es Salaam Delhi Florence Hong Kong
Istanbul Karachi Kuala Lumpur Madras Madrid Melbourne
Mexico City Nairobi Paris Singapore Taipei Tokyo Toronto

and associated companies in
Berlin Ibadan

Published by Oxford University Press, Inc.
198 Madison Avenue, New York, New York 10016

Library of Congress Cataloging-in-Publication Data
Handelman, Don.
God inside out : Śiva's Game of Dice / by Don Handelman and
David Shulman ; photographs by Carmel Berkson
p. cm.
Includes bibliographical references and index.
ISBN 0-19-510844-2; ISBN 0-19-510845-0 (pbk.)
1. Siva (Hindu deity) 2. Dice games—India.
I. Shulman, David Dean, 1949– . II. Title.
BL1218.H36 1997
294.5'2113—dc20 96-21214

1 2 3 4 5 6 7 8 9
Printed in the United States of America
on acid-free paper

In memory of
Lea Shamgar-Handelman
(1934–1995)
a woman of wonder, warmth, and wisdom,
forever loved

Preface

This book is an exploration in the mythology of the god known as Śiva, as seen through the prism of the game that occupies most of his time—the game of dice. In stark contrast to Einstein's famous dictum, Hindus maintain that Śiva is perpetually absorbed in this game, which is re-created in innumerable stories, poems, paintings, and sculptural carvings (including, in the latter category, some of the most striking visual images of this god in the entire classical tradition). We will argue that this notion of the god at play—specifically, at dice—is one of the most central and expressive veins in the metaphysics exfoliated through the centuries in many idioms and modes around him.

We began at Elephanta, in May 1992; Carmel Berkson generously guided us through the cave, allowing vast space for our own inchoate impressions and intuitions. Carmel's astounding photographs are an integral part of this book: we hope the reader will be able to sense, through them, at least something of the immediacy and power with which these images began to work on our minds. We want to express, at the outset, deep gratitude to Carmel—for the great gift of the photographs, of course, but even more for her constant support, illuminating perceptions, much-needed corrections, and greatness of spirit.

We were on our way to Tirupati, to the annual ritual cycle of the goddess Gangamma; Elephanta was a bonus, an early station on the way—an excursus, one might say, backward into the classical domain. But already, on the plane from Bombay to Madras the following morning, we were deeply immersed in speculation about the dice-game panel we had seen and its relations to the other compelling images in the cave. Gangamma then provided, somewhat obliquely, an unexpected context for these speculations. At midnight we saw a rock that was standing in the paddy field turn into a woman. We saw a predominantly masculine world shift entirely into a feminine mode. We saw guised or disguised surfaces open up to disclose the fluid depths. We saw the melting and transforming energies of heat, inside and out. It is unlikely that, without this particular range of intensities that the goddess made available that year and the next, either this book or the understandings it proposes could have taken shape.

The book has three interlocking essays, of asymmetrical lengths. The first presents the dice game proper, in the light of the texts we have collected and the visual depictions we have studied. The focus is on the mature mythology embodied in the Elephanta and Ellora panels and in narrative accounts from the early-medieval Purāṇas and poetic anthologies; here, we are looking, on the one hand, at an apparent crystallization of the myth in the western Deccan in the mid-first millenium, and, on the other hand, at an organizing conceptual logic that survives in the cult of Śiva until the present day. This logic can also be shown to have very ancient roots, as we try to show in relation to Vedic forms of the dice game. The second and third chapters take up two mythic "sequels" to the game—one being the ultimately destructive direction linked with the name of Andhaka, Śiva's blind son; the other, the reverse direction that we call *tapas*—literally "heat," but more generally, a mode of reinternalization. We argue that notions of "asceticism," so frequently associated with Śiva, with Yoga, and with Hindu religion as a whole, are in fact foreign to its inherent logic. We suggest an alternative reading of this set of practices and ideas, in line with the process articulated in the myths.

Repetition matters. It is important to see the images again and again, and to read the texts many times, listening carefully for nuance and insistence. We feel the reader, too, should be allowed to experience this mode of discovery, this manner of listening. We have thus told and retold, cited and re-cited, whole sections of the major texts, which repeat themselves at various stages of our exposition; they are all set off as extracts. Perhaps the analogy of an Indian *rāga* would be apposite: the musician makes the *rāga* come alive, fully present, by playful improvisation replete with thematic and textural repetition; and it is this repetition that effectively comprises, or manifests, the living presence. Nuance and insistence can be known only by repeated experience. We recommend that the reader let the words and images engage the imagination in this manner, echoing and mirroring their earlier appearances. Our arguments, too, loop back and spiral in relation to the recurring texts and contexts.

But these arguments have, we hope, a consistency that can also be stated in more linear terms. The conclusion restates some of the interpretations and draws out their implications for further exploration. The mythology of Śiva, perhaps encapsulated in the myth of the dice game, reworks its primary intuitions in a shocking and luxuriant range of stories. We hope to return to these themes, Gangamma permitting, in a companion volume on Śiva in the Forest of Pine.

Givat Ram, Jerusalem D.H.
February 1996 D.S.

Acknowledgments

Our thanks:

to the Swedish Collegium for Advanced Study in the Social Sciences, for a fellowship that allowed Don Handelman to complete his work on this book in the autumn of 1994

to Eric Brian, for comments on uncertainty

to Munawar R. Banatwala, at the Mitter Bedi Lab, Bombay, for skillfully printing Carmel Berkson's photographs

to Sheldon Pollock, for rushing to us a copy of Ratnâkara's *Hara-vijaya*

to Michaela Soar, for enthusiastic support and hints of Ellora

to Velcheru Narayana Rao, for reading the relevant Telugu materials with us, and for illuminating them with his intuitions

to Joyce Burkhalter Flueckiger, for melting rocks in Tirupati

to Misha Shulman, for taking careful notes and sharing the wonder in the caves

Contents

III Melting and Marrying

IV Conclusion

God
Inside
Out

I

When Śiva Plays

O Lord of Caves,
if you are stone,
what am I?[1]

1
Bhṛṅgin's Scream

Bhṛṅgin:	Where have you been?
Skanda:	At home.
Bhṛṅgin:	And what's new there?
Skanda:	The goddess beat the god at dice.
Bhṛṅgin:	What had he staked?
Skanda:	His bull, drum, ashes, snakes, the moon. . . .

Now Bhṛṅgin screams out loud,
his mind aflame
because of everything
his master lost—

no alms, no ornaments,
no qualities to call his own.

This endless scream
might just redeem
the world.[2]

1. Allama Prabhu 213, in Ramanujan 1973:153.
2. *Subhāṣitaratnakoṣa* 98, ascribed to Tuṅga.

FIGURE 1. Bhṛṅgin, detail of Śiva and Pārvatī playing dice. Elephanta, Cave 1.

Why should it? Bhṛṅgin, a haunting, skeletal figure with three bony legs, who is one of Śiva's devoted servants, has witnessed this process many times. Śiva often plays dice with the goddess—his consort, Pārvatī (see figures 1 and 2). Almost invariably, he loses to her. Frequently, both he and his partner are said to "cheat," to play deceitfully—whatever this might mean. Still the great god ends up defeated, and Pārvatī claims the various ornaments and attributes that he has staked. Sometimes she becomes angry when he refuses to pay up, or even to acknowledge that he has lost; this stubborn stance may then lead to further conflict—aggressive acts by one or both partners, sulking, quarrels, separations, even curses hurled in rage. Or, still in a playful spirit, the goddess might cover Śiva's eyes with her hands, thereby enveloping the universe itself in catastrophic darkness.[3] Nothing, in these texts, is as rich in consequence as a game.

Perhaps we should say *the* game. The dice match is in some sense equal to the cosmos, both a condensed expression of its process and a mode of activat-

3. *Aruṇācalapurāṇam* of Ĕllappanāyiðār 4.2–3.

FIGURE 2. Śiva and Pārvatī playing dice. Elephanta, Cave 1.

ing and generating that process. If one is God, there is, finally, no other game. All the more shocking, then, is the fact that he must lose. No wonder that he is sometimes more than a little reluctant to play.

The dice throws, as is well known,[4] correlate with the four *yugas*, the cosmic ages in their recursive, devolutionary sequence. Thus, time itself proceeds out of this divine game. Without the game, there would be no time, perhaps no space as well (for the dice also model the cardinal directions in horizontal alignment and in relation to the vertical vector of the zenith)[5]—in short, no world as

4. See Biardeau 1971–72:38; Hiltebeitel 1976:94–107; and cf. Heesterman 1957:153.

5. *Chāndogya Upaniṣad* 4.1–3. See n. 53.

we know it; language, sexual differentiation and identity, self-knowledge—all these, too, as we shall see, are part of the generative cycles of the game. Nevertheless, the Sanskrit poem with which we began ends in a violent protest against this same game. Bhṛṅgin, the malformed male who attends upon Śiva as leader of his unruly hosts (*gaṇas*), screams in horror at the game's result; his master has lost his vehicle, his drum, the ashes he smears over his body, the snakes crawling around his neck and hair, the moon he wears on his crest—or, more succinctly, whatever he uses to solicit alms, and to adorn himself. Note two features of this description: First, Bhṛṅgin turns up with suspicious regularity in contexts relating to the dice game; he is often a spectator at the match, or, as in the above verse, the listener who learns of its fateful conclusion. Second, Bhṛṅgin's scream is rooted in a pun, difficult to translate: *bhartṛ-bhikṣā-vibhūṣā-vaiguṇyôdvega-janmā*—literally, "born out of agitation at the unhappy issue (relating to) the master's alms and ornaments." The long compound modifies the scream (*hārava*); the pun turns on the abstract noun *vaiguṇya* "unhappy issue" but also "being without attributes or qualities (*guṇa*)." Śiva, as a result of the match, will have to give up some of his fundamental attributes or qualities, and Bhṛṅgin feels this as a keen loss. It is also striking that the scream he utters serves to carry the blessing implicit in the verse—the enigmatic promise of redeeming the world.

A preliminary set of questions emerges from the verse: If Śiva must play dice with the goddess, why should he lose? What does it mean for him to sacrifice his attributes? Is there some particular significance to Bhṛṅgin's presence at or around the game? Why does Bhṛṅgin speak or think in paronomasia? What is the power of his wordless scream? And, more generally: What is the underlying nature of this game? What kind of game is it, and how does it relate to the conceptualization of this deity, on the one hand, and of the cosmos, on the other? What does it mean to play dice with god?

THESE QUESTIONS OPEN up a range of possible approaches; our own interest is primarily in the cultural semantics implicit in the dice game Śiva plays, and in the intuitive perceptions and conceptualizations that shape its various forms and tellings. One obvious obstacle can be noted, and then temporarily avoided, at this early stage—that involving a fixed reconstruction of Śiva's game or games. It would, it is true, be helpful if we were able to set out the rules in an unambiguous fashion, and then to interpret them. Unfortunately, very few of the texts that deal with Śiva's dicing—in contrast to other, earlier forms of the dice game in India—give any details at all about procedure. By now, an extensive literature has grown up around Indian dicing, especially that of the early (Vedic and Epic) periods;[6] and we eagerly await Michaela Soar's study of the classical sources related to Śiva's dice play at Ellora.[7] We will refer here to some of this literature, and even make some remarks on certain forms of the game (there is no reason to believe that the texts refer to a single mode of play). But our main concern will be to extract the logic and metaphysics of the dicing theme as it is contextualized in Puranic sources, on the one hand, and in the famous sculptural representations at Elephanta and Ellora, on the other. In both cases, we will seek to pursue the consistent narrative relationship between Śiva's defeat at dicing and the myth of his blind and dangerous son, Andhaka, who is identified with the mysterious Bhṛṅgin.

We should state clearly at the outset: this kind of dice game is certainly not about chance, in the ordinary meaning of the word; nor is it connected to notions of statistical probability.[8] Further, it is not deterministic in any simple sense; elements of uncertainty do come into play. We see it as unfolding a tricky and subtle process, which has an inner logic as well as certain stable features, although instability and disruption tend to characterize this process as a whole. In part, the logic is built around the relations between parts and the whole in a dynamic system labeled "play"; in part, it develops a kind of sexual ontology, with crucial epistemic correlates of a somewhat paradoxical type. As already hinted, what is at stake are the continuous reorganization of the cosmos and, from both a "theological" and an intrapsychic perspective (the two largely coincide), the composition and continuous reorganization of the self.

2
The Elephanta Panels

Look at the way this process is intimated at Elephanta in the magnificent sixth-century panels. We can read these panels as a visual essay in Śaiva cosmology and psychology,[9] an essay structured around basic themes taken in a logical order, always allowing, of course, for the possibility of digressions and subsidiary concerns. We begin by walking innocently through the cave in the

6. We note, especially, the painstaking and lucid study by Falk 1986. See also the classic study by Lüders 1907; and Panduranga Bhatta 1985; Keith 1908; de Vreese 1948; Thieme 1962; Heesterman 1957:143–57; White 1989; Claus 1986; Shulman 1992; Kapferer 1988b.

7. See Soar 1988 for a preliminary statement. We wish to thank Michaela Soar for a discussion of the Ellora dice scenes and their textual implications; for bibliographic aid; and for her encouragement and kindness as we began work on this book.

8. As Hacking (1975:7) has suggested for Nala's dice game in the *Mahābhārata*.

9. "Śaiva" = pertaining to Śiva, or to the worship of Śiva (similarly: "Vaiṣṇava" = "pertaining to Viṣṇu").

FIGURE 3. View from the east entrance of the *liṅga* shrine with gatekeepers. Elephanta, Cave 1.

manner of a first-time visitor, pilgrim or tourist. If we stand at what was, in all likelihood, the original entrance to the cave shrine, on the eastern side,[10] we see (as shown in figure 3) the aniconic *liṅga* guarded by towering gatekeeper figures. This is the first major visual focus for the worshiper-devotee—and probably the original cultic center in the cave. If we begin to circumambulate the *liṅga* in the proper direction, keeping it to our right, then the very first panel we encounter is on our left—Śiva playing dice with Pārvatī. The dice game initiates the process depicted in the panels, and articulates its major parameters.

10. Note the east-west direction of the ceiling beams moving toward the *liṅga*-shrine.

Before we pursue the sequence further, let us linger a moment longer in this initial space. We face the *liṅga*; on our left is the dice; and, if we look past the *liṅga* shrine, to the right, we can just glimpse the panel that constitutes the visual and aesthetic climax offered by this cave—that of Śiva killing the demon Andhaka, his son. On our right, directly across from the dice game, as the last panel in the circumambulatory series, we find Rāvaṇa lifting up Mount Kailāsa, where Śiva and Pārvatī are sitting together—actually, in some sense driven together by the external threat coming from the demon. The dice game divides the male and female parts of the godhead; Rāvaṇa recombines them.[11] In both the first and final panels (and elsewhere inside the cave), we find the dependable Bhṛṅgin, the alarmed observer from the Sanskrit poem at the beginning of this chapter. Bhṛṅgin accompanies the god's unfolding as a shadowy, haunting presence, from start to finish. He is also there, at the breathtaking climax, as Andhaka, Bhṛṅgin's earlier form.

The visual axis is powerful and pregnant. The force of the dicing extends in a straight, diagonal line from the left wall of the original entrance, past the *liṅga* shrine, toward the point of Andhaka's slaying. This seems to be one major vector of the story. Now, proceeding in our circumambulation, we pass the following panels (on our left, the southern wall): first, Śiva as the androgyne, Ardhanārīśvara; then the great Sadāśiva, with three visible heads—the most famous and overwhelming of the Elephanta representations; then Śiva as Gaṅgā-dhara, with the Ganges, his second wife, on his head; then Śiva's wedding, as Kalyāṇa-sundara, to Pārvatī; and, directly opposite the latter, the slaying of Andhaka. We have now passed the *liṅga* shrine, and can continue to the dancing Śiva, Naṭarāja, and, across from him, the god as Yogīśvara, supreme Yogi and lord of Yogis; finally, we return to our starting point, with the Rāvaṇa panel facing the game of dice. (See figures 4–10).

This way of listing the panels, in the *pradakṣiṇā* order (keeping the *liṅga* to our right), is, of course, entirely ahistorical. Were we to attempt to articulate a possible developmental sequence, based largely on considerations of style, we would surmise the existence of several more or less autonomous, noncontemporaneous workshops represented in the cave. As already stated, the *liṅga* shrine presumably marks the point of departure. Probably, the first of the sculpted panels to emerge out of the aniconic *liṅga* was Kalyāṇa-sundara (the wedding), in close proximity to the *liṅga*-shrine itself—an initial essay in the issues of joining male and female within the godhead. Then, toward the east

11. We will return to this reading of the Rāvaṇa panel. See below, II.4. We note here that Sanskrit poets often stress the centripetal force of Rāvaṇa's attack, which drives the terrified goddess into Śiva's tight embrace: see, e.g., *Priyadarśikā* of Harṣa, 1.2; similarly, in the Tamil *Tevāram* poems of Appar 5.8.10 (Tiruvaṇṇiyūr, 5/83), among many.

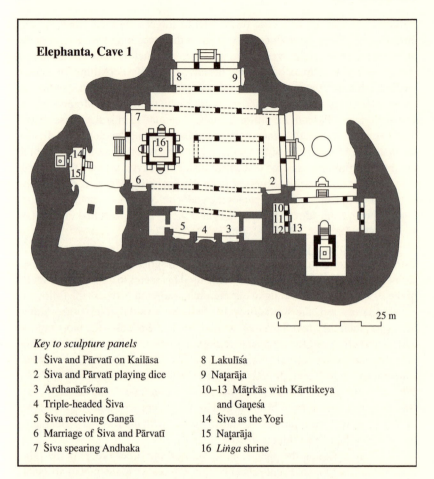

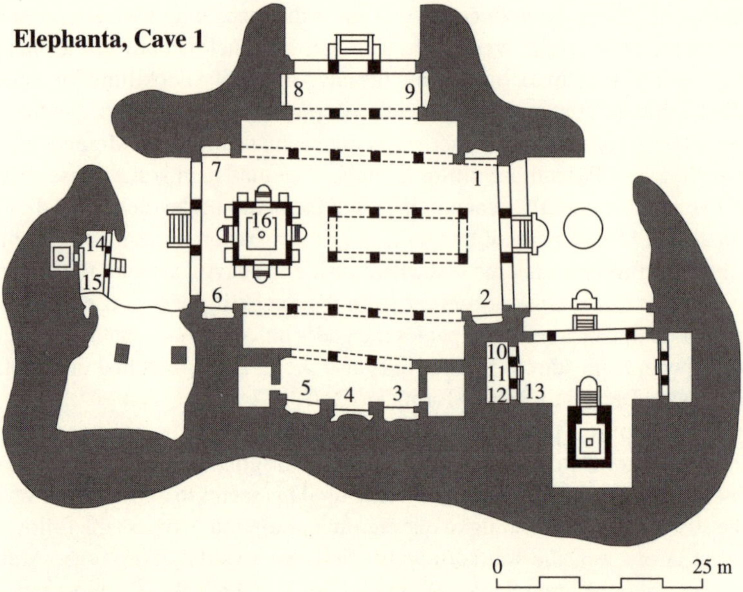

Key to sculpture panels

1 Śiva and Pārvatī on Kailāsa
2 Śiva and Pārvatī playing dice
3 Ardhanārīśvara
4 Triple-headed Śiva
5 Śiva receiving Gangā
6 Marriage of Śiva and Pārvatī
7 Śiva spearing Andhaka
8 Lakulīśa
9 Naṭarāja
10–13 Mātṛkās with Kārttikeya and Gaṇeśa
14 Śiva as the Yogi
15 Naṭarāja
16 *Liṅga* shrine

FIGURE 4. Layout of drawing by George Michell. First published in Carmel Berkson, Wendy Doniger O'Flaherty, and George Michell, *Elephanta: The Cave of Shiva,* Princeton, Princeton University Press, 1983.

and deeper back in the cave, came the great triptych of Sadāśiva, with the androgyne to his left, and the union with Gaṅgā on his right. These panels are intricately interwoven, and internally resonant, with one another; together, they constitute a set of experiments in the permutations and combinations of male-female relations. A third series—the northern panels of Andhaka, Naṭarāja, and the great Yogi—seems to reflect the work of a separate workshop (and perhaps another patron), possibly contemporaneous with the southern triptych; this series is thematically concerned with what might be called the problems of maleness in its isolated aspect. A final stage is represented by the two facing panels at the eastern entrance, the game of dice and the Rāvaṇa scene—the first taking the godhead apart; the second driving its parts back together in a problematic union. These two panels seem to have been imposed later, as a frame, on all that was already there, the organic outgrowths of several generations. The striking point, from our perspective, is that this organizing frame, added by later sculptors, presents an intelligible logic that binds together the entire set of panels, offering a "reading" that makes sense in terms of the internal processes of the Śaiva godhead. This reading has a beginning (the game of dice)

FIGURE 5. Śiva as Ardhanārīśvara, the androgyne. Elephanta, Cave 1.

FIGURE 6. Sadāśiva. Elephanta, Cave 1.

and an end (the reverse vector of reunion under the pressure of Rāvaṇa). We wish to stress, however, that this reading is in no way limited to a linear progression or a single narrative pattern; and that the various units are certainly capable of being juxtaposed or combined in a great number of meaningful ways, in accordance with the fluctuating perceptions that arise naturally as one moves through this space.

And yet the frame does create its own directionality and constraints. Stated schematically, as seen in the light of the catalytic dice-game panel, the initial sequence concentrates on Śiva's relationship with the feminine—whether as his own left half; as the gentler manifestation within the multicephalic Sadāśiva; as the Ganges; or as his primary consort, Pārvatī. The latter is, first, his partner in the game; she then appears to us fused into the god's body (or is he, in fact, fused into hers?), before we find her, poised, separate, and externalized, as his bride-to-be. More generally still, we can observe the god in process—that is, fragmenting and recomposing himself, and thus in powerful contrast to the aniconic totality/unity seemingly represented by the *liṅga*. The left (southern) panels play out his fragmentation, a possibly female-generated mode induced by the dice game, in terms of the part-whole relations suggested by the interplay of sculptured reliefs and the *liṅga*. The game itself is a form of partition that activates this entire series. On the right—that is, the northern side—the goddess temporarily disappears. Here we have Naṭarāja, dancing alone, and

FIGURE 7. Śiva receives the Ganges in his hair. Elephanta, Cave 1.

the equally solitary, male, vertically oriented lord of Yogis. The critical node of transition between these two related sequences is, once again, the Andhaka panel, directly opposite Śiva's marriage.

One could hazard further formulations: The southern panels give us Śiva in fragmenting relations with himself—above all, with his feminine parts. The northern panels reveal Śiva in other modes of relation, with for example, his devotees—Andhaka, the converted demon, and, at the end, Rāvaṇa, in perfect hierarchical subordination to the god and his consort on their mountain. There is, no doubt, a sense of the paradigmatic, sacrificial movement of devotion, which violently destroys the devotee's former, effectively hostile self. And the

FIGURE 8. Kalyāṇasundara: the wedding of Śiva and Pārvatī. Elephanta, Cave 1.

FIGURE 9. Naṭarāja, Śiva the Dancer. Elephanta, Cave 1.

image of totality, or of total innerness, embodied by the *liṅga* seems to find an answering, externalized wholeness in the destructive totality of Naṭarāja's dance. Indeed, the theme of increasingly destructive energy seems to emerge with peculiar force from the entire series. An initial fissure moves the god toward marriage, which will ultimately produce the wild son Andhaka, whom Śiva will then destroy, thereby killing part of himself; and, as the texts tell us, the god begins to dance at just this moment of destroying Andhaka—a violent dance of reabsorption and revelation. Is there a thread that ties this moment of furious energy, destructive of self and cosmos, to the inward-oriented, meditative Yogi, who faces the dancer? How does the heated, explosive dance, born out of the quandaries of engenderment, proceed to the incandescence of *tapas*, the heated innerness of Yoga?

A fissiparous whole, set in motion by play, turning destructive, and reaching toward self-knowledge through this destructive mode—surely, it is a suggestive sequence, raising more questions than it answers. We find it rearranged in the Śaiva reliefs at Ellora, which may be directly linked, both iconologically and stylistically, to the Elephanta panels. In Cave 15, for example, from the mid-eighth century, the entire northern wall is given over to the following series of reliefs (from left to right): Śiva slaying Andhaka; Śiva dancing; Śiva and Pārvatī playing dice; the marriage of Śiva and Pārvatī; Rāvaṇa lifting up

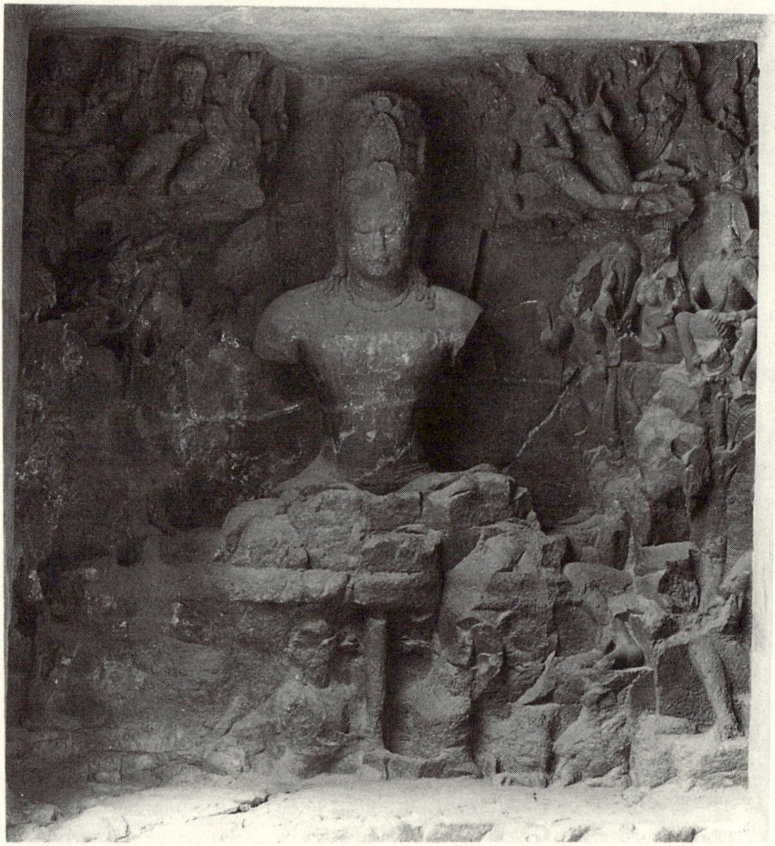

FIGURE 10. Yogīśvara, Śiva in meditation. Elephanta, Cave 1.

Kailāsa, with the god and his consort upon it. In close proximity, along the back wall, we find, as we saw at Elephanta, Śiva receiving the Ganges—his second wife—on his head. This cave spins out a further, very rich mythology, including Vaiṣṇava components (on the southern wall). But one is struck by the depth of continuity with the Elephanta themes—specifically, the relationships established between the dice game, Andhaka, and Śiva's marriage. In chapter II we examine the ways the Ellora sculptors elaborate on these relations, combining and recombining the same building blocks of myth and metaphysical psychology. We stress again that we are dealing with a nonlinear sequence, with stable thematic elements capable of varying arrangements and integrations.

Now, to proceed further, we need to see what the Purāṇic texts have to say about the process, the results, and the rationale of Śiva's game.

3
On Losing: Kedārakhaṇḍa 34–35 (= Skandapurāṇa 1.1.34–35)

Here is one medieval description of this particular game of dice, one of the most complete such versions in Purāṇic literature (we offer an extended summary, which certainly fails to do justice to this expressive text):[12]

Once Nārada went to see Śiva on Mount Kailāsa. At first, he saw two doorkeepers outside the audience room; but, realizing that they were only puppets, Nārada pushed past them and went inside. He praised Śiva and Pārvatī, who pervades the three worlds, who gave Śiva form and made him accessible, who makes the god without trans-forms [*vikāra*] undergo many transformations; he saw this goddess occupying half of the god's body. Śiva asked what the sage wanted, and Nārada said: "I came here for a game [*krīḍanârtham*]." "What game do you have in mind?" asked Pārvatī. "The game of dice has many forms—and the two of you are likely to find it more pleasing than making love."

Now she was angry: "How do you know this game, which brings evil to the wise?" But Nārada disclaimed any knowledge of dicing; he was, after all, a yogi, a servant of Śiva. Said Pārvatī: "Watch how I play with Śiva, before your very eyes, today." And she took the dice and started to play.

Soon both Śiva and Pārvatī were entirely absorbed in the game, to the sage's great satisfaction. Pārvatī began to play in tricky ways [*chalāt*], and so did he. First he beat her, and she, enraged, had to give up two of the jewels on her head.

12. On the *Kedārakhaṇḍa*, see Rocher 1986:230; on the thematic integration of the *Kedārakhaṇḍa*, and for an interpretation of the dice-game story that concludes this text, see Doniger 1993.

Śiva, noticing how she became more and more beautiful, the angrier she got, kept the game going.

She asked him what he was prepared to stake, and he said, "For you, my dear, I will wager this crescent moon, this necklace, and two earrings." They again began to play (both of them highly skilled at the dice game); and this time Pārvatī won and demanded that Śiva hand over what he had staked. Śiva merely smiled and said something true: "I wasn't really beaten by you, dearest; look at things from the right perspective. No living being can ever overcome me. You shouldn't talk like this. Play dice as much as you want—I will always win."

Pārvatī replied, "I did beat you. There is nothing surprising about that." She took him by the hand, and repeated: "There is simply no doubt about it—you have lost. You just don't realize it."

Still he refused to pay up. "You speak out of egoism [*ahaṅkāra*]; please reconsider." Pārvatī laughed: "It is quite true—there is no one who can beat the great god—except me. I have won at this immaculate game."

Nārada, who had overheard this heated conversation, now broke in. "You are speaking nonsense," he said to the goddess; "you are talking about the supreme lord of the universe and its inner being, invincible, formless, formed and beyond form. How could you beat him? You do not know Śiva, since you are only a woman."

This infuriated Pārvatī. "Shut up," she screamed; "your fickle and unstable nature makes you talk like this. Śiva was born through my grace, born and set securely in his place."

Nārada fell silent, but Bhṛṅgin spoke up: "You should not talk so much. Our lord is not given to mutation [*nirvikāra*], but you are yoked to a feminine state. You came to Śiva after giving in to Desire; don't you remember how Śiva burnt away Desire's body, and burnt the forest on the Mountain that is your father?"

Now she was angry indeed: "Bhṛṅgin, you are a dull person, with a divided mind [*bhedabuddhi*]. I have Śiva as my inner being, and he always abides in me. How can you, through the power of language, articulate the notion of separate existence between the two Śivas [i.e., between him and me]?"

Bhṛṅgin answered in anger:"Once, at your father Dakṣa's sacrifice, you gave up your body because you could not bear to hear Śiva being reviled. Today, in your confusion, you don't even recognize that you are reviling him yourself. You don't remember that you were born from a mountain, and tortured yourself for Śiva's sake; you have no affection for him at this moment. There is nothing higher than Śiva in the cosmos, and you should make an effort to feel affection for him."

Pārvatī cursed Bhṛṅgin to be without flesh, and she said: "You are talking like a ghoul [*piśāca*]. Who am I, and who is Śiva? You certainly don't know. You speak with a divided mind. And who are you, anyway? To whom are you connected? I will curse you, and what will Śiva do then?"

Then Pārvatī removed with her hand the snake Vāsuki that Śiva wore around his neck, along with many other ornaments of his—the crescent moon, the elephant's hide, the serpents Kambala and Aśvatara, and, finally, tricking him with words, his loincloth. Bhṛṅgin and the other servants averted their eyes in shame. Śiva, too, was ashamed, and spoke in hostile tones to Pārvatī: "All the sages, along with Brahmā and Viṣṇu, are laughing at this joke. What have you done? You were born in a good family. If you know for a fact that you beat me, then at least give me back my loincloth."

But she merely laughed. "Why do you need a loincloth? When you went into the Pine Forest, beguiling the wives of the sages, pretending to beg for alms, you were clothed only in space. You were such a pure, rarefied sage. Those sages worshiped you, and they made your loincloth fall, so you might as well let it go. After all, I won it at dice."

Śiva was so enraged that he opened his third eye and directed it at Pārvatī. Still she went on smiling [and said]: "Why are you so intent on staring at me? I am not Death, or Desire, or Dakṣa's sacrifice, or the Triple City, or Andhaka. Why bother with this blazing gaze? It is all for nothing that you are becoming Virūpâkṣa—'Ugly Eyes'—in front of me."

As she went on in this vein, Śiva began to think about going away to some deserted place, where a man could be happy by himself—free, devoid of attachments, his thoughts under control, beyond desire and passion, aware of ultimate truths; in short, both happy and wise. So he left her and went to the Siddha wilderness. His companions—Bhṛṅgin, Vīrabhadra, Nandin—followed him, but soon he sent them away and continued alone. Pārvatī, for her part, went into the women's quarters, in a foul mood.

She was tormented by this separation and found no joy anywhere. She thought only about Śiva. Her attendant Vijayā said to her, "You won Śiva by self-mortification; it was wrong to play dice with him. Haven't you heard that dicing is full of flaws? You should forgive him. Go quickly, before he is too far away, and appease him. If you don't, you will be sorry later."

Pārvatī replied, entirely truthfully: "I won against that shameless man; and I chose him, before, for my lover. Now there is nothing I must do. Without me, he is formless [or ugly—*virūpa*]; for him, there can be no separation from, or conjunction with, me. I have made him formed or formless, as the case may be, just as I have created this entire universe with all its gods. I just wanted to play with him, for fun, for the sake of the game, in order to play with the causes of his emerging into activity [*udbhava-vṛtti-hetubhiḥ*]."

She took the form of a tribal woman [*śabarī*], dark and lovely, with bright red lips, a splendid neck, a curvaceous body staggering under the weight of two magnificent breasts, her waist thin but hips and thighs fleshy and golden, with bangles on her arms and peacock feathers in her hair. Carrying a bow in her hands, a quiver on her back, she seemed to be reviving Desire, while the very bees [*bhṛṅgin*] and peacocks in that wilderness were overpowered by love.

She went to where Śiva was sitting, deep in meditation on the Self, his eyes closed—he who is one and many, without limit, fashioned only from his own understanding. Confused by the humming of the bees, he woke up and saw her, and wanted her. As he reached for her hand, she vanished. Now Śiva, Destroyer of Desire, was overcome, in his turn, by the pain of separation; he who knows no delusion was overwhelmed by delusion. He called to her, "Who are you, and to whom do you belong? Why are you wandering in this wilderness?"

She said, "I am looking for a husband who is omniscient, who fulfills all needs, who is free and without mutations, the lord of the worlds."

Said Śiva, "That's me! I'm the right husband for you. Think it over."

The Śabarī agreed. "Yes, you are the husband I have been seeking. But I have to tell you—you are lacking in virtue [or qualities, *nirguṇa*]. A woman won you long ago, by intense mortifications, yet you abandoned her in a flash, in the wilderness. You're hard to like [*durārādhya*], and you shouldn't say what you just said to me."

Śiva replied, "I didn't abandon that woman. Or if I did—what can I say today? Even knowing this wretchedness of mine, you should still do as I say."

Pārvatī laughed: "You're an ascetic, detached, without passion, delighting only in the Self, free from duality, a murderer of Desire. I see you as a living incarnation of Virūpâkṣa/Śiva. I cannot approach you."

Śiva took her hand and asked her to be his wife, but Pārvatī insisted that he ask her father's consent. He agreed. She brought him to Mount Himālaya. Śiva pleaded that the girl be his, and the Mountain said, "What are you saying, great lord? This isn't right. You are the one who gives everything in the three worlds."

Nārada arrived and said, "Listen: union with women always leads to mockery for men." Now Śiva was enlightened, and agreed: "You're right. Uniting with women is the downfall of men. I have been acting like a ghoul, infatuated with her. I'm leaving for another part of the universe." And he went somewhere where even Yogis cannot go.

But Nārada knew that Śiva had no support [*nirālambam*], so he advised the goddess and the Mountain and others to praise him. The mountains prostrated themselves and sang Śiva's greatness. Drums sounded and the gods rained flowers, as the Lord of Yogis returned to reign in state with Pārvatī.

Playful, ironic, often verging on parody, this myth is powerfully integrated into the thematic texture of the *Kedārakhaṇḍa*, to which it provides a fitting closure. For our purposes, its usefulness lies in the expansive vision of the dice game in its characteristic unfolding. Certain of the features intimated in the Sanskrit verse at the beginning of this chapter recur here in much fuller form. Thus, Śiva loses to the goddess, and Bhṛṅgin protests vocally (and pays the price); the presence or absence of Śiva's attributes (*guṇa*) is, again, a basic issue, obviously linked to the game. Once the game is begun, there seems to be no escaping it, or its consequences. These consequences appear to be heavily colored, for both players, by anger, antagonism, and the experience of separation.

Indeed, in general, we could describe the course of the game as a process of increasingly stark division. Śiva and Pārvatī begin as one, fused into a single, androgynous being at home on Kailāsa. Nārada, a compulsive busybody and troublemaker, seduces this conjunct divinity into playing dice—which requires an initial act of separation into two competing players. Dicing, he says, is even more fun for a couple than making love (and note that the androgyne is precisely that form of sexual existence in which it is impossible to make love).[13] After a mild protest by Pārvatī, the two embark on the game, and are soon entirely absorbed by it; they also begin to "cheat," or to play deceitfully (*chalena*). Śiva's early winnings prove ephemeral, and when he starts to lose—as lose he must—he tries to subvert the game and renege on his pledge. Pārvatī stubbornly insists on her victory, whatever the metaphysical implications of this might be (both Nārada and Bhṛṅgin, and, of course, Śiva himself, blandly and blindly assert that the male godhead can never be beaten). The atmosphere becomes more and more acrimonious, as Pārvatī sticks to her conviction; when the god fails to cow her even with his fiery third eye, he becomes discouraged and plans a retreat. The result is an extreme form of separation—the male being isolated, lost in self-absorption, far away in the wilderness; the goddess, still defiant and ill at ease in the harem. Her seductive disguise as the Śabarī tribal woman clearly demonstrates the utter vacuity of Śiva's claims to self-sufficiency—she is evidently right in saying that he needs her (even more than she needs him); that thus, she need do no more than persist in her secure mode of being in order to manipulate him; that she imparts form to him and propels him through transformations (*vikāra*) without reference to his own wishes. She has no regrets about the game—she was playing for fun, and in order to observe "the causes of his emerging into activity"; and this emergence is precisely what has occurred. The god, previously inert, has indeed been activated, divided, driven away by the conflict generated in the game. Although by any usual standard, Pārvatī must be seen as the ultimate victor in this confrontation—in effect, she puts Śiva to a test reminiscent of the trial-by-disguise that he makes her undergo in other texts, when she is subjecting herself to physical torture in order to win Śiva as her husband[14]—the story ends with another fruitless attempt by him to escape or deny her power over him. We see them at the end, as they were at the beginning, very much together, hymned as a unity of sorts by the mountains and the gods. Notice, however, that the motivating tension within the story remains entirely unresolved; the conclusion feels almost artificial, even disappointing, however necessary it may be; the question of Śiva's relationship with his female partner, and that of the relative autonomy of both figures, go essentially unanswered.

To restate this perspective: the dice game is an arena of inner division within the godhead, activated in play and thereby separated into masculine and feminine parts, which are driven away from one another. The goddess leads the way

13. See *Subhāṣitaratnakoṣa* 82, and *Saduktikarṇâmṛta* 139; see also, nn. 148–149.

14. See chapter III.

into the game, and thus forces the male divinity into the process of bifurcation; she also identifies herself with the power of playing and with the implicit devolution of the godhead into form. It is very striking that, by a symmetrical reaction, Śiva adopts a stance that is generally suspicious of, or inimical to, this arena; he seems, on the whole, reluctant to undergo the process that the game entails. He is hesitant, obstructive, angry, a hostile player unwilling to abide by the rules. Categorically denying the very possibility that he might lose, he is, in effect, rejecting the necessity of his inner division—and, by this very act, contributing to the process of actualizing this division. This is instructive: the dice game now fits the wider pattern of Śaiva myth, in which a negative stance on the part of the god (who, for example, refuses to create, or seeks to prevent Prajāpati/Brahmā from embarking on a disastrous creation) always produces the positive result that he is attempting to preclude.[15] In the dice game, as elsewhere, Śiva utters a stubborn no—and finds himself dragged, reluctantly, deeper into the destructive cycle.

Why is he so reluctant? It is not a matter of division and fissure alone. The dice game also diminishes the god. Division, here, implies a downward movement within the hierarchy of being. Śiva has to give up his ornaments and attributes—that is to say, parts of himself—to be transferred to the increasingly autonomous goddess. It is as if the world itself were shifting into a feminine mode, in which the goddess is enhanced in power and attributes through the simultaneous impoverishment of her husband. It is to this that he most objects—the self-loss and self-diminution that flow out of the game. The god resists this result, resists change in his inner composition, will not give in to the power of the dice. Nonetheless, once he has begun to play, the game overpowers him and instigates movement within him. The dice activate a process in which the female takes the male apart; he stakes pieces of himself that go to her; his control (over himself and his world) disintegrates; and he is forced to confront elements of his former being that have broken loose and are now in movement, thereby bringing the concomitant anxiety and rage that, apparently, not even the god can avoid. Perhaps one should say *especially* the god. As the prime player in the game of the cosmos, Śiva suffers the fate of any player who is helplessly caught up in this inherently destabilizing game.

Somewhat surprisingly, this must mean that Śiva acts, within the confines of the game, from a position of diminished understanding. We might imagine that when God plays dice, he will know the outcome in advance, and will thus effectively control the game. There may indeed be some level on which, or certain contexts in which, this statement could be true. In general, however, the opposite case is much more likely, as in our story. Another description of the Śaiva dice game, this time from the *Kāśīkhaṇḍa*, actually tells us explic-

15. See Shulman 1986; Kramrisch 1981a:19–26.

itly: "Although God is omniscient, he understands nothing at all [from within the game]."[16] Despite his desperate protestations to the contrary, Śiva cannot enter the game as a totality, permeated with total knowledge. For a whole being to play, it has to break itself apart into players—as the androgynous divinity divides into male and female halves to begin the game. What enters the game is that part of the totality now called "Śiva," which is pitted against the split-off "Pārvatī" part. Through this act of self-devolution, the part gains autonomy and loses its former plenitude of knowledge (which was, in any case, unarticulated and, presumably, not present to awareness). If anything remains of the former whole, it can only be identified, now, with the game itself. This whole is now in process, active, exploring the interrelationship of its parts, unstable, self-divisive, self-diminishing on the level of any individual piece.

There is a paradox here: entering the game allows the godhead to explore itself, but only as a part; the self-knowledge that can be gained—that may even be said to constitute a telos of the play—emerges out of the self-diminution inherent in this frame. One wonders if, in a Śaiva universe, all self-knowledge is not marked by this same paradox. This is knowing from a position of self-loss and partial obscuration. Knowing oneself entails the loss or veiling of other, possibly more complete kinds of knowledge. We see this result lucidly expressed in the highly ironic interchange between the ascetic Śiva and the seductive Śabarī-Pārvatī. The latter asks for an omniscient husband, and Śiva immediately volunteers for this title; he is also supposed to be free of inner mutations (*vikāras*) and the vicissitudes of form. But it is precisely such *vikāras* that he has been made to undergo through the dice game, while his omniscience is hardly in evidence here—indeed, the authors take the trouble to tell us that this god, who should be free of delusion, is in fact entirely under the sway of delusion, a victim of ignorance and desire. Pārvatī's taunting pun—"You are lacking in virtue/qualities"—only confirms his paradoxical devolution, which is then demonstrated anew by the god's further flight from his only real support (*ālamba*). The myth ends here, in this version, with the sense of a temporary and tenuous reconstitution of the broken unity. But the image of the Śaiva god that we are left with is alive with paradox and trauma—a deity who is active, and therefore diminished; whose self-knowledge reflects this process of circumscription and partial self-loss; who is subject to the game, and, in this context, largely dependent on a female component that has extricated itself from his control, and that is fast feminizing the entire cosmos and evoking desire; and who might be said to be moving toward his devotees by assuming time-bound forms and, from an existential situation of his own frustrating partiality, to be seeking their love and their desire. This is how the Śabarī encounters

16. *Skandapurāṇa* 4.88.10: *devaḥ sarvajña-nātho 'pi na kiṃcid avabudhyati*. See the further discussion in sections 8 and 11.

Śiva in the wilderness, and how we find him at Elephanta, in the majority of the panels "subsequent" to the dice game—in a state of movement; entropic; unbalanced; reflexive; and violently hungry for a prior wholeness (including a level of feminine being) that continuously eludes him.

Diminution; fragmentation; the occlusion of knowledge, which also constitutes self-knowledge—these are the standard features of this process. They seem to combine in the general direction of what we might have called "engendering"—that is, the assumption of a sexual identity. "Before" the game, the godhead is androgynous, an amalgam of male and female elements—already sufficiently separated to be identified as such, yet fused together in a holistic mode. In this, the two genders share the primary feature of the existential state before play begins, a state of infinite density and interconnectedness, in which no discontinuities exist. Time and form—conceived precisely as constituting such discontinuities within god's being—come about only in the course of play, as its main consequences. What this means for the godhead, among other things, is that labels such as "male" and "female" now have urgent significance. These words are in no way metaphorical, as, from an external perspective, we might imagine them to be. In the Sanskrit texts, to describe god as "he" or "she" entails a series of metaphysical implications. Indeed, in some sense, the whole story of the dice game is an extended essay on having identity of a sexual nature—on the internal constitution of such an identity; the economy of energies that it displays; and its effects on consciousness and agency. And what is true on the level of the godhead is also, it appears, true for human beings.

There is another way to think about the godhead's transition into play. If the point of departure is a state of total density within being, in which everything in the cosmos is connected simultaneously to everything else—before time appears—then the separations and ruptures that result from play can be seen as devolving simultaneity into a slower, but also a cooler and more objectified, mode. Look at one of the most common terms for "form"—*mūrti*—which so often appears in descriptions of the game. *Mūrti* derives from the root *mūrch*, whose primary force has to do with congealing, coagulating, solidifying. This is what happens to the Śaiva godhead: as gaps open up inside him, pieces of him begin to freeze into solid objects that exist in time. Gender is, perhaps, the very first movement of self-objectification, the first characteristic of a given *mūrti*. These frozen entities do not, of course, remain static; rather, their changing contours reflect the ongoing process of temporality itself. The famous grammarian Patañjali offers the following definition: "Time is that through which growth and diminution in congealed forms can be observed" (*yena mūrtānām upacayaś câpacayaś ca lakṣyante taṃ kālam āhuḥ*).[17] Temporality is thus tied

17. *Mahābhāṣya* 1.409.21–23 (on Pāṇini, 2.2.5); see Cardona 1991:448.

to the waxing and waning of congealed solids, objectified forms perhaps delimiting or containing a more original, subtle, or fluid substance or state.

But objectification *always*, in this metaphysical framework, has another aspect, critical to our discussion, an aspect relating to the movement from inside out. To freeze into form is to become externalized, to cross the newly formed border that now separates the god's inner being from what has poured out of him via the spaces that have opened up within his prior density. Indeed, in a way, these spaces *are* themselves gaping externalities, sucking innerness outward toward slower and less subtle existential modes. The deeper issues of the dice game are located precisely here, at this point of crossing, where it is the holism of the inside that, ultimately, is at stake. Density, simultaneity, wholeness—these are inner qualities, at odds with the porousness, linearity, and fragmentation of the exterior. Our task is to pursue this contest, this constant alternation in cosmic state, in relation to the game that puts the godhead into play.

4
Minor Victories

Is it true that Śiva always loses when he plays dice? This is an empirical question with a relatively straightforward answer. In the texts we have examined, Śiva does not, and apparently cannot, win a game. He can, however, win a single round:

> "I'll pay up what I owe you,
> all the kisses you won at dice.
> But what's the rush?
> You clever man, your eagerness
> is misplaced. Under our terms,
> I have a period of grace,
> a hundred days and nights."
>
> That's what she said, while Śiva
> was already blinking his eyes—
> the sun and moon—
> and at every blink a day
> was over.
>
> He's busy, this god, who really should
> protect you.[18]

18. *Karpūracaritabhāṇa* 1.

Pārvatī has. it seems, staked a series of kisses—probably a long series—before the game could begin; and she has lost. But she is in no hurry to pay up; by the terms of the wager, she has a hundred days and nights before the debt is due. Alas, she has failed to reckon with the fact that the god's two eyes provide the external measures of time itself; every blink causes a combined solar and lunar eclipse, which means that a day has already passed. In other circumstances, as we will see, the goddess herself produces exactly this result, playfully blinding the god, thereby wreaking havoc on the orderly progression of time, and ultimately triggering the destructive objectification of the god's blindness in the form of the dangerous, demonic Andhaka. In the verse just quoted, however, the god's vision is eclipsed only momentarily—by a hundred blinks of the eye—in the interests of his achieving the lover's prize that he has won from Pārvatī. Still, even here, this erotic recombination, emerging from the dice game, remains a tantalizing promise, the fulfillment of which is not described.

The theme itself is well known. Lovers divert themselves with games of dice, gambling for ever-escalating stakes:

> First they played for an embrace,
> then a delicious kiss.
> Now he is asking her again
> to name the stake.
> She is silent, but as her hand,
> moist and trembling,
> moves toward her token,
> from deep within, the hidden hunger
> rises to her tingling cheeks.[19]

So the male can, in principle, win, which is what the female here seems to want. The poet Murâri offers yet another way to think about this kind of contest:

> Embraces, kisses, the full
> and playful festival of love—
> these are the stakes, and Desire himself
> provides security for the bets.
> Win or lose, delight
> is certain. Still, since they are
> so young, at heart each one
> would kill to win.[20]

19. *Subhāṣitaratnakoṣa* 605, attributed to Rājaśekhara.

20. Ibid., 606.

And yet all of this is a far cry from the kind of victory we might expect from God. Even if the Śaiva dice game occasionally comes under the sway of images derived from the poetry of romantic play, the process, in general, moves, inexorably, in the direction of the god's defeat. Moreover, this vision of the game seems to resume a widespread pattern related to Hindu marriage rituals, which require the newlyweds to play a series of games with one another—partly, no doubt, with the aim of encouraging some initial contact between these two relative strangers. In all such rituals, the bridegroom invariably loses, and the bride then graciously concedes—in the interests of domestic harmony.[21] We have also heard a guide at Elephanta, standing before the dice-game panel, say that Pārvatī, "although she knew that she could not be defeated, accepted defeat—thus bringing out her greatness. This is what you see in many families, isn't it?"[22]

Very often, the two parties to the game begin to abuse one another verbally, as in the *Kedārakhaṇḍa* version. In essence, these arguments reflect the god's reluctance to accept defeat; technically, Pārvatī is always right about her victory. In the Tamil *Kantapurāṇam*, for example, Śiva challenges Pārvatī to play, and appoints Viṣṇu as arbiter; as the game heats up, Śiva begins to lose but, laughing aloud, claims the opposite is the case, and even demands that Pārvatī pay up what she staked. In anger, she turns to Viṣṇu for support; he, however, although perfectly aware that Śiva has lost, says, "The Supreme God is the *only* one who can win at dice."[23] Pārvatī is so furious at this answer that she curses Viṣṇu—who speaks, she says, without any real awareness, or in crooked ways, although he is fully present and has watched the game carefully; the curse will turn him into a serpent in Tiruvālaṅkāṭu, in the Tamil land. Here, it is the arbiter who pays the price of violent dislocation, out of solidarity with the male player in his inevitable drift toward defeat. More often, however, one or both of the *players* will undergo forms of far-reaching displacement as the game unfolds. They quarrel, and their conflict rapidly degenerates to the point of breakdown, until the game itself is abandoned, imploded from within. This rupture then leads to even more radical forms of separation. In the south In-

21. Velcheru Narayana Rao (personal communication) reports that his grandmother used to say about Sītā, the prototype of Hindu womanhood, that she *always* won in the games she played with Rāma but was never given the chance to enjoy the victory.

22. The guide went on to say: "He can never ever win, nor can she." (Elephanta, February 5, 1994.)

23. *cūt'uṭaip por/ vĕllun takaiyoṉ paraṉ*: *Kantapurāṇam* 6.14.172. This passage (6.14.158–74) is one of the more elaborate descriptions of the game in Tamil, and includes technical terms for the various throws of the dice. It appears to be connected to a local tradition of Tiruvālaṅkāṭu.

dian tradition, the goddess often finds herself exiled to the earth because of the tensions articulated by the game of dice:

> Śiva and Pārvatī quarreled, made up, garlanded one another, listened to the Veda, chatted, sang to the accompaniment of the vīṇā, played at various pastimes—including dice. They won, they lost, they exchanged ornaments. . . . Then Pārvatī asked Śiva, "Just who are the sun and the moon, really?" He told her they were his two eyes. So she hid these eyes with her hands: at once the entire cosmos was as if anointed with a melted-down mass of darkness. To atone for this act, Pārvatī was sent to earth as the dark goddess Kālī.[24]

Pārvatī's playful blinding of her husband is, elsewhere, the immediate cause of Andhaka's birth and, as such, the logical continuation of the dice game.[25] Here, the same act projects the goddess from the divine sphere into the human world of constricted existence; only through further violence and conflict will she eventually be able to regain her place within the godhead's androgynous whole.[26]

Loss and separation, then, are the fundamental outcomes of the dice game. They are accompanied by intense anxiety—felt, above all, by the male divinity, who sees his female persona slipping away. In several of the dice-game panels at Ellora, Śiva grabs Pārvatī's arm even as she turns away (see figures 11 and 12), as if desperately trying to hold her back. At Elephanta, too, she is already clearly caught up in the business of separation, moving into her own domain, away from the god. She is often angry, infuriated by what she perceives as Śiva's cheating, which he will not acknowledge.[27] In any case, the male deity is utterly unable to prevent her from leaving. The dice game unfolds according to its own logic: the dice themselves, so the *Kathāsaritsāgara* tells us, are "endowed with the freedom to pursue their effect" (*sva-kārya-datta-svātantrya*).[28] The result is a recurrent moment of great pathos: the god is despoiled, and the cosmos is at risk. At the Madhukeśvara temple in Mukhalingam (northern Andhra Pradesh), a panel shows Śiva and Pārvatī at this point of the game. Pārvatī's servants are carrying away the weapons and ornaments she

24. *Aruṇâcalapurāṇam* of Ĕllapanāyiðār, 4.2–3. Cf. *Skandapurāṇa* 1.3.2.17.30; *Tiruvāvaṭuturai kovil katai*, cited by Mahalingam 1972:250–51; *Kāñcīmāhātmya* 23–34, cited in Shulman 1980:171–72. For earlier references to Śiva and dice in the Tamil tradition, see, e.g., *Tevāram* of Appar 5.4.32 (*vaṭṭaṉ* < *vaṭṭu*, "playing piece").

25. See our discussion in chapter II, section 3.

26. Shulman 1980:179–80.

27. Soar 1988:80–103, citing the *Śivâlaya-māhātmya.*

28. *Kathāsaritsāgara* 110.55. In the continuation of this verse, however, the dice are called "unstable" (*lola*), and "under control" (*vaśagata*)—of the game?

FIGURE 11. Pārvatī turns away from the game. Detail of Śiva and Pārvatī playing dice. Elephanta, Cave 1.

has won from her husband. "To the right of Śiva are found three *Śivagaṇas* carrying trident with disappointed faces. To the left of Pārvatī is seen the bull, the mount of Śiva, reluctant and helpless for being pushed and pulled away by the attendants of Pārvatī. It turns back its head and cries in vain for Śiva's help."[29] Similarly, when Ratnâkara, the author of the *Haravijaya*, mentions the

29. Masthaniah 1978: 79. Cf. Donaldson 1987:II, plate 2600, and III, plates 3645–48 (the Madhukeśvara panel is divided into its two halves). Plate 3645 shows the tempestuous dice game from the seventh-century Svarṇajaleśvara shrine, where Śiva's "right hand is stretched toward the oblong chess board while the left hand is uplifted and placed near his face, possibly displaying distress at having lost the game" (3:1349).

FIGURE 12. Śiva and Pārvatī at dice. Ellora, Cave 15.

dice game (at the close of a long introductory chapter that begins with the god's playfulness [*krīḍārasa*] and culminates in his cosmic dance), it is to show us Śiva in this rather helpless and potentially unhappy mode:

The goddess had beat him,
and the troops were dragging off
his reluctant, aged bull,
which dug in its hooves, leaving deep marks
all over that mountain.

> The moon, too, that belonged on his head
> had been staked and lost, and was now
> bewildered. This game, in short,
> was most perturbing.[30]

This is how Śiva spends his time (*iti samayam anaiṣīt*, 64)—watching his familiar accoutrements being torn away from him, in a newly uncertain world—though he remains, according to Ratnâkara, "unfamiliar with separation from Pārvatī" (*acala-kanyā-viprayogânabhijñaḥ*, 64). She is still there beside him, ready to play. Yet the separation that lies in store—when the androgynous Śiva-Pārvatī amalgam will split in two in order to allow the god to do battle with Andhaka—may already be intimated here, in this early statement of playful competition.

The tone of all these passages, and of their iconographic counterparts, is remarkably consistent. Somewhere there must surely be counterexamples (our readers can supply them from their own knowledge or experience). Panduranga Bhatta, citing, at second hand, a Kannada *Viśvakoṣa*, tells us that Pārvatī once defeated Śiva at dice; she then lost to Kumāra, and Kumāra then lost to Gaṇeśa. Viṣṇu, wanting to help Śiva out of his depression, arranged a rematch on the holiday of Dīpâvali; this time, Śiva entered into the dice, made them produce the desired result, and won.[31] This is more like what we might have expected from God—a nonarbitrary determination, from within, of the dice throws and their results.[32] Note that the sequence of losses still runs consistently from higher-order beings to lower-order ones, as the major myths of dicing we have cited would lead us to expect. But this story is closely tied to ritualized gambling on Dīpâvali, as the conclusion makes clear: Although Pārvatī was at first angry about her loss, she was appeased when Viṣṇu explained matters to her; she then promised that those who gamble on Dīpâvali would have a prosperous year.[33] Śiva's victory is thus used to underpin Pārvatī's boon; in effect, we are dealing with a context in which the game is rigged, the result predetermined, if one performs the ritual correctly. As we shall see, this pattern is reminiscent of the ancient Rājasūya dice game and

30. *Haravijaya* 2.63: *śailâtmajā-vijita-tad-gaṇa-kṛṣyamāṇa-vṛddhokṣa-niṣṭhura-khurâhata-mandarâdriḥ/*
tasya glahī-kṛta-vimugdha-kirīṭa-candra-khaṇḍaḥ kadācana durodara-vibhramo 'būt//

31. Panduranga Bhatta 1985:50. Panduranga Bhatta also quotes *Caturvargacintāmaṇi*, to the effect that Śiva played with Pārvatī on Dīpâvali, and lost.

32. See Kapferer 1988b.

33. Panduranga Bhatta 1985.

its contemporary analogues. Ritual dicing is meant to effect a causal sequence and to control its results. In general, however, there is only one way to achieve this goal—by keeping the god, or the central figure, for all intents and purposes, *outside* the game.

5
How to Play

We can no longer avoid the question: Just what game are they playing? There are several possible answers; however, if we are dealing only with Śiva's dice game—in sharp contrast to the difficult issues that arise whenever more ancient forms of Indian dice play are discussed—the great bulk of the evidence, both textual and iconographic, points to one form or another of the game known today, throughout north India, as *chaupar* (in the Tamil south, *cŏkkaṭṭāṉ*; in Telugu, *sŏkaṭālu*). *Chaupar*, well described by Brown,[34] is the origin of the game the modern West calls Pachisi, or Parcheesi (from Hindi *pacīsi*, "[relating to] 25," a throw in the game). A game board, usually made of cloth, consists of two intersecting axes with a large empty square at their central point of meeting. Each of the four "arms" of this cross has 24 squares, in 8 rows of 3. Players move their pieces or tokens (*sāri*)—usually eight each—counterclockwise around the board in accordance with the throws of the dice (*pāśa*, *pāśaka*); the latter are usually oblong in shape, made of ivory, and marked with dots that always add up to 7 on opposite sides (1 and 6; 2 and 5). Cowrie shells can be used in place of actual dice. The object is to assemble all one's tokens in the empty middle square before the opponent can do so. Pieces that are "bitten" by the opponent in his movement through the board are sent back to the beginning; some boards have "safe" squares in which the token is not susceptible to this kind of attack. Each throw of the dice normally affects only a single token. Various rules apply to the final progression down the center of the fourth "arm" and into the middle space. The tokens themselves are often of carved wood perforated by several empty holes—perhaps, as we shall see, an iconic expression of the internal processes unfolding within the players. It is also of some importance that the game progresses via the radical dispersion of fragmented self-representations, toward a point of ultimate reintegration in the empty central space.

Most modern visual depictions of Śiva's game with Pārvatī seem to show some variant of the basic *pacīsi* board;[35] and when the dice game turns up in folktales

34. Brown 1972, citing, among others, the '*Ain-i Akbari* and Richard Carnac Temple.

35. Thus, e.g., the board in the Basohli *Rasamañjari* illustration of Śiva playing dice with Pārvatī (seventeenth century) at the Metropolitan Museum of Art.

and folk epics (for example, in the Panjabi Rāja Rasālu story,[36] or the Chattisgarhi tale of Bandhīya Rāja[37]), it is usually *chaupar*, in some form, that is meant. There are, nonetheless, other options: It sometimes appears from descriptions of play that a single throw of the dice can determine a round—the same impression we get from reading about the fateful dice game in the second book of the *Mahābhārata*. In these cases, we may well be dealing with a different game altogether, one in which large numbers of dice were thrown at once; it has been argued that an "even," or an "odd," result was the determining factor.[38] When the *Mahābhārata* dice game is painted or sculpted today, however, we inevitably find the *pacīsi-chaupar* board.[39] In Cave 21, at Ellora, the carved dice board used by Śiva and Pārvatī is rectangular, rather than square, with no sign of the intersecting axes. For the Ellora sculptors, then, and possibly for the texts with which they were familiar, the dice game must have followed another pattern.[40] Two alternatives are still actively in use in South Asia. The first, called *jñāna-chaupar* or "the game of karma," is the source of the familiar game of Snakes and Ladders. Here the dice regulate movement from the lower reaches of the board, by way of various dangers, traps, and potential bonuses, toward the higher ontic realms of the cosmos at the upper limit of the board. This game has been exhaustively described for Tibet;[41] more than any other, it is closely linked to divination, the dice disclosing, in external clarity, the karmic-existential state of the player in his every move.[42] The second possibility is some variation on the very widespread Mancala series (*cĕnnĕ* in Tulu, described at length by Claus).[43] Here we find a series of 14 empty pits or holes in which seeds or other tokens are deposited in turn, in accordance with rules that limit and regulate this "sowing"; distributing one's tokens, without having a remainder, is a major theme or goal. Units of four are critical: in the highly ritualized form of the game, a pit with

36. Ions 1970:44–64.

37. Flueckiger 1987 and 1996:72.

38. See discussion by Keith 1908; de Vreese 1948; this reading remains unlikely. See also Shulman 1992.

39. For example, see Beck 1982:201.

40. Similarly, many medieval carvings of the dice game show us a rectangular board with 24 squares (two rows of 12); see, e.g., Donaldson 1987:3, plates 3645–48, from Orissa.

41. See Tatz and Kent 1977; Shimkhada 1983.

42. Cf. Hoernle, cited by Brown 1972.

43. Claus 1986; and cf. Arnold 1985:52–53 (our thanks to Michaela Soar for this reference). See section 13. We wish to thank Peter Claus for demonstrating the rules of *cĕnnĕ*, and Purushottama Bilimale for introducing us to the game in practice, for explaining its major types and subtypes, and for patiently tolerating our early inept attempts to play.

three seeds in it can be completed if, and only if, the player has one seed left in his hand; in this case, the four seeds can be extracted as "winnings," leaving behind an empty hole. In this perspective, there is an equivalence of sorts between the number that represents completion (four) and the empty hole; the latter suggests the reintegration of the fragmented holism which starts the game, when each hole contains an initial four seeds. To the extent that the board depicts the internal state of the player, one could say that the ideal winner is, paradoxically, full of emptiness—that is, of complete, fully reintegrated, and, therefore, empty holes. By way of contrast, to be left with a residual, unbalanced number of seeds in a pit is to lose; in particular, the most ominous state is that of a pit with only one seed (in Tulu, *jĕppĕ* "sleeper"). Indeed, this result—a single seed in an empty hole—means the end of the player's turn, a moment of exhaustion and stasis. There is reason to conceptualize the fateful remainder, the single token in a pit that augurs defeat, as a kind of inverted or extruded hole, an inward space turned inside out; we will return to this image. One could also describe the game's process more generally, in highly abstract terms, as a movement from external holism—four seeds in every pit—to dynamic disruption, fragmentation, and incremental recomposition of the shattered whole, in a manner that transfers the fragmented and unbalanced unity from the board outside into the player's self; or, in the opposite, winning move, as the emptying out of the player's residual self-fragment (one seed in hand) into the pit with three seeds, thus reconstituting, from within, the external whole. But this abstract formulation does an injustice to the remarkable proliferation of subtypes of the game, each with its motivating logic; we might note that in the ritualized *cĕnnĕ* of Tulu Nad, the *loser* has to marry[44]—as if the inherent telos of the game were to produce precisely this result, in which the blocked isolation of the self-extruding loser is redressed through an erotic and generative further move. We shall see that such an eventuality is deeply integrated into the mythic materials relating to Śiva's game of dice. Moreover, this game, though usually played without dice today, is, in some ways, recognizably continuous with the oldest forms of dice games in the subcontinent, attested in the Vedic sources; we will examine closely, at the conclusion of this chapter, one story in which Śiva and Pārvatī play *cĕnnĕ.*

Notions of emptying, reassembling, calculating, and, especially, redistributing the tokens in an ordered sequence have been common to all major forms of Indian dice play since the most ancient times. Already in the famous "gambler's lament" from the *Ṛg Veda*, we hear of a game played with nuts, which have to be divided up without a remainder; the winner in this holds up

44. Purushottama Bilimale, personal communication, Mysore, January, 1995; and see Claus 1986:270–71.

his empty hands to show he has held nothing back.[45] These dice nuts are "honeyed" (*mádhvā sámpṛktāḥ*), "deluding" (*nikṛ́tvānas*), "heated/heating" (*tápanās tāpayiṣṇávaḥ*)[46]—that is, dangerous, elusive, in some sense crooked; the danger seems to reflect the state of imbalance marked by being left with (or *as*) a remnant, especially the lonely remainder of one. This is no less an internal state than an external one. If Harry Falk is right, the corresponding ritual game, linked to proto–Śaiva Vrātya bands, could produce not a winner, only a loser—the single player who ends up with this fatal residue of one, the *kali* result.[47] The actual technique of distributing the dice nuts (Skt. *vi-ci*) remains obscure, though it is clear that units of four were basic to this process,[48] as they are in the various forms of *cĕnnĕ*-mancala today. We have no intention of entering the debate about the technicalities of play, but there is still reason to notice the metaphysical tone that attaches to these ancient images. Movement in the course of play, which might even seem random, sooner or later becomes a burdensome imbalance or excess, in which a remnant—the last nut or token—can no longer be resumed or contained. A stubbornly resistant piece of inner reality remains excluded—or extruded—this being the conclusive sign of its owner's defeat.

In this sense, the Vedic game is actually remarkably close to our Śaiva myths, which also, in effect, produce a clear loser (and no clear victor). And it is perhaps not entirely coincidental that the failing hero of the Śaiva game is historically and developmentally linked to Rudra, the divinity who emerges from the ancient Vrātya game in the form of Kali—the loser. But for our purposes here, it is enough to stress the delusive, slippery nature of this game, in both its ancient and modern forms, as it is perceived in the texts; the powerful and evocative images of filling and emptying holes on the board, of parceling out tokens in symmetrical groups of four, and of the fateful asymmetry that brings the game to an end; and, above all, the devolutionary direction that seems to inhere in it. There is, however, another, countervailing set of images and conceptions, which applies to a very different type of dice game, known to us from sources rooted in the context of Vedic sacrifice. Highly ritualized forms of the game are constructed so as to produce a predictable result, known in advance. The emblematic example of this type is the dice game enacted (rather than "played") at the Vedic ritual of royal consecration, the Rājasūya.[49] We discuss

45. See Falk 1986:181–87.

46. *Ṛg Veda* 10.34.7.

47. Falk 1986:108–17.

48. Ibid., 126–33.

49. See the analysis by Heesterman 1957:143–57; more recently, Falk 1986:163–74, including a close study of the related case of the Agnyādheya dicing.

this form of dice play and its internal logic in section 8. Suffice it to say, at this point, that the king must always win in this well-defined arena, and that he achieves this result by not truly entering into the game.[50] Or the game may be set up in such a way that the central or senior figure *must* win, as one sees in accounts of the Agnyādheya dice game.[51] A similar achievement—certain victory—is arranged for the head of the family at the ritual dice play in North India during Diwali in modern times.[52]

Underlying both of these types—the devolving structure of the Śaiva game and its ancient analogs; and the ritualized dice play, with its fixed sequence and result—lie profound issues relating to notions of continuity and wholeness. Both proceed from a troubling sense of radical discontinuity in the texture of cosmos, of god, of self; but where the Śaiva pattern sees this discontinuity as normative and, it seems, irreversible, the ritualized models produce, or actually reproduce, a world governed by continuous transitions across precisely corresponding domains. *Chāndogya Upaniṣad* 4.1–3 (the *samvarga-vidyā*) offers perhaps the finest articulation of this latter vision:[53]

> These 5 and the other 5 are 10, that is the *kṛta* result. That is why food is tenfold in all the cardinal directions. Virāj is an eater of food: she sees all. . . . Just as all the lower throws come together in the winner, who has won by the *kṛta* result, so whatever creatures do that is right comes together for him.

The Upaniṣadic play with the symbology of dicing seems to require 6-sided dice cubes, marked from 1 to 6 in such a way that opposite sides of the cube always add up to 7 (1 + 6; 2 + 5; 3 + 4)—as one can still see in Indian dice in use today.[54] The numerical combinations that emerge from a throw of two dice are correlated to homologous combinations in the realms of cosmic space (the cardinal directions); time (the seasons of the year, or the cosmic ages); language (the Vedic meters, with their fixed number of syllables and caesuras);[55]

50. It is true that the version in *Kātyāyanaśrautasūtra* (15.7.5–20) makes the king participate in the second moment of dicing (for the killing of a cow), as noted by Falk (1986:167). The standard sequence, however, clearly obviates the king's involvement in play.

51. See Heesterman 1993:194–95 and Falk 1986:136–63.

52. Crooke 1894:346.

53. See the brilliant analysis by Falk 1986:119–26.

54. Our impression, however, is that 3 and 4 are generally lacking from the modern dice.

55. Falk convincingly stresses the overriding role of the Virāj meter—40 syllables in its fullest form, conforming to two dice standing on the single "eye" marker (*ekapada*); this leaves 20 exposed "eyes" on each die. Another line of development extends from this perception: Virāj is that "feminine" movement within the holistic deity that produces creation itself, in the form of this deity's self-diminishment (*Ṛg Veda* 10.90, the famous Puruṣa

the elements that comprise the universe, or the human body, or consciousness—and so on, in a nearly inexhaustible chain of interconnectedness and parallel diffusion. A throw that leaves both dice with one eye exposed on top (thus standing on, and hiding, the 6) is homologized to the universe, with the sun at the zenith, and to another form of the Virāj meter—that is, language in its supremely ordered, controlled, and powerful form. A vision of this sort requires, or privileges, knowledge of a technical kind conducive to the goal of perfect internal harmony and resonance. The levels of the cosmos echo in precise alignment with the consciousness of the ritualist "who knows thus," and who is thus himself whole, contained, and symmetrical[56]—nothing like the unbalanced deity, spinning out of control in an outward direction, in a state of precarious excess and fragmentation, as we have seen him in the myth.[57] Indeed, the ritual dicing seems intended to prevent or heal just this problematic state of internal rupture and uneven movement, with its untidy remainders and losses. In this case a ritual structure leaves nothing to chance, and the dice game begins to look more like the determining framework we might once have expected from a mode of playing with, or in, the god. But to begin to understand the nature of this "solution," and of the intradivine processes that properly constitute the problem, we have to explore the more fundamental notions of play that are embedded in Hindu cosmology.

6
The Boundary between Not-Play and Play

Indic cosmology is imbued with playful properties of ludic paradox. These playful qualities of fluidity and processuality are embedded in cosmogenesis—indeed, in the first difference, the first boundary, made in this cosmos. This very first boundary is that between not-play and play and constitutes the paradoxical distinction between self and other. The passage from not-play to play is a key to the logic of the organization of this cosmos, to its use and tolerance of paradox and ambiguity, and to the role of ludic forms of play and games in the evolution and transformation of cosmos. More generally, the logic of paradox and, therefore, of process, in the passage from not-play to play needs to be

hymn); and one thinks of the critical *Virāṭa* section of the *Mahābhārata*, where Yudhiṣṭhira, the central hero, becomes a disguised master of dice. But to explore the rich texture of the Virāj materials would require a different study.

56. See the discussion in Shulman 1994, in relation to the story of Nala.

57. And yet we note that even the ritualists' cubes must stand on one side, which is blocked or hidden—an invisible remnant that informs the remaining totality.

examined here as a prelude to discussing the significance of this passage in Indic cosmology. As we will argue here in detail, the shift to play in Indic cosmology entails the evolution, but also the destruction, of cosmos.

In a pioneering article titled "A Theory of Play and Fantasy," first published in 1955, Gregory Bateson made three elementary points that are relevant to our argument: first, that the invocation of play creates a boundary between not-play and play; second, that this boundary is paradoxical; third, that this same invocation of play also overcomes the paradox it creates, enabling passage into the reality of play. Bateson highlighted the problematic relationship of not-play to play by using Whitehead and Russell's (1927) theory of logical types. This enabled Bateson to posit play as an abstraction different from that of not-play. The logic of play, argued Bateson, frames it differently from that of not-play.

We emphasize that Bateson's problematic was epistemological—that is, his concern was the character of the relationship of not-play to play as a puzzle in the realities of communication. In his view, this relationship privileged neither not-play nor play. Neither reality was inferior to the other. Not-play and play were organized according to premises that were different. But more than this, their respective premises radically contradicted one another, creating what Hofstadter has called a tangled hierarchy.[58] At issue was not the contents of these domains (whether one was real and serious, and the other, illusory and pretend). Instead, the problem of their difference was located in the very nexus of their interaction, in the logic of the frame (or of what we call the boundary) between not-play and play.

Bateson argued that this kind of frame has a peculiar, paradoxical character. He wrote that "it is our hypothesis that the message 'This is play' establishes a paradoxical frame comparable to Epimenides' paradox".[59] As we commented, this invocation, or metamessage, of play—which Bateson called "This is play"—does three things simultaneously: it creates the frame, or boundary; it creates the paradox of the frame (or boundary); and it overrides this paradox, opening the way into play. The paradox referred to is of the self-referential variety. So, Epimenides the Cretan stated that all Cretans were liars. A more condensed version of this kind of paradox would simply say, "This statement is false." If the statement is true, then it is false; but if the statement is false, then it falsifies itself. Playfully, we could replace the period that ends this sentence with the sign for infinity, at least for a time.

Among the examples that Bateson used to illustrate this paradox is one closer in substance to the issue of play—the example of the bite and the playful nip. The playful nip looks like a bite, but it signifies something quite different. It is

58. See Hofstadter 1980.

59. Bateson 1972:184.

a bite, and it is not a bite, at one and the same time. It is a different bite, perhaps an imaginary bite, a bite that does not exist, yet does, for it is consequential as a bite that wasn't.[60] Or, one may say that the playful nip is a bite on its way to becoming what it isn't. Simultaneously, the playful nip is not only a bite and a nonbite, not only one thing and another (a problem in static classification), but also a bite in process, in transformation to something else. Something looks like what it isn't, and indeed it is that.[61] This kind of formulation has significant implications for the boundary between not-play and play, and we will soon get to this.

In his 1955 article, Bateson addressed the logic of self-referential paradox as a structure and process (and, therefore, also as temporal). Bateson depicted a self-referential paradox in terms of a rectangular frame within which was written, "All statements within this frame are untrue," followed by two alternatives within the rectangle, "I love you" and "I hate you." This rectangular frame is misleading if one thinks that it models a paradoxical reality that one enters into, on the other side of the boundary. Quite the contrary, this depiction models the interior logic of the frame itself. In other words, it models the boundary, or the threshold between realities. Likewise, the depiction models the paradoxical interior of the boundary between not-play and play. We emphasize that the realities of play are not necessarily paradoxical in relation to themselves, but that play is paradoxical in relation to not-play.[62]

Bateson did not address the interior features of ludic worlds, cosmic or otherwise, and how these realities are put together. However, he did demonstrate imaginatively and incisively the problematic character of the paradoxical passage from not-play to play. Nevertheless, he quickly disregarded the signifi-

60. Handelman 1990:69.

61. A play on this problem in transformative perception is found in the forms painted by Magritte—a frame within the frame of the painting conceals exactly those forms that would be beneath the former frame if its forms did not exist.

62. Some scholars make paradoxical boundaries, like that between not-play and play, unproblematical. Three examples will suffice. Goffman (1974:40–46) supposedly built on Bateson's idea of the play frame in order to analyze the shift from not-play to play. Goffman grotesquely turned this into a problem of mechanics: strips of play, made to mimic strips of not-play, were laid like lumber, strip on strip, through simple redefinitions in social conventions. Buckley (1983:389) conflated the contents of play realities with the paradox of the play frame, and thereby argued that Bateson considered the realities of play to be paradoxical from within. Goffman and Buckley reduced play to forms of not-play, making each continuous with the other. Schechner (1988:16) argued that the "Batesonian play frame is a rationalist attempt to stabilize and localize playing, to contain it safely within definable borders." Schechner complemented Buckley by conflating Bateson's argument on passages to play with the substance of play within play frames. All three ignored the logic of passages to play.

cance of this paradoxical passage for an epistemology of the ludic by invoking the metamessage "This is play." This metamessage enables us, with speed and ease, to override the paradox of passage from one kind of reality to another, on a routine and mundane basis, without paying heed to the magnitude of our accomplishment.

This is where Bateson stopped. Having found the way out of paradox, Bateson did not look into paradox; yet there he would have found hints of how play works and what play can do. Instead, with the solution for the passage to play in hand, Bateson did not pursue what paradox, and paradox as boundary, intimate about the ludic. However, our reading of Bateson is of an implicit invitation to peer into the paradoxical composition of this kind of boundary in order to consider the relevance of paradox for play, and, particularly, for the ludic in Indic cosmology.

Most boundaries we are familiar with in daily life either are traversed routinely or close off special domains of experience.[63] Both are commonly marked by thresholds, whether these are thresholds of space (physical and visible); of time (counted and felt); or of sociality (known and normative). For our purposes, the presence of all such boundaries can be summarized as shifts in social definition, from some segment of continuity to its discontinuity, where this discontinuity is the location of a boundary. Here, the sides of the boundary are adjacent to and contiguous with one another. Regardless of how forceful these boundaries are, whether because of their pervasiveness, or because of the hegemonies of power they signify, there is nothing inherently problematic about them. They separate alternatives in an either/or fashion. These boundaries are constructs that retain their shape through either consensus or imposition. They are always subject to contestation, to redefinition and change. These boundaries are not relevant to the themes pursued here.

Boundaries that are made of the stuff of self-referential paradox are quite distinct. Such boundaries likely symbolize locations of a potential crossing between different realities. In this regard, the passage to play is analogous to the classic problem of paradoxical movement between contrasting levels or domains of cosmos, from one reality to another, a movement that Eliade called paradoxical passage (for example, to go where night and day meet; to find a gate in a blank wall; to pass between two boulders that constantly clash together)[64]—in other words, simultaneously to do one thing and to do its contrary, the impossible.

Such points of passage are made of paradox. The interior of the boundary between not-play and play is constituted as a severely restricted and highly

63. See, for example, Zerubavel 1991.

64. Eliade 1964:483–86.

redundant world, one that is formed through self-reference, contradiction, and infinite regress, a world that encloses itself within itself.[65] This tiny world of paradox is itself a simulation of the passage between realities. In its most rudimentary form, this miniscule world consists of two alternatives ("I love you," "I hate you"; this is not-play . . . this is play; and so on). These alternatives are governed by self-contradiction, such that each leads to and negates the other, which, in turn, leads to and negates the other, and so forth. According to Bateson, "Norbert Weiner used to point out that if you present the Epimenides paradox to a computer, the answer will come out yes . . . no . . . yes . . . no . . . until the computer runs out of ink or energy."[66]

Paradox is generated because each alternative exists on the same level of abstraction, where each is given the same value as the other and lacks the capability to dominate or to cancel the other. The paradox seems like an impassable trap. Ironically, the very conjunction and interaction of these contradictory alternatives make this kind of paradox a nexus of potential crossing between levels of abstraction or between alternative realities.

Rosalie Colie has pointed to several premises of self-referential paradox that are especially relevant to the interior of the paradoxical boundary of neither/nor. She notes, first, the closed structure of this sort of paradox. "The perfect self-contradiction is a perfect equivocation."[67] Moreover, "it tells the truth and it doesn't . . . its negative and positive meanings are so balanced that one meaning can never outweigh the other, though weighed to eternity." Indeed, such a paradox has no formal ending.[68]

Not only is this sort of paradox totalistic, but, inside itself, it breaks down and resynthesizes the contradictions that are the basis for its very existence. Thus, not only does such a paradox deal with itself both as form and as content, as subject and object, but it also collapses these distinctions. Subject turns into object, object into subject. So, too, the means of a paradox are always its ends as it turns endlessly in and upon itself.[69] Phrased in terms of change, this kind of paradox transforms itself continually, its structure is also its process, and its process its very structure. The stability of a self-referential paradox is transformation. The ongoing, internal collapse of categories and their resynthesis indicate that paradox ultimately insists on a unity of being. Paradox, comments Colie, folds "all its parts into one unbroken [whole]. . . . Paradox is

65. Hughes and Brecht 1984:1.

66. Bateson 1980:130.

67. Colie 1966:6.

68. Ibid., 21.

69. Ibid., 518.

self-regarding, self-contained, and self-confirming; it attempts to give the appearance of ontological wholeness."[70] Given its powerful momentum toward wholeness and totality, toward seamlessness and self-separation, this kind of paradox creates a powerful demarcation, a forceful boundary.

Yet inside this special boundary there is another aspect of importance. A self-referential paradox is "profoundly self-critical,"[71] since, within its strictures, it is continually calling itself into question, making itself problematic. A self-referential paradox operates at the "limits of discourse,"[72] calling into question those categories that are thought out in order to express human thought. Playing on the Latin term for mirror, *speculum*, Colie adds that a self-referential paradox is "literally, speculative, its meanings infinitely mirrored, infinitely reflected in each other."[73] This is infinite regress, but also an imaginative search of the parameters of the in-between conditions of boundariness—that is, of being, in between. "Like a tight spring, the implications of any particular paradox impel that paradox beyond its own limitation to defy its own categories."[74] Self-limited, it denies limitation. Just as a paradox bounds itself off and closes itself in, so, too, it has the potential to open itself, to become a nexus of passage, of crossing through the impassable. Paradox may function as a gateway.[75]

These premises of the self-referential paradox compose the boundary between not-play and play. In turn, the paradox generates qualities that are of direct relevance to an epistemology of the ludic, one that tells us how play can act on the evolution and transformation of cosmos, but only where such premises are embedded at a high level of cosmic organization.

Thus, paradox is not only full of movement but is, in fact, made up wholly, and only, through movement. Once set into operation, it seems to go on forever, nearing a metaphor of perpetual motion. It is a fiercely dynamic medium, one that is highly processual.[76] Its being is always a becoming, to paraphrase Gadamer,[77] and it is conducive to spherical thinking, rather than to lineal thought.[78] Just as it contains and collapses distinctions—between ends and means, structure and function—so it actualizes the perfect praxis of idea and

70. Colie 1966:518.

71. Ibid., 7.

72. Ibid., 10.

73. Ibid., 6.

74. Ibid., 11.

75. Yusa 1987:191.

76. Slaate 1968.

77. Gadamer 1988:110.

78. Yusa 1987:194.

action.[79] There seems to be no such phenomenon as a static paradox, or one that is stable without being continually unstable. Indeed, the paradox of self-reference is highly systemic in its self-reproduction through self-transformation.

The only way out of this sort of paradox (aside from waiting for entropy to degenerate the structure) is to make a choice. The passage through paradox is an issue of agency. In this, the self-criticism of paradox is significant because it spells out alternatives even as it attributes equal values to these alternatives. Self-doubt evokes a reflexive stance that may break the dynamic deadlock of the paradoxical boundary.

Choice requires hierarchy, a hierarchy of value, the preference of one alternative to another. This preference is an index of a change in value, one that breaks the dynamic deadlock. Passage through this kind of boundary is always a discourse on a change in values. Phrased differently, there is no movement between realities without a change in values. The capacity to change values is a prerequisite of moving between levels of abstraction, whether this is seemingly as simple as an act of imagination, as in the ludic case, or as complex as training in self-transcendence. The passage through paradox demands this capacity. This is the significance of Bateson's metamessage, "This is play." It is a message of passage through paradox because it makes a choice—it puts the value of play above that of not-play. One cannot play without changing values, without changing the value of reality, without changing realities.

Qualities of play have strong affinities to these qualities of paradox. The paradoxical boundary, the passage from not-play to play through neither/nor, cryptically prefigures many of the qualities of play realities. Especially important is the powerful thrust of processuality. The passage to play makes a structural difference, but one that is related intimately to processuality. Processuality speaks to the flexibility and malleability, to the fluidity and changeability, that pervade and inform so many realities of play. At the same time, the paradoxical passage from not-play to play creates self-transformation through two degrees of abstraction. One is the level of the paradox itself, the level of neither/nor, where not-play and play interact, lead to, and turn into the other. The second is the movement between levels or realities, through the metamessage that enables choice, and so enables exit from the paradox and entry into play.

Every invocation of play activates the impassable yet fluid boundary that is passed through. Every invocation of play activates premises of self-transformation. Every invocation of play puts things in motion. This formulation suggests the following correspondence between play and cosmos: The higher, the more abstract, the level of cosmos at which these qualities of play are embedded and legitimated, the greater the influence of these qualities on

79. On the idea of perfect praxis, see Handelman 1991.

the organization of that cosmos. Therefore, where the invocation of the ludic is embedded in cosmos at a high level of abstraction and generality, its fluid, transformational qualities are manifest at all levels of cosmos. The boundaries throughout such a cosmos are more malleable, and the entire cosmos may approximate more closely a holistic system of self-transformation.

In such a cosmology, the presence of the ludic is what may be called a top-down idea. Here, qualities of play are integral to the operation of the hierarchical cosmos, from its very apex, throughout its levels and domains. In this regard, to be involved in conditions of play, to partake of the qualities of play, is to be in tune with cosmic processes and their self-transformations. To be in play is to reproduce, time and again, the very premises that inform the existence of this kind of cosmos. Generally speaking, these are the relationships between the ludic and Indic cosmology. The processual qualities of the ludic—fluidity and malleability, movement and change—are deeply and centrally embedded, under a variety of rubrics, in Indic cosmologies and cultural ideologies. As one commentator has noted, "The most striking aspect of play activity in India . . . is its tendency to set in motion, to propel the society forwards by an incessant circulation."[80]

It is worth noting here that in cosmologies where premises of the ludic are not embedded at a high level of cosmos, and are not integral to the workings of cosmos, the phenomenon of play seems to erupt more from the bottom. Bottom-up play means that the ludic is often formulated in opposition to, or as a negation of, the order of things. This is the perception of play as unserious, illusory, and ephemeral, but it is also the perception of play as subversive and as resisting the order of things. These descriptions apply to the roles of play in, for example, mainstream monotheistic cosmologies, where the relationships between God and humankind are organized generally in terms of rupture, of absolute difference and hardened boundaries, and of opposites. There, the premises of play have a role neither in cosmogony nor in the organization of cosmos. Bottom-up play has deep roots in monotheistic cosmologies. In related

80. Lannoy 1971:195. During the past two decades, an increasing number of scholars have pointed to the significance of ideas of processuality in Indian life. Thus, stasis is undesirable (Das 1985; Ostor 1980); personhood, relationships, and matter itself are perceived as fluid, shifting, and mutable (Daniels 1984; Marriott 1989:17–18; Trawick 1990); so, too, relationships between humans and gods are more continuous (Parry 1985). Even Dumont's (1970) seemingly rigid structuralism is relevant here, given his great insight that a hierarchical system based on difference (he discussed caste) is extremely flexible, elastic, and internally expandable, so long as hierarchical relationships are maintained continuously throughout the system. None of these studies conceptualize processuality as play, yet qualities of play are very close to the ethos of processuality that informs much of the recent scholarship on India. Process as play, and play as process, are embedded deeply not only in cosmology, but also, more indirectly, in Indian cultural ideologies.

societies, the bottom-up entry of the ludic into routine living is often a battle for presence, a struggle over space and time devoted to other practices, and a confrontation over legitimacy, apart from those special occasions and places that indeed are set apart. So play often is perceived to lurk within the interstices and to spill over from the margins. Although the effortless, quicksilver qualities of play are always the same, the ontic and epistemic statuses of these qualities differ radically between cosmologies that embed such qualities at the top of the cosmic hierarchy and cosmologies that locate such qualities nearer the bottom.[81]

7
Metaphysics of the Fluid Indic Cosmos

Ancient Indo-European cosmologies, including those of India, made change integral to their operation. Bruce Lincoln discusses two complementary Indo-European visions of cosmic creation. In one, the body of a primordial being became the raw material from which the cosmos was made. In the other, the elements that comprised the phenomenal cosmos became the material from which the body of the first man was made. Lincoln argues that each vision was a phase in an encompassing process whereby "whenever the cosmos is created, the body is destroyed, and . . . whenever the body is created, the cosmos is destroyed."[82] Cosmos and body, macrocosm and microcosm were alternative forms of one another, each broken down and transformed into the other.[83]

81. Even within the carnivalesque world created by Rabelais, the most playfully subversive is more a bottom-up phenomenon. Thus, although both Gargantua and his son, Pantagruel, are bottom-up characters, the circumstances of their respective births highlight this trait in Pantagruel, the more playfully subversive of the two. Gargantua cannot come into existence naturally through his mother's birth canal and must find another aperture. Forced higher, he emerges through her left ear (Putnam 1955:69)—in other words, through her head. For all his excesses, he becomes a scholar and a subsidizer of a utopian, humanistic community. Covered in fur, Pantagruel is born from his mother's belly, killing her in childbirth (Putnam 1955:237). Pantagruel is even more subversive than his father. Within the entirety of this carnivalesque world, the playful is graduated in increasing degrees of subversion, from top to bottom—in keeping with Western monotheisms. We also question the view that the development of Protestantism was a necessary condition for the emergence of play as subversion and resistance in Western cosmologies (e.g., Norbeck 1971; Turner 1974). Though this was a significant contributing factor, such conceptions of play are associated more with cosmologies that are not self-transformative and that include Western monotheisms, as these developed long before the Reformation.

82. Lincoln 1986:33.

83. Ibid., 40.

In this kind of cosmos the only constancy was that of change. The cosmos operated by transforming itself—indeed, by reabsorbing itself. It constituted a cultural milieu within which ideas of play as cosmic process gained prominence.

Numerous Indic cosmologies are predicated on conceptions of a holistic, encompassing cosmos that goes through processes of internal differentiation by which the cosmos evolves, externalizing its planes and levels and manifesting shape and substance. So, too, cosmic processes contract and internalize, erasing differences and distinctions and returning to the holism of more homogeneous encompassment. This kind of cosmos is organized hierarchically in terms of two axes: One may be called vertical, extending from the zenith of the cosmos to its nadir; and the other, horizontal, extending from the innermost being or middle of the cosmos to its outermost externalizations. Within the cosmic whole, these two axes often are isomorphic to one another, so that the apex of the cosmos is equivalent to its innermost, contracted middle, and its nadir is equivalent to its most externalized and expanded manifestations. The whole, however this is understood, includes all its own parts, reproducing itself through them. Yet, unlike monotheistic cosmologies that invoke the absolute division and segmentation between the whole and its parts, between god and humankind, the levels of Indic cosmology are continuous with one another, processually transforming the cosmos from zenith to nadir, from deep within itself to its outermost externalizations, and back once more.

In the most ancient Sanskrit text, the *Ṛg Veda*, the cosmic Self is the undifferentiated, unreflective unity that "breathes or pulsates by itself, though without breath."[84]

> Then [before the beginning]
> there was neither death nor no-death,
> no sign of night or of day.
> The One breathed, breathless,
> through its own impulsion,
> and there was no Other of any kind.[85]

The cosmic Self is identified with the encompassing entirety of the cosmos, so that nothing exists beyond this. The Self is homogeneous and, therefore, utterly lacks any discontinuity or internal gaps. We propose that this total absence of discontinuity in the cosmos, at its most encompassing level, is akin to an extreme density of being. This thick density of the cosmic Self speaks to its

84. Miller 1985:53.

85. *Ṛg Veda* 10.129.2 (my translation, D. S.).

lack of any sense of self-awareness and motivation, and to the nonexistence of otherness. Moreover, the total absence of discontinuity points to the simultaneity of time and space and, therefore, to their nonexistence—in other words to what may be called no-time and no-space. Like the distinction between self and other, those of time and space depend on the existence of gaps and boundaries in the substance of the cosmos. We will expand on these points as they take on major significance in our discussion of cosmic processes in Saiva myths.

At some moment, for no particular reason, the cosmic Self began the directional process of differentiating itself, thereby creating the cosmic level of gods who, in turn, gave shape to human agency. Of special significance is the paradox of self-reference that is embedded in that initial moment of differentiation as (and, indeed, when) the cosmic Self became to itself simultaneously one thing and another, Self and Other.

Following the first movement of the cosmic Self, evolution continued ceaselessly through extremely lengthy periods. Nonetheless, all evolution—the externalization of cosmic distinctions—was entropic. Eventually, the process would reverse and contract itself, destroying the phenomenal cosmos and returning to the sentient but undifferentiated and unreflective cosmic Self, then beginning another cosmic cycle. The ordering of this world was never at rest, never static—but, rather, one of ongoing "becoming." The fundamental rhythms of these cosmic processes were analogous to those of expansion and contraction, externalization and internalization, or, in the language of the *Ṛg Veda*, weaving forth, weaving back.[86] Expansion and externalization connote descent and evolution through the creation of a hierarchy of increasingly material levels of phenomenal reality. Contraction and internalization refer to contrary processes that ascend to a condition of cosmic holism, effacing all differences. In this cosmos, "everything is in constant motion . . . but this constancy of movement is itself the stability of cosmic order."[87]

To this we add that in terms of cosmic evolution, in the *Ṛg Vedic* version, the horizontal axis seems to exist prior to the vertical. Initially, holism is identified with an inside rather than with an apex. In this regard, holism is, first and foremost, an internal quality, since only the inside exists. The generation of difference is from the inside out. The external is generated from within the whole that knows nothing external to itself. The vertical axis comes into being only as innerness externalizes itself.

Ideas of play were made central to this cosmogony, especially in relation to the puzzle of why the cosmic Self, utterly without desire or need, bothered to create the phenomenal universe. The concept of *līlā* answered this conundrum.

86. Miller 1985: 58.

87. Ibid., 289.

Līlā is a Sanskrit noun that means play or sport—in the sense of diversion, amusement, fun. It also connotes effortless, rapid movement.[88] The philosophers absorbed this term for their own purposes. Thus the *Vedānta Sūtra* describes the creative activity of the Divine as mere *līlā*, "such as we see in ordinary life."[89] Śaṇkara, the great teacher of nondualism, commented on this passage:

> Just as inhalation and exhalation proceed from their own being, without aiming at any external purpose, so God's activity, too, proceeds from his own being in the form of play, without aiming at any other purpose.[90]

Līlā is the motive that is without motive—spontaneous action wholly for its own sake.[91] The Divine makes and regulates the cosmos with which he is identified out of neither need nor necessity, "but by a free and joyous creativity that is integral to his own nature. He acts in a state of rapt absorption comparable to that of an artist possessed by his creative vision."[92] In *līlā*, in play, the Divine takes spontaneous delight in his own self-transformation and, therefore, in that of the cosmos with which he is homologous.[93] By providing the motive, as it were, for the ongoing creation of the phenomenal cosmos, *līlā* embeds the metamessage "This is play" both at a high level of cosmic organization and deep within the cosmos, the location of its first movement. Play undoubtedly has top-down significance in this cosmogony, and thus pervades its evolving, fluid universe.

Earlier, we commented that a paradox of self-reference was embedded in the initial movement, the very first moment of differentiation within the homogeneous cosmic Self. Through that movement of *līlā*, the cosmic Self became to itself, simultaneously, one thing and another—indeed, self and other. In this cosmos, this paradox was integral to the beginning of self-definition through difference, to the very creation of the conscious self through the division between self and other. Therefore, this division into difference opened a gap in the density of being between self and other. This was the creation of self-alienation, of fragmentation and estrangement from self, of the distancing from self and, so, knowing oneself as otherwise, because this was inherent in the creation of other from self, self from other.

88. Huizinga 1970:51.
89. *Vedānta Sūtra* 2.1.33; Thibaut 1962: 356.
90. Śaṇkara on *Vedānta Sūtra* 2.1.33.
91. See, e.g., O'Flaherty [Doniger] 1984:230.
92. Hein 1987:550.
93. Zimmer 1984:24.

This division of Self into self and other was also the process of the creation and hierarchization of cosmic holism and encompassment. Until its initial division into self-awareness and alienation, the cosmic Self had, as it were, a single plane of existence, without boundaries that could differentiate higher and lower dimensions. The distinction and separation of self and other created a level that derived from, but that was beneath, that of the undifferentiated Self. The higher level of the Self encompassed the lower level of distinctions between self and other. In other words, just as the higher levels evolved and exfoliated into lower ones, so those lower ones would contract, lose their distinctions, and fold back into the higher levels, until the highest level potentially absorbed the entire cosmos into its undifferentiated holism. The principle of encompassing holism was a hallmark of Indic cosmology from its earliest formulations.

The paradox of self-reference opening in the gap within the cosmic Self, and then within the gap between self and other, also constituted the very first boundary of this cosmos, that between self and other. So, too, this boundary created time (temporal discontinuity) and space (directional discontinuity). This boundary was created through *līlā*—that is, by the equivalent of the metamessage "This is play." Indeed, this is the boundary between not-play (the undifferentiated cosmic Self) and play (the creation of the other, and the definition of self through the other). *Līlā* also constituted the first passage through this boundary, just as this passage constituted the creation of cosmos. In this cosmology, *līlā* (play) is implicated in many of the rudiments of the creation of being and cosmos—of self and other, of the boundary between them, and of time and space.

The metamessage "This is play" imputes to the comprehensive organization of this cosmos all of the qualities of play that are embedded in the paradoxical passage from not-play to play. As noted earlier, these are the qualities of malleability and fluidity, movement and change. Movement, one may say, is the mysterious choice of the cosmic Self. It is the passage from inaction to action, from immobility to mobility. Processuality is encoded in this paradoxical passage, and cosmic action and movement are identified with play. These qualities of play are attached to all differences among levels, to all boundaries, putting them in play in the cosmic system. But even more than this, play (and its derivative, game) is the medium of division in this cosmos, the medium of separation, of fragmentation, and of alienation. Just as the holistic cosmic Self divides through play, so, too, in many later myths, play takes apart self, cosmos, and cosmic relationships. One may well argue that in Indic cosmologies, the ludic always differentiates and is implicated in some sort of devolution and diminishment of holism (unless these processes are carefully controlled against, as in the Vedic Rājasūya ritual that we discuss later).

IN OTHER DESCRIPTIONS of cosmogenesis in which play is not mentioned explicitly, but in which processuality nonetheless has attributes akin to the playful, the initial act of self-consciousness again involves a paradox of self-reference in relation to the first boundary between self and nothing/something. So, too, cosmogenesis emphasizes innerness, even when the self is not the sole form or null form that has cosmic existence. To illustrate this notion more concretely, we address in detail one of the richest of all surviving Vedic cosmogonies, from *Bṛhadāraṇyaka Upaniṣad* 1.4. This text begins with the presence of *puruṣa*, the cosmic male:

> At first all this was only self, something like a male person. He looked around and saw nothing other than self; so he said—in the beginning—"I am." That is how the name "I" came to be. That is why when someone is addressed, he first says, "That is I," and then adds whatever other name he may have. Being there before all this, he had burned up [*auṣat*] all forms of evil; that is why he is called *puruṣa*—a male. Anyone who knows this burns up whoever seeks to be there before him.
>
> He was afraid. That is why a person who is alone is afraid. Then he considered: "Since there is nobody other than me, whom do I fear?" Then fear left him—was there anyone he could have feared? Fear only comes into being when there is a second.
>
> But he felt no joy. A person who is alone has no joy. He longed for a second person. He assumed the measure of a man and woman in tight embrace. He made his self fall [*apātayat*] into two, and that is how husband and wife [*pati/patnī*] came into being. That is why anything that is one's own is really but a fragment broken in half, as Yājñavalkya used to say. That is why this open space is filled up with a wife. He came together with her, and from that human beings were born.
>
> She considered: "How can he come together with me after producing me from himself? I had better hide." She became a cow, and he became a bull and joined her: cattle were born. She became a mare, and he a horse; she was a female ass, and he a male ass that joined her: solid-hoofed animals were born. She became a she-goat, he a he-goat; she a ewe, he a ram, which joined her: goats and sheep were born. In this way he externalized everything, whatever exists in pairs, right down to the ants.
>
> He knew: "I am this outpouring [*sṛṣṭi*], I have externalized all of this." That is how the cosmos emerged outside. Whoever knows this comes into being in that externalized cosmos.
>
> He rubbed together, emitting fire from his mouth and vagina and hands. So both of these have no hair inside them, and the vagina is also without hair inside. When people say, "Worship this one or that one"—one god or other—that is all externalized out of him, and he is all the gods. Whatever is wet he emitted from seed, and that is Soma. All of this is either food or an eater of food: Soma

is food, and fire is the eater. But Brahman—the fullness of language—was over-externalized, in that he emitted the great gods, and in that, mortal himself, he emitted immortals. This is an over-externalization [*atisṛṣṭi*]: and whoever knows it comes into being in that over-externalized cosmos.

Then none of this was yet divided. It became divided through name and form: "This is a name, this has that form." Even now, it is by name and form that everything is divided: "This is a name, this has that form." He entered here up to his fingernails, as a razor lies in its sheath, or the all-bearing fire in its container. They cannot see him, for he is not whole. When breathing, he becomes breath; speaking, speech; seeing, eye; hearing, ear; thinking, mind: these are his action-names. One who thinks of them one by one does not know, for he is not whole as he becomes them one by one; but if one thinks this is self, then all of them become one in this. This self is the footprint of all that, for by this, one knows all that, as one might track down someone by his footprint. Anyone who knows this finds fame and renown.

This, the self, is more dear than a son, or than wealth, or than anything else, for it is more internal. . . .

In effect, the text begins *before* the beginning, with a powerful sense of prior movement—an internal split or boundary—within the godhead. The first division here is between self and nothing, self and the absence of self. There is no other, but there is a vacuity of space/time, empty of any being. Thus, something (the self) exists in relation to its negation (vacuity). So, too, nothingness (emptiness) exists in relation to its negation (again, emptiness). But there also is the intimation that initially *puruṣa* was not the sole form of the cosmos:

Being there before all of this, he had burned up [*auṣat*] all forms of evil; that is why he is called *puruṣa*—a male.

Fire—for that matter, heat in general, as we shall see—is a dense but fluid destroyer of categories, of boundaries that define categories of being. These categories are existential externalizations of phenomenal existence. The intimation is that the godhead had divided previously; that self-division (e.g., externalization of the whole) was "evil" in the sense that all fragmentations of the whole are evil;[94] and that the godhead had melted down (e.g., burned) the boundary it had created between self and other, thereby reintegrating itself. Yet this recoalescence had left a paradoxical remnant—emptiness, the negation of self, the cancellation of the selfhood that now existed together with self. This is the context of the self's declaration of a self-reference, "I am." Moreover, at this juncture the feeling of the cosmic self in relation to its contrastive nega-

94. Cf. Kapferer 1988a, on Buddhist Sri Lanka.

tion was one of fear. At first sight, this seems rather distant from the ludic impulsion of the *Ṛg Veda.*

> He was afraid. That is why a person who is alone is afraid. Then he considered: "Since there is nobody other than me, whom do I fear?" Then fear left him—was there anyone he could have feared? Fear only comes into being when there is a second.

The cosmic self faces the void—his self-definition, his boundary of being, exist not through another (i.e., through one who offers a contrastive perspective on selfhood), but only through their self-nullification. The cosmic self knows his self through its absence; "I am" slips smoothly, as it were, into "I am not." The latter offers no explicit basis for the reconstitution of selfhood. Not being (like not-play) is, here, the alternative to being (like play). If being can externalize to fill the void that it has created out of self-differentiation and destruction of the other (where the void is itself also a form of the self-destruction of holism, and therefore "evil"), then this void can empty the self of its being, vacuuming out the self's innerness so that there is no self-reconstitution—hence the fear of the cosmic being.

We have seen how the ludic impulse is pervaded with uncertainty—indeed, how this impulse is the very motion of indeterminacy. Here we stress that the uncertainty of play and that of terror "are not necessarily genteel kissing cousins, but intimate, perhaps incestuous, bedmates. The play of forces is never more exhilarating nor frightening than when boundaries are breached and identities blurred."[95] The phenomenologist Eugen Fink argues that "play can contain within itself not only the clear apollonian moment of free self-determination, but also the dark dionysian moment of panic self-abandon."[96] Terror and play are both forceful modes of introducing uncertainty, and their affinities are undeniable. Play and fear are always confrontations with being, with questioning the nature or shape of self-identity.

The recognition of uncertainty is that of the deep flux of unpredictability, especially through relatively short durations[97]; of processes of change—indeed, of the capacity of changeability itself. Uncertainty and play are cognate in phenomenal knowledge, existential feelings, and bodily senses.[98] Uncertainty may be valorized as beneficial (true, moral, sacred), as harmful (evil, immoral, demonic), or as neutral (amoral, indifferent), but all of these index an organic

95. Handelman 1990:67.

96. Fink 1968.

97. As so-called chaos theory also argues: see, e.g., Kellert 1993.

98. Handelman 1990.

cosmos that has the profound self-knowledge of indeterminacy. One should never forget that the Indic cosmos is not mechanistic, but is organic, alive. In this cosmos the metamessage, "This is play" can be rephrased as "This is uncertainty"—the self-recognition of processuality and creativity. The paradoxical passage to play, as seen above, is the passage to realities pervaded by uncertainty, whether in cosmogenesis or in dice games, as we shall see.

The cosmic being in the *Upaniṣad* is afraid of the uncertainty of the void, implicit in a sense of the potential void within himself, and, so, of play and its division into the gaps of otherness and separation. Uncertainty puts in question the determinacy—or, one may say, the validity—of the phenomenal and its existential being. Ironically, the cosmic self loses fear of the void when he recognizes its emptiness as an externalization of himself—one that has no being, no agency, but that is a self-spaciousness that he can fill with the phenomenal existence of otherness, with someone different from himself. Yet this otherness again is threatening.

> Fear only comes into being when there is a second.

> He felt no joy. A person who is alone has no joy. He longed for a second person,

even though he feared this. Just as the unselfconscious, paradoxical impulse to play, described for the utterly dense Cosmic Self of the *Ṛg Veda*, leads to its fragmentation and separation, so here, too, the already self-conscious cosmic self, paradoxically defined in terms of his existing potential for self-emptiness and self-nullification, will move in the same direction.

> He assumed the measure of a man and a woman in tight embrace. He made his self fall [*apātayat*] into two, which is how husband and wife [*pati/patnī*] came into being. That is why anything that is one's own is really but a fragment broken in half, as Yājnavalkya used to say. That is why this open space is filled up with a wife. He came together with her, and from that human beings were born.

Fleetingly, there is, in this text, the image of the cosmogonic, evolving androgynous externalization of the self on its way to a greater fragmentation ("He assumed the measure of a man and a woman in tight embrace"), which then separates and congeals further ("He made his self fall into two"). The female embodies and accentuates otherness, disguise, illusion—all that in later, Purāṇic texts will be identified with the powers of *māyā* associated with Śiva's active female part (e.g., Pārvatī). In the *Upaniṣad*, the female's desire for illusion, for taking on increasing otherness, is the direct consequence of the self's attempt to fill the external void that he fears, and that he tries to fill with the substance of an other self. In this text, the otherness of the female's capacity for illusion, of the male self's current potential for viewing himself externally through a myriad of angles of division, leads directly to the self's ongoing fragmentation, externalization, and congealing. "Evil" is the direct consequence of the creation of otherness, of the need to empty oneself in order to fill oneself by creating difference (e.g., externalization and descent). By the same token, hiding also depends on otherness, on the externalization of parts of the self as gaps or holes. One cannot hide within the self (in its nonexternalized fullness). It is only after the female has emerged, as an autonomous force, that self-disguise and masking become necessary options. In a sense, they now play at hide-and-seek—although it is primarily he who does the seeking, while she enacts an innate affinity with being hidden:

> She considered: "How can he come together with me after producing me from his self? I had better hide." She became a cow, and he became a bull and joined her: cattle were born. She became a mare, and he a horse; she was a female ass, and he a male ass that joined her: solid-hoofed animals were born. She became a she-goat, he a he-goat; she a ewe, he a ram, which joined her; goats and sheep were born. In this way he externalized everything, whatever exists in pairs, right down to the ants.

"She"—the female fragment—hid in the guise of various others, and he joined her time after time. Presumably, each of these others is an act of imagination that externalizes space within the self, ironically enlarging the void that it is trying to fill by creating more and more internal divisions and separations—the host of beings, from cattle to ants—within itself. Each of these acts of imagination is classified by name and form, and, therefore, is consciously known—a point of critical importance to this text. Increasingly, the self empties itself—inside out—into the nullification of itself, filling this self-generated emptiness that cannot be filled, except by time-filled illusions or shapes of self. It is very striking that imagination per se is a kind of hole or absence: Such an opening of space through self-extrusion is the creative impulse at the core of Hindu notions of being. The self-conscious imagining of difference—moving from the tight joining of the androgynous figure to separate human genders, and then to a host of beings—is the externalization of the cosmos. By this logic, anything formed, solid, or visible—a living person, a carved image, a temple—is first a consolidated, congealed gap. But this externalization seems to expand the cosmos beyond the void that accompanies the cosmic self, the emptiness filled by the woman and her disguises, her hiding from her self and from his (and, therefore, their ongoing creation of difference and otherness).

The female's guising, through the invention of form, is playful, *māyā*-like, and it produces the differences of the phenomenal cosmos through an ongoing, hierarchical process, from cattle to the lowly ants. But more than this, the human cosmic pair experience the existential interiors of each form as they externalize these. They imagine and create each being, each thing, from its own inside. Therefore, all of these beings of the cosmos, from inside to out, from top to bottom, share affinities of existential knowledge and know one another in some sense, even though they are so phenomenally different. Their differences are characterized by homologic connections that will enable them to contract into one another. All are connected beings of the cosmos, from outside to in, from bottom to top.

> He knew: "I am this outpouring [*sṛṣṭi*], I have externalized all of this." This is how the cosmos emerged outside.

But now Brahman becomes "over-externalized" [*atisṛṣṭi*],

> in that he emitted the great gods, and in that, mortal himself, he emitted immortals. This is an over-externalization.

The imagining of the cosmos (in itself, ludic creativity)—that is, the creation of its spaciousness—spirals and expands in all directions, as it were, from the cosmic self, upward (the great gods) as well as downward (the ants). In a word, the expansion of the cosmos extends at least through four dimensions. The early gods, regardless of their great encompassment, are themselves reifications who attain or prove their hierarchical positioning by defeating and subsuming their opponents. The imagining of overexternalization (like that also of externalization) has to do with the symbolic potential of language for going far beyond the literality of its words, to imagine shapes and relationships that supersede its linguistic forms. In the *Upaniṣad*, Brahman consciously imagines immortality, and thereby brings it into being out of himself, but in space (the upward direction, as it were) that encompasses him as well. Once immortality is reified existentially (as distinct, for example, from the unconscious, phenomenal existence of the *Ṛg Vedic* Cosmic Self before its ludic division), it supersedes the mortal being who created it, making him part of its own externality.

In this formulation, immortality, no less than mortality, is a cosmic creation. Gods, like humans, are artifices of cosmic construction, and the horizontal axis of the inner to the other contains within itself the vertical axis of top to bottom. Yet ultimate innerness, like ultimate apicity, sometimes seems to elude god no less than immortality eludes the great bulk of humanity. The cosmos teeters uncertainly on its axes and will cease to exist if one stops imagining it, stops playing with it—for then the cosmos returns to its densest, homogeneous innerness. Yet the cosmos imagined and played with also will cease to exist if it is emptied utterly, and innerness turns wholly into otherness. The self must exist for the cosmos to exist—and this, nonetheless, seems to be a function of the deep innerness of being: *"This, the self, is more dear than a son, or than wealth, or than anything else, for it is more internal."* This also explains why the self must be active in order for it, and itself as the cosmos, to exist; why this activity generates differences and, ironically, the destruction of selfhood through otherness; and why the most powerful process of reintegrating a holistic selfhood is a process of innerness, rather than the clash of exterior forms, or their interpenetration and fusion. Through all of this, the power of the self to impart identity through imagining itself creates all beings—gods no less than ants.

In later Hinduism, the character of play (*līlā*) became embedded within deities themselves. Here, *līlā* is related to their capacity to manifest themselves within the human world. Their shifts among levels and their abrupt appearances among humankind are the embodied effects of cosmic processes in the world.[99] Their appearances are paradoxical. Prominent among these conundra is the paradox of the infinite god who is "embedded in finite form" at the human level of the cosmos.[100] This puzzle plays on the simultaneous difference, yet nondifference, between god and humankind and on their simultaneous separation, but non-separation, from one another. To humankind, deity is, at one and the same time, transcendent and immanent, unknowable and knowable [*bheda/abheda*].[101]

For example, the god Kṛṣṇa is a human form (*avatāra*) of the god Viṣṇu. Kṛṣṇa contains the entire cosmos within himself. He is a child who is full of spontaneous, mischievous fun, playing with his own shadow, stealing butter, eating dirt. He is a beautiful youth playing the flute, frolicking with, and seducing, the village girls.[102] He is the misshapen, monstrous, primeval Jagganāth. As Dimock comments, all of these Kṛṣṇas are real and all are really Kṛṣṇa—

99. Although we do not discuss the Indian concept of *māyā* here, its associations with gods and their capacities to transform phenomenal worlds are strongly resonant with the idea of *līlā*/play. The Sanskrit term *māyā* derives from the same Indo-European root as Greek *mētis* (see Burrow 1980), "cunning intelligence." In cosmology, Mĕtis was a primordial female deity. Among the connotations of *mētis* are: fast or incessant movement, swiftness, mobility, shimmering sheen, the power of metamorphosis, and multiplicity. Gods and humans endowed with *mētis* were able to dominate (or perhaps manage?) uncertain, fluid, rapidly changing situations. See Detienne and Vernant 1978:5–23. In Śaivism, *māyā* is understood as female.

100. Dimock 1989:164.

101. Ibid., 192; Handelman 1987.

102. See Hawley 1981; Kinsley 1975.

each form is the infinite, essential godhead.[103] These forms are his play, his *līlās*, because "the full deity [who is the cosmos] is in constant motion and therefore of ever-changing form."[104] The deity simultaneously encompasses the cosmos and appears within it in a different form, as a part of himself.

Similarly, Śiva is simultaneously higher and lower, transcendent and immanent in his play, his *līlās*.[105] "All the time that Śiva made love with Satī [his wife], it was just his divine play, for he was entirely self-controlled and without emotional excitement the whole time; . . . when Satī died, Śiva, the great Yogi, wept like a lover in agony, but this is just his divine play, to act like a lover, for in fact he is unconquered and without emotional excitement."[106] These playful transformations of god within himself—of god slipping into the gaps within himself, as we explain later—are crucial to an understanding of the relationship of god in cosmic dice games as a part of himself, the cosmic whole.

As we mentioned in relation to the cosmic Self, the motion of *līlā* intimates motive in the creation of the phenomenal universe. Moreover, the appearance of *līlā* is that of the Divine, the manifestation of cosmic process on different levels of the universe. In both instances, this presence of play (like that of fright) is necessarily one of boundaries. In the first instance—that of creation—*līlā* points to the making of boundaries—that is, to the forming of those differences among phenomena that define and constitute the world. In the second—the transformative manifestation of deity—*līlā* accomplishes passage through boundaries. As we commented earlier, because the idea of play, of *līlā*, is often embedded at a high level of cosmic organization, it influences the fluidity and permeability of boundaries. Play, the creative imagining of the cosmos in its multitude of externalized differences, bursts from deep within the cosmos, and barriers to passage are transmuted more into way stations. The playful, continuous movement of cosmic forces among levels relates directly to the transformative character of the entire cosmos.

This concern with the fluid character of boundaries has a long history in India. Finding the correct balance in the substance of boundaries was an ontological problem of ancient Indian cosmogonies. There was an emphasis on malleability and change, on the necessity of making adjustments to the quality of boundaries, because their creator was imperfect in his creations. Thus the parts of the cosmos might be insufficiently differentiated from one another, and, therefore, too similar to one another (*jāmi*). These boundaries were overly

103. Dimock 1976:113 and 1989:165.

104. Dimock 1976:113; Handelman 1987; see also Handelman 1995.

105. See Dessigane, Pattabiramin, and Filliozat 1960.

106. *Śivapurāṇa* 2.2.24.16, 2.3.4.32–40, cited in O'Flaherty 1973:147.

soft and shapeless, and so the parts they bounded became joined indiscriminately, losing their distinctiveness and producing cosmic chaos. Or, the parts might be excessively differentiated from one another, thereby lacking all connectivity and, therefore, separated and dispersed without any cohesion (*pṛthak*). These boundaries were overly rigid, preventing all interaction between parts and, again, producing cosmic chaos.[107]

Apart from the ontic need to create the correct balance of separation and connection in boundaries between the levels and domains of the cosmos, two concepts were crucial to the integration of the ancient Vedic universe. In one way or another, the ramifications of these concepts also reverberate in later Hindu cosmologies. One concept was *nidāna*, meaning a rope, tie, or bond. The other, *bandhu*, indexed relationships that can be formulated as follows: "X is so 'bound' to Y that X is Y."[108] The cosmos was tied together and made whole by connections of homologic identity (*bandhu*), while knowledge constituted the capacity to tie together these connections. In this cosmic infrastructure, everything was connected to everything else, and therefore, all relationships were mutual in their causal effects. Given the hierarchical character of the cosmos, these connections of homologic identity were bound together most tightly within its deepest innerness and at its highest levels. The more such bonds were tied closely to one another, the deeper and higher were the degrees of encompassment that they signified in the hierarchically organized cosmic whole.

These continuous levels of the hierarchical cosmos may be conceptualized, as we commented above, in terms of the graduated density of their cosmic connections. These connections are extremely dense at the deepest and highest levels of the cosmos, where there is little or no differentiation, no externalization of self, nor creation of other. These connections become correspondingly less dense as cosmic levels externalize and descend. A most important corollary of this conception of cosmic density is that at the deepest and highest levels of holism and encompassment, everything exists simultaneously. In this tightest, highest, and most internal of cosmic weaves, time, space, and self do not exist. To paraphrase Henri Bergson, everything happens at once, and therefore, there are no discontinuities.

At these levels of encompassment, the simultaneity of everything means the existence of what may be called the "total knowledge" of the cosmos. In Vedic cosmology the totality of knowledge was more impersonal but, nonetheless, integral to the being of the cosmos. In later forms of Hinduism, the totality of knowledge was lodged in supreme deities, like Śiva, who were identified with

107. See Smith 1989:50–69.

108. Knipe 1975:43.

the cosmic whole. Total knowledge is possible at these interior, high levels of encompassment because there are no gaps, no tears or lacunae, in the extreme denseness of cosmic homologies. Space and time exist only in and through such gaps, in and through the distance between here and there, between one connection and another, across a boundary. Without these gaps in cosmic density, there is no before and after, no past and future, and no region of openness or spaciousness that can be called space. At this level of deity, every place is the same and all possible events are known everywhere. Given the simultaneity of total knowledge at this level, nothing is indeterminate or unexpected. All tenses exist simultaneously. This level is the omnipotence of the godhead.

As levels of the cosmos externalize and descend, the extremely tight density of cosmic connections loosens. One may say that tears open in the tightly knotted cosmic weave. As the unified, homogeneous godhead fragments, externalizes itself, and divides into self and other, time, space, and language come into existence. Thus the gap, the distance between self and other, is spatial and linguistic—someone is positioned separately from someone else, in communication, across this gap, with that other; while the rupture between self and other opens into temporal and linguistic pulsations that constitute the past (their unity), present (their division), and future.

> Time is that through which growth and diminution in congealed forms can be observed.[109]

Patañjali is referring to increases and decreases in the externalization and concretization of externalized forms. Since the godhead, the highest encompassment of the holistic cosmos, constitutes the cosmos on all its levels, so does the godhead's total knowledge of the determinate universe. But total knowledge does not exist for beings such as lesser gods, the *asura* antigods,[110] or humans whose natural locations are on more exterior, lower levels of cosmic organization, and whose ascent within and burrowing into the cosmos should therefore not exceed those levels of affinity to which they belong. Like their own existence as parts within the cosmic whole, their knowledge of cosmic connections and of their own futures are, correspondingly, occluded and limited.

The descent into time is a descent into difference, into periodization, in a relation to otherness that may only be temporal since the other is external to, but also a part of, self—in other words, they remain connected. The descent

109. See n. 17; Cardona 1991:448, citing Patañjali 1.409.

110. We discuss the existential character of these beings in chapter II. At this point, we note simply that the *asuras* are the great rivals of the gods; that they tend toward violent externalization, often cutting off the softer parts of their own bodies; and that their cosmos tends to be rigid and static.

into time entails slowing down, counting, congealing, forming—a movement into lineality, into gender, into relationships. "The universe of all there is is divided by time through its inhibiting and permitting particular acts to occur. . . . For if time did not inhibit and also let go of such inhibition, stages of evolution [i.e., externalization, contraction] would become intermixed, without their due sequence."[111] The externalized, multiformed cosmos is bursting with the porousness of time, with a host of differentiated activities, just as the more externalized deity bursts forth with a multitude of arms, legs, heads.[112]

During "routine" operations of the cosmos, there are probably no unexpected occurrences for the cosmic encompassment, since he exists simultaneously at the zenith and core of the cosmos and on all its graduated levels as lesser forms of himself.[113] How then does this kind of cosmos generate the unusual (for example, new forms of being) on its higher levels, perhaps with destructive consequences that reverberate throughout its being? Cosmic dice games and other ludic processes are significant media for creating new forms of existence and unanticipated outcomes in mythologies, Śaiva and other ones.

Virtually every time that Śiva enters the game of dice as a player, he loses the qualities of holism, of his absolute identity with the cosmos, and leaves the contest diminished. Thus the highest form of god, of the totality of cosmic being and knowledge, consistently loses at dice and other ludic forms, fragmenting, shedding parts of his self and diminishing the cosmos with which he is identified. What then is the epistemological status of the ludic process in Indic myth (and ritual)? In other words, what does the ludic do to the cosmic process? We are certain that the dice game is not a mirrorlike reflection of the cosmos.[114] Rather, the dice game is what we call a "model" of cosmos, which acts on the very cosmos that it simulates in order to create something new, perhaps unexpected, within the determinate order of the universe. The dice game is a strange loop that ruptures cosmic holism, with unusual consequences. Neither Śiva nor his supporters expect to lose, but the consequences of his losses are predictable to the extent that they are destructive and catastrophic for cosmic order.

We gloss the consequences of Śiva's losses as the Andhaka outcome—after his flawed, black, blind son created through ludic process; a destroyer of the moral universe; decimated, in turn, by his father and turned into the even more diminished, skeletal Bhṛṅgin, who cannot even stand upright without support. Yet unlike Andhaka (and the problems of evil that he raises), Bhṛṅgin, the virtual dead end (indeed, the endgame) of gender externalization and devo-

111. Cardona 1991:448–49.

112. Handelman 1987:157–60.

113. See Kapferer 1983.

114. As, e.g., Hiltebeitel 1987 argues.

lution, is brought back into the moral order of the cosmos. Śiva makes Bhṛṅgin the chief of his grotesque, flawed followers, the *gaṇas*. Śiva thus embraces the hierarchical ordering of the cosmos, from its innermost dense connectivity to its outermost fragmentation.

8
Generating the Expected: The Rājasūya Dice Game and the Modeling of the Cosmos

We argue that in Indian cosmology, play is top-down. The ludic, in general, and dice games, in particular, open gaps in the dense interconnectivity of the cosmos. Higher-order figures (including the greatest of deities) lose their total knowledge of holism when they enter models of their own cosmos—that is, when they enter games as players. These games set the cosmos in motion. Nonetheless, higher-order beings commonly lose in these games. This outcome is destructive for the cosmos. The holistic cosmic encompassment undergoes division, fragmentation, externalization, and evolution, often against its own desire. The modeling of a cosmos limits and externalizes itself through play, thereby generating unanticipated consequences. The first step in understanding how this occurs is to discuss a case in which it does not—in other words, the conditions under which a game produces exactly the expected and desired outcome.

The Rājasūya, "king-engendering,"[115] constituted an annual series of Vedic rites for the cosmic regeneration and rebirth of kingship. In these rites, the king as embryo was made homologous with the encompassment of cosmic holism through the manipulation of *bandhu* connections. Yearly, the universe was recreated so that the king incorporated the cosmos. There is no need here to discuss the rites that preceded the dice game, except to note that each ritual complex in the series was constructed as a homologous model of the cosmos; that the king had an active role in the operation of these models;[116] and that through these operations, the king and the cosmos were reborn as homologous images of one another.

Toward the end of the sequence of rites, the enthronement of the king was accompanied by a game of dice. The game was probably played with dice made of nuts of the *vibhītaka* tree. The king mounted the throne, which was addressed as the womb of kingship and the navel of the world. Four gutters homologized with four world streams that originated at the throne and that divided the uni-

115. Heesterman 1957:86.
116. E.g., ibid., 120.

verse into quadrants, with the throne/navel/cosmic mountain at the center.[117] As we have commented, there are powerful identities here and in later Indian cosmologies between the center and zenith of the cosmos—both are homologous with cosmic encompassment. Thus the king was reborn, simultaneously, in the middle of the cosmos and at its zenith.

The Rājasūya game was put together through the complex integration of homologies among elements of the universe. Seated on the throne before the game began, the king was handed five dice, homologized spatially with the five cardinal directions (including the zenith) and the quadrants of the universe they demarcated. Four persons actually played the game—a Brahman, a Kṣatriya, a Vaiśya, and a Śūdra. Each player represented one of the elementary *varṇa* categories of the Indian system, themselves homologized with parts of the human body, from head to foot. The form of this body in turn was homologized with the shape of the cosmos. So, too, the number five was homologized temporally with the great world periods of cosmic duration (*yugas*). The player who won a round always handed five dice, correlated to the cosmic regions, to the enthroned king.

Heesterman has suggested that the rounds of the game won by the *kṛta* throw (itself implicating cosmogony) homologized the powers of the macrocosm (wind, fire, sun, moon, water) with those of the somatic microcosm (breath, voice, eye, ear, thought) within the being of the king.[118] As the embryonic cosmos, the king contracted and internalized this universe within himself, and then externalized this once more, creating division, difference, and descent.[119] The Rājasūya dice game was undoubtedly a model or simulation of the cosmos, constituted through ties of homology, and operated to give rebirth and regeneration to this universe.

We need to explicate our usage of the concept of model to characterize divine dice games and other cosmic contests in India. The term *model* is common in English-language usage. In its dictionary rendition, for example, a model may refer to "a standard, an example used as a canon," and to "a representation or pattern in miniature . . . of something to be made on a larger scale."[120] These definitions contain two aspects—thinking and doing—that often are attributed to the concept. A model is good for thinking with (a standard, a canon) or for doing with (a miniature of something to be made). This usage parallels the broad distinctions between "knowing that" and "knowing how," which are made by Gilbert Ryle;[121] and those between "models of" and "models for,"

117. Heesterman 1957:149.

118. Ibid., 155.

119. See also, the discussion in Falk 1986:163–74.

120. *Concise English Dictionary*, 1982.

121. Ryle 1975:27–32.

which are made by Clifford Geertz,[122] who based his usage on Ryle's. In these instances, models abstract reality in coherent ways by selecting, simplifying, and condensing various of its aspects and relationships. Models also provide directions for the reformulation of these abstractions into action. The most frequent usage of model in anthropology is that of "folk model"—the mental or cognitive commonsense constructs through which people grasp and account for their worlds.[123] Our usage is more restrictive, and bears a limited correspondence to what Max Black calls an "analogue model," one that "shares with its original not a set of features or an identical proportionality of magnitudes but, more abstractly, the same structure or pattern of relationships."[124] We would qualify the necessity of "sameness" in structure and pattern, and add that what is crucial is how these are made to work in contrast to the template from which they derive[125] We will isolate and emphasize several primary features of this kind of model.

First, the model necessarily is a reduction and simplification of the cosmos and subsumes in its composition certain aspects of the latter. Therefore, through stipulated homologies, the model retains its connectivity to the cosmos that it models. Thus, as Heesterman shows, the structure of the Rājasūya dice game is constituted as a limited selection of cosmic principles that are stipulated to connect to and to effect one another. However, though the Rājasūya dice game is homologous with the cosmos it models, it is not fully isomorphic with this cosmos.

Of special significance here (yet given little attention in other scholarly references to the Rājasūya) is that the king—the holistic, divine encompassment who activates and regulates the cosmos outside the game—does not enter the dice contest as an active player. Handed the dice of the cardinal directions at the outset, he accrues the fruits of the game before it begins, just as he is handed the winnings (the parts of the cosmic whole) of each round of the contest. From the perspective of the king (the cosmic whole), all unpredictability is eliminated from the game, and, therefore, the king cannot lose. Again, from the perspective of the cosmic whole, the player who actually loses in the game is of no relevance, since the king always wins. The hierarchical encompassment of cosmic holism is never put at risk here, since the embryonic cosmos is not in play, but is expanded and externalized into difference by the results of the game. Put otherwise, in the Rājasūya game, god does not enter within the partial simulation of himself that is the game.

122. Geertz 1973:93ff.

123. For example, Holy and Stuchlik 1981.

124. Black 1962:223.

125. See Handelman 1990:23–40, 116–35, for a more general discussion that applies the concept of model to certain forms of ritual.

An alternative strategy of ensuring the outcome is exemplified by the ancient Vedic Aśvamedha ("horse sacrifice") ritual. In these rites, the king's horse was set free to wander for a period of one year. This was a form of ritualized conquest, since the accompanying king's army had to make certain (by force, if necessary) that the rulers on whose land the horse trod gave fealty to the king. If the year of wandering ended without a defeat for the king's army, the horse was returned and sacrificed, after which the officiating priest declared the king a cosmic ruler.[126] The wandering of the horse was preceded by a gigantic dice game that "symbolically encompasses every possible permutation of family, social, political, and cosmic relationships or ties."[127] But here again the king himself was not a player. The purpose of this ritual dice game was to eliminate (by sacrifice) the only throw of the dice (the *kṛta*) that could defeat (whether by luck, fate, or destiny) the king and thereby thwart the success of the horse's wanderings and eventual sacrifice. In this dice game, "every possible counterstroke to the royal horse—in the year of wandering that is to follow—is played out and neutralized in advance,"[128] thereby ensuring the victorious conclusion: horse sacrifice and the king's enthronement as divine ruler.

Neither the Rājasūya nor the Aśvamedha dice game was fully isomorphic with the entirety of cosmic connections and encompassment, nor could they be, since their intention was to generate cosmic process, but only in particular ways. Something of cosmic significance is always missing (and necessarily so) in the ways these microcosms are constituted. More bluntly, if these games were isomorphic with the full density of cosmic connectivity and encompassment, then they could not function as games, as contests, since where there is no-time and no-space, without the division of self and other, nothing takes place that is not simultaneously taking place. As we will show, the cosmic dice game can have existence only on a lower level of cosmic density and encompassment. For that matter, the dice game is itself a lower level phenomenon, a gap that opens in cosmic density, and that, like all such gaps, acquires shape through its own evolving interaction with other evolving connections and any lack of these.

The cosmic, mythic dice games (unlike the ritual games of the Rājasūya and Aśvamedha) are not a *deus ex machina*, a hard, rigid form of game that is stuck into the evolving plasticity of cosmic form, and that molds the cosmos around its rules. The cosmic games, like the other gaps in the cosmos, are all relatively soft shapes whose forms twist and turn (perhaps in Möbius fashion) as they congeal, and whose shapes may be effected by a variety of cosmic con-

126. White 1989:284.

127. Ibid., 300.

128. Ibid., 302.

nections and disconnections. While the androgyne ruptures into new forms, the dice game is twisting into its labile shape. Śiva and Pārvatī are each given a name and gender—in a process which puts them further and further away from one another, negating, step by step, any return to wholeness, or any move toward sexuality. So, too, the cosmic game is given a name and form. It is more a game than it is anything else. It is played as a game, with definite rules, though the players manipulate the soft margins of these strictures even as they congeal into hard, fixed edges of externalized existence.

Second, whatever its stipulated limits, the game model is a domain governed by rules that enable it to be activated and played as a total world in and of itself, without any intervention by external agencies. The logic of the model is that of a system of interrelated connections and interdependent parts that moves in accordance with rules of play. The operations of the model (the game) have an effect on the cosmos only because the model and modeled are not isomorphic. From the view of an external, higher-order observer, the model is only a version, or a part, of the cosmos it models. But from within itself, the model fills the world of its participants, assuming a totality of discourse. God, outside the game, is the most dense level of cosmic encompassment, and, therefore, has omnipotent knowledge. Inside the game, god, within a model of himself as the cosmos, is limited without knowing this. For the model behaves as if it were the cosmic whole; and once in operation, it contains all the information necessary to continue to a conclusion whose nature is stipulated at the outset. So, within its rules or parameters, the Rājasūya game contains the agency necessary to generate and to complete a universe that indexes cosmic regeneration. More than this, its rules prevent any other outcome.

Third, the model is teleological. The goals of the model, and the means to attain these, are contained within the model itself, and are specified at the outset of its operation; they generate cause-and-effect relationships between rules, practices, and the outcome. Without doubt, the relationships postulated within the dice game are causal ones. The model is a maker of change that, should the rules stipulate this, is neither haphazard nor aimless. The Rājasūya and Aśvamedha games preview hypothetical futures that will be brought into being, and provide procedures that will actualize these acts of cultural imagination. As von Wright comments: "Teleological explanations point to the future. 'This happened in order that that should occur.'"[129] Since on the more exterior, lower cosmic level of the model, this future existence does not yet exist, the model must have predictive capabilities. Put otherwise, the Rājasūya and Aśvamedha dice games contain their futures within themselves, and control processes of causality that actualize these futures.

129. von Wright 1971:83.

The dice in Indian games take different shapes—nuts, cubes, rectangles. But regardless of their form, the dice themselves are little models of the cosmos, within the modeling of the dice game. Thus, a model is embedded within a model, as one can see from descriptions such as the following, offered by the familiar sage Nārada on the occasion of another visit to Śiva on Kailāsa (here, Nārada, "driven by longing," is hoping to extricate the god from the dice game in which he is engrossed, together with the goddess):

> God of gods, your game is the entire cosmos. The squares on the diceboard are the twelve months. The pieces in play are the thirty lunar days—the lit and unlit, the black and the unblack. The pair of dice are the summer and winter paths of the sun. Externalization [*sṛṣṭi*] and reabsorption [*pralaya*] are the names of the two stakes—victory and defeat. If the goddess wins, that means externalization; if Śiva wins, that means nonexternalization [*asṛṣṭi*]. The rules of the game are fixed. That is why I say: Everything there is, is play—this whole cosmos that belongs to the two of you. The goddess cannot beat her husband, and the god can't overcome his *śakti*. And I have one more thing to say to the Mother: Although god is omniscient, he understands nothing at all [within the dice game?], since he remains very far removed from both honor and disgrace. His very being is play [*līlātmā*]. . . . Since he is in the center of everything, he is utterly impartial [literally, centered]. . . .[130]

The dice (here, "paths of the sun," spatially and temporally correlated to the dynamics of the cosmos) are *always* what we call "modular detonators," which, through their action, must generate causal connections. Yet these connections are those allowed by the dice game's modeling of the cosmos. Just as the model is not isomorphic with what it models, so, too, the operations of the model are constrained by its values—in other words, by its limits or parameters. So, for example, the Rājasūya dice game cannot generate an unexpected form of cosmic encompassment, one not called for by its rules or program, nor can it destroy the cosmos. Moreover, the variously enfolded models are not isomorphic with one another; each is its own, different reduction of the cosmos. Homologies between models at different levels—for example, those articulated in *bandhu* connections—are ultimately limited in scope, and can never transcend, or do away with, the game (except in the hands of the trickiest players, as discussed in section 12).

Fourth, the outcome generated within the model impacts on that which is modeled. The dice game, and the dice embedded within the game, are constituted through homologies. Since the dice model the cosmic process, their action effects the dice game. And since the dice game models the cosmic

130. *Skandapurāṇa* 4 [*Kāśīkhaṇḍa*].88 5–12.

process, its action effects the cosmos. Dice games transform the cosmos. Nonetheless, one important qualification should be made here (and will be explained later): the dice game and the dice seem to influence the momentum of the cosmos in opposite directions. The dice game exists on a lower level of cosmic density and integration precisely because its structure (however pliant) forces the cosmos to tear itself open, to rip a hole or a gap within itself. The game, as a model of the cosmos, necessarily builds into itself contradictory forces that it should resolve or synthesize. The game pits at least two sides against one another, and through play, their opposition should be resolved into a winner and loser. At the level of cosmic holism, above that of the game, there are no contradictions or oppositions, but, rather, a more cohesive integration. Brought into existence, the game disconnects the cosmos, forcing it into opposing sides. The game's momentum drives the existence of the cosmos into its own widening gaps—its lower, more fragmented, discrete, and alienated levels, where more and more congealing part-beings, like ourselves, take shape. On the other hand, within the values of the game, the play of the dice makes connections, pushing upward and inward in a quest for higher integration, and bringing forms into existence even as the game itself drives the cosmos downward and outward, making these forms of lesser, more alienated value. Thus, in their own embedded processes, the dice game and the dice reproduce the simultaneously opposed momenta of cosmic forces.

The logics of ritual dice games in India are designed to circumvent the inexorable tearing apart, disconnection, and externalization of the universe that cosmic dice games invariably cause. Thus, the parameters of the dice game in the Rājasūya enable it to create cosmic holism and encompassment that can be imparted to the embryonic world ruler, while those of the Aśvamedha obviate the possibility of a negative outcome in the wider ritual sequence, thereby ensuring the king's installation as the universal sovereign. These ritual dice games reveal one major condition of their capacity to model their own play and outcomes as holistic, rather than as disintegrative: the zenith and center of cosmic encompassment must not enter the game as a player. God must not enter a model of himself (that, by definition, limits him). The game's ability to generate holism and integration requires that the whole not enter into itself as a limited part of itself. Then the extreme density of total knowledge—of no-time, no-space, no division between self and other—is preserved on a higher, more interior level of encompassment than that of the game. But once god enters his own game—a set becoming a member of itself—he limits and occludes his own knowledge, thereby creating conditions in the determinate cosmos that are fraught with uncertainty, in keeping with the lower cosmic level of the game. This is what occurs in the great dice game of the *Mahābhārata* epic, discussed below. In the light of this instance, we will be able to state more generally that when higher-order beings or cosmic levels oppose lower-order beings or levels in dice games, the former almost invariably lose, or else the game itself is disrupted.

Two further cautions should be noted, in view of the preceding discussion. In these ludic processes of gaming, a part must not be equated with, or treated as, a reflection of its whole—unlike the whole-part relation *outside* the game. Regardless of how complex the stipulated homologies between part and whole are, the two should never be confounded when they are brought together within ludic models. The cosmos of the dice game is never that cosmos within which the game is embedded. However, one should also note that the whole in relation to itself as a part, the part in relation to itself, the part (indeed, the very shaping of cosmic dice games) in relation to the whole—all these are in-process,[131] in greater and lesser degrees of movement and momentum, of congealing differences and melting togetherness. The cosmos of the dice game, and that in which the game is embedded, are never stable constants in relation to themselves and to one another.

9
Generating the Unexpected: The Mahābhārata Dice Game

The *Mahābhārata* tells of the conflict between two groups of kinsmen—the five Pāṇḍava brothers and their cousins, the Kauravas. Crucial to the escalation of their quarrel is the dice-game challenge that Duryodhana, a Kaurava, issues to Yudhiṣṭhira, the leader of the Pāṇḍavas. Prior to this challenge, Yudhiṣṭhira had been consecrated as the Dharmarāja, the universal sovereign, a status fraught with the cosmic meaning of holism and encompassment. Van Buitenen has argued persuasively that this ritual sequence—consecration, followed by a dice game—indicates that the authors of the epic used the Vedic Rājasūya as a template.[132] Later versions of the epic sometimes suggest that this *Mahābhārata* game was organized as a model of the cosmos.[133] Yudhiṣṭhira, who, in the earlier sections of the narrative, never evinces the slightest interest in dicing, feels compelled to accept the challenge, and plays against the Kaurava representative, Śakuni. Engrossed and obsessed with the game during round after round, Yudhiṣṭhira cannot break its grip on his being and ultimately loses everything, including himself. The five Pāṇḍava brothers and their wife, Draupadī, are forced from their kingdom into lengthy exile; and the fragmen-

131. See Handelman 1981.

132. Van Buitenen 1972:78.

133. See Beck 1982:200, citing a modern commentary on Villiputtūr Āẏvār.

tation and destruction of social and cosmic order gather direction and momentum, ending eventually in an utter holocaust and the annihilation of all.[134]

The *Mahābhārata* dice game upends the template of the Rājasūya by contravening a basic premise of the latter. The holism of hierarchical encompassment must not enter the gap in its own cosmic density—the game—thereby becoming a part, a self-limiting fragment, of itself. When this occurs, the causal effect is that of the destruction of cosmic and social order. Just as the Rājasūya dice game generates cosmic integration by subordinating the contest to the ordering premises of cosmic connectivity, so the *Mahābhārata* dice game makes connections that disconnect order by contravening these premises. Much of what can be said more generally about the operation of such cosmic games falls within these parameters of discussion. Here it may be helpful briefly to survey a few additional (mainly epic) texts that reveal the powerful tendencies of Indic dice games and other contests to upend the cosmos and impart to it the spin of fragmentation.

In the Tamil folk epic *Aṇṇaṉmār katai*, the twin male heroes play six games of dice. Each of these games is followed by some new misfortune; and the sixth leads eventually to the heroes' death. Brenda Beck comments that although the connection between dice games and misfortune is never made explicit in this epic, their relationship is one of cause and effect.[135] This also holds for the further examples cited later in this chapter. The Tulu story of two sisters, Mayage and Maipage, echoes the destructive effects of gaming, especially when the players outside the game are of a different status. The younger sister defeats the elder one at *cĕnnĕ*, inverting qualities of seniority, leadership, and propriety in social order. In a state of fury, the elder one crushes the younger's head with the *cĕnnĕ* board and then takes her own life.[136] The Punjabi narrative of Raja Rasālu tells of a young prince who, for reasons of which he is unaware, is forced to leave his father's kingdom. The prince plays the dice game, *chaupar*, with the "Beheader," Rāja Sarkap, all of whose opponents have paid for their loss with their heads. Rasālu defeats Sarkap, but this great victory leads eventually to his own beheading.[137] In a Chattisgarhi (Madhya Pradesh) narrative, Princess Subanbali plays Bandhīya Rāja at dice; he has already defeated and imprisoned many kings. In yet another inversion of status, he loses everything in this game, including himself. Subanbali trusses him, takes him to her father's kingdom, and marries him.[138]

134. See discussion in Shulman 1992.

135. Beck 1982:143.

136. Claus 1986:285–89; on *cĕnnĕ*, see section 5.

137. Ions 1970:44–64.

138. Flueckiger 1987:9–10 and 1996:72.

Although dice are not a prominent form of competition in the Telugu epic of Palnāḍu, on one occasion when the heroes play this game, their perception is occluded and they are surrounded by the armies of their enemies.[139] However, of major significance in this epic are two other forms of contest. One is a cockfight between two great enemies—Brahma Nāyuḍu, the hero and an avatar of Viṣṇu; and Nāyakurālu, a widow and an *avatāra* of the local goddess, Aṅkamma. Aṅkamma herself is born from the perspiration of the sexually aroused Pārvatī, as an alienated Śiva separates from her.[140] The other is the play of spinning tops. Nāyakurālu challenges Brahma Nāyuḍu to the cockfight. He at first refuses to contest with a woman, but is eventually forced to accept the challenge. In a strategy reminiscent of the Aśvamedha dice game, which excises all possibility of loss from its ritual complex, Nāyakurālu coopts every cock, chick, and egg, so that not a single combatant will be left to Brahma Nāyudu and he will lose by default. Nevertheless, a powerful cock, also described as Viṣṇu incarnate, is found for him.[141]

During the contest, Nāyakurālu disguises three powerful wizards as devotees of Viṣṇu; Brahma Nāyuḍu, who is "able to see uninterruptedly behind himself . . . the seer of the human world, Viṣṇu incarnate,"[142] is unable to see through their disguise to their true being. His perception blocked and his power weakened, he loses the contest and his land to Nāyakurālu, and goes into exile. Like the *Mahābhārata* dice game, the cockfight activates the great conflict between these two when Brahma Nāyuḍu, a lower form of Viṣṇu, enters the contest.[143]

The motif of the top is associated with Brahma Nāyuḍu's birth and his escape from Nāyakurālu's first attempt to kill him; later, it is connected to the

139. Roghair 1982:337. There are three other significant contests in the epic of Palnāḍu. In one, the 66 heroes are challenged to a dice game by Kṛṣṇa, who wagers his pearl necklace. The heroes wager their heads, and agree to carry them to Kṛṣṇa's domain. Kṛṣṇa "interferes with the dice" and the heroes are beaten (ibid. 142). But despite the pressures that Kṛṣṇa puts on them, they refuse to accept the outcome. Instead, they behead themselves for Śiva, and he comes to their rescue. In this instance, god enters the game as a player and controls the outcome; but the losers do not accept his interference, and he is unable to force them to do so. In a second case, the armies of their enemies surround six of the brothers while they are engrossed in dice, their perceptions apparently dulled (ibid., 337). In a third, two heroes hold a contest in which their horses must jump the width of a river. Viṣṇu (as Brahma Nāyuḍu) intervenes to affect the outcome (ibid., 280). This is the only contest we have found in which god intervenes and the outcome is accepted by the contestants—but here god is not a player. For an additional example of the occlusion of the protagonist's clarity of perception during dice play, see Handelman 1995:301.

140. Roghair 1982:195.

141. Ibid., 222, 235.

142. Ibid., 236.

143. Ibid., 143.

death of his son, Bāluḍu. At his birth, Brahma Nāyuḍu descends to the serpent world, where the serpent maidens give him a marvelous top of silver with strings of pearl. During his play one day, this top bounds away and lands in a cave. Years later, when Bāluḍu and his brothers are on the edge of manhood, they want to play tops; Bāluḍu seeks his father's serpent top in the cave. As he lifts it, it cries out for a human sacrifice—a demand that Bāluḍu fulfills by dying in the epic battle.[144] The play of tops leads directly to the hero's death in a devastated universe. Before he dies, Bāluḍu reminds his father that the cockfight catalyzed the entire disaster.[145]

Let us cite an example from another generic domain, a folktale based on a classical tale from the *Pañcatantra* tradition, expanded, here, to incorporate the theme of dicing in a manner which allows the central protagonist to move into and out of the game—with decisive consequences for his self-knowledge and survival in each of these modes:

A Shepherd's Pilgrimage

A brahmin once started out on a pilgrimage to Kashi [Benares]. A shepherd who was grazing his sheep on the mound asked him, "Sāmi, where are you going?"

"I'll go where I want to. You stay with your sheep," said the brahmin.

"O brahmin, sir, please tell me where you are going," begged the shepherd.

The brahmin replied, "I'm going to Kashi."

"If you're going to Kashi, I'll come with you," said the shepherd.

"What will you do with the sheep?"

"Oh, nothing. They'll graze their fill and then they'll go home. People there will look after them. Let me go with you."

"All right, you can come with me," said the brahmin.

So they walked toward Kashi together. After a little while, the shepherd asked, "Sāmi, where is Kashi?"

"You'll see it, you'll see it. Don't be in such a stupid hurry."

"Ayyo, then show it to me. Where is it?"

"Don't behave like an impatient demon. Just come with me. You are a shepherd. You won't be able to see the goddess of Ganges anyway."

"You said you'll show me Kashi. Where is it?" asked the shepherd.

"It's not too far. Come and see the bank of the Ganges," said the brahmin, showing him the holy river.

"Then where is Kashi?"

"Here, you idiot, right in front of you. This is Kashi. And this is the river Ganges. And don't you talk to me now. I've to take my bath," said the brahmin.

144. Roghair 1982:294.

145. Ibid., 359.

"Ayyo, why are you doing this to me? I was grazing my sheep and you said you would show me Kashi. Here you show me this river, this water. You are a phony brahmin. Do we have to come this far to see a bit of water? Don't we have water in our village tank?" scolded the shepherd.

The goddess Ganges heard this and found it terribly amusing. Everyone was overawed by Her river, the Ganges, holiest of rivers. Here was someone who wasn't even impressed by it. So she laughed aloud, and came straight up out of the river. She held him by the chin affectionately, asked him to open his mouth and show her his tongue. When he put out his tongue, she called him a poor dear fool and wrote magic letters on his tongue and blessed him: "May you understand the language of all eighteen million beings. And you'll be crowned king in three days. But if you tell anyone about this, may your head break into a thousand pieces!"

And then she vanished.

The brahmin, meanwhile, dipped and dipped in the holy water of the Ganges and didn't get even one glimpse of the goddess. But the idiot shepherd had understood everything in a flash in that moment. He left the brahmin behind and walked on by himself. He listened to the birds and understood what they said. He listened to the ants and understood what the ants said.

He soon walked into a city where the reigning king had just died. According to custom, they had sent out the royal elephant with a garland. While the people of the city stood in the streets anxiously waiting for the elephant to pick the next king and garland him, it wandered toward the shepherd, who was standing there watching the fun, threw the garland round his neck, picked him up and placed him on its back. The people cheered and led him to the palace to crown him king. They even found a princess for him and asked him to rule the kingdom.

One day he asked his queen to play pachisi. As the two of them sat down to play and started rolling the dice, a line of ants was forming close to where they sat. The ant in front of the line saw the couple playing dice, and turned around. The whole line scattered at once and began to move away. The ant-in-chief asked the one in front why the line was moving away. It replied, "Oh, look, the king is sitting there. I felt a bit shy."

The chief ant replied, "Why do you have to be shy? Let's march right in front of him. What can he do to us?"

The king heard it all. He understood every word of it, and burst out laughing. The queen asked him why. He said evasively, "Because I'm going to win and you're going to lose."

She said, "I know that's not why you laughed. Tell me the truth."

He said, "Well, I could tell you. But if I did, my head would split into a thousand pieces."

"Even if your head should split into a thousand pieces, you should tell me. Yes, you must," said the queen, pouting.

"Do I really have to tell you? Don't you want me to stay alive?"

"Live or die, but you must tell me why you laughed the way you did."

tion and self-alienation of the deity—as a module that gen-
nentation.

time that Śiva enters the game of dice, slipping into the gaps
ses the qualities of his holism, of his absolute identity with
nsequences of his losses are destructive for cosmic order.
ghest form of god, of the totality of cosmic being and knowl-
loses at dice and other ludic forms, thereby losing parts of
hing the cosmos with which he is identified? The effects of
ne androgyne give insight into this problem.

iva androgyne exists at a very high level of cosmic holism,
ady a loss of unified selfhood and a shift toward the distinc-
l other. A recognized theme in Sanskrit poetry defines the
ne" (*śṛṅgārâtmakârdhanārīśvara*), whose two parts, though
e each tormented by frustration—since the fullness of nor-
d them:

> I'll grant you, golden goddess:
> ne has the joy
> of embracing you forever,
> without pause,
> since he carries your supple body
> mixed into his.
> Still, inside of him
> that three-eyed god
> s ever burning with sorrow,
> for he will never see the gentle light,
> alive with loving,
> n *your* eyes.[148]

it has been observed, is precisely that form of union in which
lity is impossible.[149] As a result of these difficulties, among
pieces of the amalgam are sometimes said to be pulled
splitting. In the following verse, Pārvatī angrily articulates
such surgery, while her halfway-husband resists:

> 'You enemy of Love, give someone else
> the gracious gift of half your body.

mṛta 139 [Bhagīratha].

n by O'Flaherty [Doniger] 1980: 319.

"Then I'd rather die. Make arrangements for the funeral. Order seven cartloads of sandalwood for the cremation fire," said the king. And she ordered at once seven cartloads of sandalwood and made a fire in a pit.

Before he threw himself in the fire, he thought he should circumambulate his capital city. As he walked through the city in a ritual procession, his eyes fell on a he-goat and a she-goat grazing on an old fort wall. The he-goat said, "Get me those leaves that have fallen there. I can't reach them."

The she-goat replied, "I can't. It's too close to the edge. I may fall and die."

The he-goat said, "If you die, I won't become a widower. I'll get another she-goat. I'm not like the foolish king of this country who is ready to fall into the fire, because he can't tell his wife what's on his mind. Why can't he throw her into the fire and get himself another queen?"

The king stopped there for a minute and heard what the he-goat had said. He turned to his wife and asked her, "Do you really want to hear why I laughed?"

"Yes, what else?" she said.

"If I tell you, I'll die!"

"Then die if you must. Tell me first and then die."

By this time they had come to the pit of fire. When they reached the edge, instead of jumping into it himself, he seized her and threw her into the blazing fire. Then he got himself another queen and lived for a long time.[146]

For all the deceptive simplicity of this tale, it is very much to the point of our argument. Outside the dice game, the shepherd-king has total knowledge, symbolized by the languages of all beings in the universe and his kingship. He encompasses his queen, who is subordinate to him. Within the game, he easily succumbs to her wiles, agrees to his own diminishment, and accepts his own death, even though these are not wagers in the game. It is sufficient that the king has entered the game, the limited model of his cosmos. Within these strictures of the possible, he becomes a diminished being, his self-knowledge is occluded, and he loses to his wife even without the play of dice. She emerges superior from the game, and plans the destruction he has ordered for himself. But outside the game, on his circumambulation that will lead to his death, he again is the encompassing being of total knowledge who overhears the commonsensical advice of the he-goat, immediately acts on his own holistic superiority, and kills his wife, living happily ever after, as it were. Once again, the superior being inside and outside the game represents quite different compositions, clearly distinct moments of the cosmic process.

The ludic processes at work in these examples begin to reveal the epistemological status of the dice game and other contests in Indian cosmology. The game has a positional and processual value. The game has no essential ethos

146. Ramanujan, in press. The prototype of this story is well known; see Becker 1989.

in and of itself. Thus the dice game is not merely a lower level of order, one that automatically is subject to the same forces that generally characterize the cosmic process. Instead, the game is posited in the following ways. So long as god or other higher order beings do not enter the game as players, the game is a part of the cosmic whole that is encompassed and controlled by the latter. The momentum of the game, and its effects on cosmos, drive upward and inward, toward increasing internalization, integration, and holism. This is the Rājasūya model, of which the Aśvamedha game is a variant. On the other hand, the game is a part that is simulated as the cosmic whole but is independent of the latter, thereby subjecting the whole to the modeled constraints of the part's fragmentary nature. The game then refracts the gaps torn open within the cosmos, within which the conditions of the contest take shape. When god enters the game, the simulation of the cosmic whole, he is constrained by parameters of its modeling. The momentum of this game, and its effects on the cosmos, now drive downward, toward increasing externalization, alienation, and destruction.

Thus the game may be a module of certainty in harmony with a cosmos of total knowledge. This is the ritual model of the dice game, in which the rules are fixed and predictable, if only in that they exclude loss for the superior being. Or, the game may be a module of uncertainty that opens the cosmos toward new shapings. This is the cosmic, mythic, and epic model of the dice game, in which the rules of the game are pliable, and are themselves in the process of being shaped by the playing of the players, who, are, in turn, in the process of being shaped by the rules. Given these modular characteristics, the dice game, like other such contests, is once again a strange loop that plays with relationships between whole and part, between internalization and externalization. This loop may appear at virtually every level of the cosmic order, and it can be designed to accelerate connectivity or disconnectivity. In either instance, it is an activator of the cosmic process, not merely its expression or reflection. To explore further these relationships between whole, part, and the cosmic process, we return here to the dice game in Śaiva myth.

10
The Elimination of the Androgyne Outcome

Of all Indian deities, Śiva has the most intimate relationship with dice games. His being, his self, and, therefore, the cosmos, are often shaped by his participation in dice and other forms of play. Our arguments on the relationships between play, *tapas*, and cosmic process are powerfully exemplified in the myths of Śiva and his consort, Pārvatī. Śiva's dynamic of externalization (and,

so, that of his cosmos) passes fron
separation of genders (as Śiva and P
(Ardhanārīśvara), who is lower than
densely connecting male and femal
we argue that if the androgyne ente
ping open the gap between genders
over, through the logic of its play, t
the higher order integration of the a
lowing cosmogenesis, Śiva's attemp
are consistently circumvented in a v

In Śaiva cosmology, the god Śiv
universe and existing on all, or throu
the Vedic Self, the highest form of Ś
self deep within the zenith of its own
is characterized by the extremely hig
so, by the simultaneity of time and
knowledge of the cosmos. But when Ś
ity and totality of his knowledge are o
at this point: In the first book of the *M*
Śiva, "a handsome youth, on a lion-t
playing at dice on a Himalayan peak.
perhaps playing against himself. So l
does not (and, we would say, *cannot*)
view is the foretelling of the *Mahābhā*
does Śiva show Indra five replicas of h
Indras will be reborn as the five Pāṇḍ
lifelines of the *Mahābhārata*. The reve
science—emerges only after the god sto
Śiva thus embodies profoundly differe
are related to holism and to its premise
of the dice game, this god is a limited,
whole.

The highest level of the cosmic who
which gender and the erotic are absent,
ings are partial creatures of time and sp
the cosmic weave, no gaps that open t
spaciousness. However, in cosmogonic
cosmic self begins to divide, taking the
female half. It is at this level that the di

147. *Mahābhārata* 1.189, translated by va

cosmic externa
erates cosmic f

Virtually ev
in his cosmos,
the cosmos. Th
How is it that th
edge, consister
his self and di
the dice game

Although th
for Śiva this is
tiveness of se
"love-sick and
welded togeth
mal loving is

The andr
conventiona
others, one
powerfully t
her motivat

148. *Sad*
149. See

"Then I'd rather die. Make arrangements for the funeral. Order seven cartloads of sandalwood for the cremation fire," said the king. And she ordered at once seven cartloads of sandalwood and made a fire in a pit.

Before he threw himself in the fire, he thought he should circumambulate his capital city. As he walked through the city in a ritual procession, his eyes fell on a he-goat and a she-goat grazing on an old fort wall. The he-goat said, "Get me those leaves that have fallen there. I can't reach them."

The she-goat replied, "I can't. It's too close to the edge. I may fall and die."

The he-goat said, "If you die, I won't become a widower. I'll get another she-goat. I'm not like the foolish king of this country who is ready to fall into the fire, because he can't tell his wife what's on his mind. Why can't he throw her into the fire and get himself another queen?"

The king stopped there for a minute and heard what the he-goat had said. He turned to his wife and asked her, "Do you really want to hear why I laughed?"

"Yes, what else?" she said.

"If I tell you, I'll die!"

"Then die if you must. Tell me first and then die."

By this time they had come to the pit of fire. When they reached the edge, instead of jumping into it himself, he seized her and threw her into the blazing fire. Then he got himself another queen and lived for a long time.[146]

For all the deceptive simplicity of this tale, it is very much to the point of our argument. Outside the dice game, the shepherd-king has total knowledge, symbolized by the languages of all beings in the universe and his kingship. He encompasses his queen, who is subordinate to him. Within the game, he easily succumbs to her wiles, agrees to his own diminishment, and accepts his own death, even though these are not wagers in the game. It is sufficient that the king has entered the game, the limited model of his cosmos. Within these strictures of the possible, he becomes a diminished being, his self-knowledge is occluded, and he loses to his wife even without the play of dice. She emerges superior from the game, and plans the destruction he has ordered for himself. But outside the game, on his circumambulation that will lead to his death, he again is the encompassing being of total knowledge who overhears the commonsensical advice of the he-goat, immediately acts on his own holistic superiority, and kills his wife, living happily ever after, as it were. Once again, the superior being inside and outside the game represents quite different compositions, clearly distinct moments of the cosmic process.

The ludic processes at work in these examples begin to reveal the epistemological status of the dice game and other contests in Indian cosmology. The game has a positional and processual value. The game has no essential ethos

146. Ramanujan, in press. The prototype of this story is well known; see Becker 1989.

in and of itself. Thus the dice game is not merely a lower level of order, one that automatically is subject to the same forces that generally characterize the cosmic process. Instead, the game is posited in the following ways. So long as god or other higher order beings do not enter the game as players, the game is a part of the cosmic whole that is encompassed and controlled by the latter. The momentum of the game, and its effects on cosmos, drive upward and inward, toward increasing internalization, integration, and holism. This is the Rājasūya model, of which the Aśvamedha game is a variant. On the other hand, the game is a part that is simulated as the cosmic whole but is independent of the latter, thereby subjecting the whole to the modeled constraints of the part's fragmentary nature. The game then refracts the gaps torn open within the cosmos, within which the conditions of the contest take shape. When god enters the game, the simulation of the cosmic whole, he is constrained by parameters of its modeling. The momentum of this game, and its effects on the cosmos, now drive downward, toward increasing externalization, alienation, and destruction.

Thus the game may be a module of certainty in harmony with a cosmos of total knowledge. This is the ritual model of the dice game, in which the rules are fixed and predictable, if only in that they exclude loss for the superior being. Or, the game may be a module of uncertainty that opens the cosmos toward new shapings. This is the cosmic, mythic, and epic model of the dice game, in which the rules of the game are pliable, and are themselves in the process of being shaped by the playing of the players, who, are, in turn, in the process of being shaped by the rules. Given these modular characteristics, the dice game, like other such contests, is once again a strange loop that plays with relationships between whole and part, between internalization and externalization. This loop may appear at virtually every level of the cosmic order, and it can be designed to accelerate connectivity or disconnectivity. In either instance, it is an activator of the cosmic process, not merely its expression or reflection. To explore further these relationships between whole, part, and the cosmic process, we return here to the dice game in Śaiva myth.

10
The Elimination of the Androgyne Outcome

Of all Indian deities, Śiva has the most intimate relationship with dice games. His being, his self, and, therefore, the cosmos, are often shaped by his participation in dice and other forms of play. Our arguments on the relationships between play, *tapas*, and cosmic process are powerfully exemplified in the myths of Śiva and his consort, Pārvatī. Śiva's dynamic of externalization (and, so, that of his cosmos) passes from undifferentiated encompassment to the separation of genders (as Śiva and Pārvatī) through the figure of the androgyne (Ardhanārīśvara), who is lower than the former, higher than the latter, and still densely connecting male and female in one being, one flesh. In this section, we argue that if the androgyne enters the dice game, he/she is torn apart, ripping open the gap between genders and alienating one from the other. Moreover, through the logic of its play, the dice game itself prevents any return to the higher order integration of the androgyne. Later, we will argue that, following cosmogenesis, Śiva's attempts to get back to holistic encompassment are consistently circumvented in a variety of ways.

In Śaiva cosmology, the god Śiva is the cosmic whole, encompassing the universe and existing on all, or through all, of its levels, planes, and axes. Like the Vedic Self, the highest form of Śiva is one of undifferentiated being, the self deep within the zenith of its own middle. On its upper levels, this cosmos is characterized by the extremely high density of its cosmic connections, and, so, by the simultaneity of time and space and, therefore, by the god's total knowledge of the cosmos. But when Śiva enters the dice game, the simultaneity and totality of his knowledge are occluded. One minor instance will suffice at this point: In the first book of the *Mahābhārata*, the god Indra is brought to Śiva, "a handsome youth, on a lion-throne seated, young women about him, playing at dice on a Himalayan peak."[147] Śiva seems engrossed in the game, perhaps playing against himself. So long as Śiva is absorbed in the game, he does not (and, we would say, *cannot*) tell Indra his future, although this preview is the foretelling of the *Mahābhārata* narrative. Only on leaving the game does Śiva show Indra five replicas of himself within the mountain peak. These Indras will be reborn as the five Pāṇḍava brothers, who will set forth on the lifelines of the *Mahābhārata*. The revelation—a reflection of the god's omniscience—emerges only after the god stops playing. Inside and outside the game, Śiva thus embodies profoundly different moments of cosmic process, as these are related to holism and to its premise of total knowledge. Within the model of the dice game, this god is a limited, lower version of himself as the cosmic whole.

The highest level of the cosmic whole, that of no-time and no-space, from which gender and the erotic are absent, is a nonhuman level, since human beings are partial creatures of time and space. On this plane, there are no rips in the cosmic weave, no gaps that open through time into space—indeed, into spaciousness. However, in cosmogonic terms, one level below, as it were, the cosmic self begins to divide, taking the form of the androgyne, a male with a female half. It is at this level that the dice game first appears, in processes of

147. *Mahābhārata* 1.189, translated by van Buitenen 1973:371–72.

cosmic externalization and self-alienation of the deity—as a module that generates cosmic fragmentation.

Virtually every time that Śiva enters the game of dice, slipping into the gaps in his cosmos, he loses the qualities of his holism, of his absolute identity with the cosmos. The consequences of his losses are destructive for cosmic order. How is it that the highest form of god, of the totality of cosmic being and knowledge, consistently loses at dice and other ludic forms, thereby losing parts of his self and diminishing the cosmos with which he is identified? The effects of the dice game on the androgyne give insight into this problem.

Although the Śaiva androgyne exists at a very high level of cosmic holism, for Śiva this is already a loss of unified selfhood and a shift toward the distinctiveness of self and other. A recognized theme in Sanskrit poetry defines the "love-sick androgyne" (*śṛṅgārâtmakârdhanārīśvara*), whose two parts, though welded together, are each tormented by frustration—since the fullness of normal loving is denied them:

> I'll grant you, golden goddess:
> he has the joy
> of embracing you forever,
> without pause,
> since he carries your supple body
> mixed into his.
> Still, inside of him
> that three-eyed god
> is ever burning with sorrow,
> for he will never see the gentle light,
> alive with loving,
> in *your* eyes.[148]

The androgyne, it has been observed, is precisely that form of union in which conventional sexuality is impossible.[149] As a result of these difficulties, among others, one or both pieces of the amalgam are sometimes said to be pulled powerfully toward splitting. In the following verse, Pārvatī angrily articulates her motivation for such surgery, while her halfway-husband resists:

> "You enemy of Love, give someone else
> the gracious gift of half your body.

148. *Saduktikarṇâmṛta* 139 [Bhagīratha].

149. See discussion by O'Flaherty [Doniger] 1980: 319.

I can't stand it anymore—
that River-Woman [Gaṅgā] on your head,
or the way you worship Mistress Twilight [Sandhyā]
twice every day."

She's trying to get out, riddled
with rage, to split her body
away from his, while his long arm—
  may it protect *you*!—
is holding her back, desperately wrestling
with her firm, full breast.[150]

Only one breast, of course, and a single arm. Such descriptions are fairly usual; even in a moment of epiphany, when the male and female parts of this god fuse together at the height of a general festival of erotic unions—as we see in Ratnâkara's *Haravijaya* (21)—it is the paradoxical and unhappy concomitants of this fusion that the poet chooses to express.[151] The motivating impulse is a feeling of terror at separation, sparked by Pārvatī's observation of the female *cakravāka* bird, which is condemned by fate to be torn away from her loving mate every night from sunset to dawn (*Haravijaya* 21.34).[152] Śiva, too, is afraid of disjunction (*viyoga-bhītimān*, 21.35)—so he absorbs the goddess into his own body. But she has her doubts, from the very beginning: "frigid" Gaṅgā will burn her out of jealousy, and she will hardly be able to worship Śiva properly with only one hand to cup in greeting (21.36). Indeed, the newly experienced frustration is mutual:

Each eye, alone—
half of a pair, drawn into the whole—
closed under long curling lashes,
since from this moment on
the cherished face of the beloved
could only be imagined.[153]

150. *Saduktikarṇâmṛta* 140 [Mayūra].

151. *Haravijaya* 21.34–56. David Smith (1985: 130, 258–60) argues that this moment is the climax of the long poem's depiction of the Śaiva godhead.

152. On the *cakravāka* in relation to the love of Śiva and Pārvatī, see chapter III, sections 3 and 4.

153. *niveśitasyântarasīmni cakṣuṣo nimīlitârāla-karāla-pakṣmaṇaḥ/ vidhīyate bhāvanayâiva tat-kṣaṇaṃ priyânanâmbhoruha-darśanotsavaḥ//* 21.40.

This is one side of the equation: what could once be known and seen with the reasonable fullness of distance is now divided, blocked, obscured; the eye that has been taken, literally, into the other's body can no longer even perceive otherness properly. There is also, however, a complementary dissatisfaction at the lack of a *total* fusion and interpenetration:

> In the very middle of her body,
> her skin folded back in gentle lines
> as if frowning in fury, for she was too slender
> to enter fully
> the *other* half.[154]

Pārvatī, an exemplar of classical feminine beauty, has a waist that tapers into nothingness; hence, she is simply too thin to be able to pervade the whole of the bisexual being into which she has been absorbed. For her, so the poet tells us, this failure means frustration—the wish is for an unambiguous fusion and interpenetration. Still, neither part, female or male, is quite comfortable in the altered circumstances of combination; and neither loses its own integrity as a defined and partly autonomous entity.

Nonetheless, selfhood and gender in the androgyne are still continuous, rather than being discrete and different. If, on occasion, we see the incipient genders seeming to pull toward separation (for example, by trying to walk in different directions),[155] more often, they are seen as flowing without interruption into one another. It is in this fluid and continuous form that we have already encountered the androgyne at the beginning of the dice-game myth from *Kedārakhaṇḍa*:

> Once Nārada went to see Śiva on Mount Kailāsa. . . . He praised Śiva and Pārvatī, who pervades the three worlds, who gave Śiva form and made him accessible, who takes apart the god without trans-forms, via many transformations; he saw this goddess occupying half of the god's body. Śiva asked what the sage wanted, and Nārada said: "I came here for a game." "What game do you have in mind?" asked Pārvatī. Nārada replied: "The game of dice has many forms—and the two of you are likely to find it more pleasing than making love."
>
> Soon both Śiva and Pārvatī were entirely absorbed in the game, to the sage's great satisfaction. Pārvatī began to play in tricky ways, and so did he. First he beat her, and she, enraged, had to give up two of the jewels on her head. Śiva, noticing how she became more and more beautiful, the angrier she got, kept the game going.

154. *niṣiddha-dehârdha-niveśa-vibhramaṃ kṛśatva-yogaṃ prati baddhakopayā/ sa-bhaṅgura-bhrū-latayêva kevalaṃ vali-cchalān madhyabhuvā vyavasthitam//* 21.45.

155. E.g., Kramrisch 1981b:163.

> She asked him what he was prepared to stake, and he replied: "For you, my dear, I will wager this crescent moon, this necklace, and two earrings." They again began to play (both of them highly skilled at the dice game); and this time Pārvatī won and demanded that Śiva hand over what he had staked.

The androgyne governs the universe from the zenith of Kailāsa, the cosmic mountain and axis mundi. The fused androgynous shape is close to full holism, to the deeply internalized uniformity of self, to the simultaneity of time and space, and to the total knowledge of a dense level of cosmic integration. The androgyne is also relatively passive, quite without desire or other emotions, doing little except staying in place at the apex of cosmic encompassment. The cosmic androgyne embodies the fluid fusion of genders, the less-than-clear borders between them, the unproblematic status of this fluidity, and the complex being's self-awareness of its shifting bisexual qualities. Contrast this with King Iḷa, the first human androgyne, who lives entirely in the world of time and space and is consequently forced to divide, sequentialize, and spatialize his androgyny. Iḷa must alternate genders. He/she is either male or female, changing sex every month. Moreover, he/she is never able to remember his/her previous self.[156] Iḷa exists on a lower level of encompassment and holism than does the cosmic androgyne, one on which the fused embodiment of gender and the being's self-awareness of this are much more limited. Iḷa is a less fluid being, whose self or selves are characterized by gaping holes in her/his androgyny, while each of her/his engendered selves appears, in turn, as if it were alone, independent of its other. In other words, each of Iḷa's engendered selves is highly externalized and congealed in the world of time and space.

Iḷa appears remarkably close to Winnicott's psychoanalytical discussion of the internal organization of the male and female in men and women: "The other-sex element may be completely split off so that, for instance, a man may not be able to make any link at all with the split off [female] part."[157] Like the human Iḷa, but unlike the higher level of divine integration, the female is integrated within the male but is dissociated, split off—congealed within the male but consciously unknown to him. Winnicott argues that the female can be known in her "purest" sense when she is a fully dissociated part of the male. The "essential" bisexual moment is that of dissociated genders within the same being.

The *Kedārakhaṇḍa* dice game models a cosmos in which holism is impossible. Nārada entices the androgyne into the game by offering the dice contest as a more pleasing alternative to making love. The contrast is instructive, as we shall see. Pārvatī, in response, snatches the dice and begins to play against Śiva, who joins in. To do this, the androgyne must split completely, tearing,

156. Kramrisch 1981:236–37.

157. Winnicott 1971:77.

separating, and externalizing into distinct selves and genders. The continuousness of the androgyne ruptures abruptly into difference. The game forces sides, division, a contest. In the first instance the cosmic whole divides against itself, into a contest between self and other. This rupture entails a shift in hierarchy. The goddess who passively occupied a part of Śiva's body was subordinate to him. Now she is a fully autonomous player. Śaiva thought posits the female principle, Śiva's *śakti* or female force (e.g., Pārvatī), as the activator of the more inert male principle, Śiva. The female principle is the energetic force in the creation and externalization of the phenomenal world. In this myth, it is Pārvatī's response to Nārada that ruptures the inert androgyne and activates the dice game.

In contrast to the hierarchical cosmos, the game model is an egalitarian one, insisting on equal sides. This separation of sides opens into the game board, itself an opening within the gap in cosmic density. The game board constitutes spaciousness in which are embedded empty holes of possibility; these will be filled by the pieces of the players, set in motion by the modular detonations of the dice. The pieces echo the fragmentary forms of their players. Often the midpoint of the board—for example, in pachisi—is itself a null point characterized by emptiness. This separation of sides is the engenderment of space. Moreover, the game operates through taking turns and corresponding moves. In other words, one thing happens before another, while another happens after the other. The game creates time by dividing the simultaneity of infinity into segments, and by imparting sequential pulsations (for example, the throws of the dice) to these divisions.

As Śiva and Pārvatī become engrossed in the game, they begin to "cheat." Cheating, or trickiness, in play is frequently said to characterize Indian cosmic and epic dice games, but what cheating actually means is not at all clear. Although all these games have rules, rarely, if ever, is a player penalized for cheating, despite vociferous accusations that this is going on. Moreover, those players accused of cheating do not deny this; sometimes take pride in it; and seem to understand their actions as integral to their playing skill. If cheating is not a transgression of the game rules, as we understand this, then perhaps it has something to do with the actual externalization and shaping of the rules. We might ask, in this vein: What comes first, cheating or the rules? It would seem that rules attempt to close the gaps that the game as an idea has opened up. They reflect a felt absence, where the gaps of formlessness generate and influence forms.

The dice game comes into existence only as gaps open within the cosmos. The cosmic dice game, we would argue, is itself such a gap, a locus of fluid uncertainty that is between externalizing, congealing forms of gender, and the space and time of their generative interaction. The game models the innermost being of god, the apex of the encompassment of the cosmos, as spacious—indeed, even as empty and, therefore, as open to potential reconfigurations that were not possible within the simultaneity of the dense cosmos. Indeed, as we argue later, regardless of the game's outcome, this innermost emptiness cannot be filled with the fullest density of *bandhu* connectivity. The protagonists play for holism; yet this outcome is not possible, given that within the parameters of the game, one wins and the other loses, accentuating their congealing distinctiveness and separation. Within the empty innerness of the game, Śiva and Pārvatī play for the dense simultaneity of cosmic encompassment. They do this with two kinds of tokens. First there are the dice themselves, each of them a model of cosmic connectivity, of *bandhu* linkages. Modeling connections, the dice *always* make these connections happen, as we see from the ritual texts that set forth the rich correlations and homologies between the dice throws and various levels and components of the universe. The dice are agents of holism. The other pieces, representing the players directly and, as such, moving through the dice board, are fragments of the whole that are operated on by the dice, by cosmic processes of *bandhu* connections. There is, thus, extreme tension between the dice and the game, a tension unresolved by the game's outcome, as god falls, or is pushed into, the slippery holes that open within his being.

To put this differently, these lower level gaps are realities that are coming into existence and congealing into form. The game itself is such a reality, an externalizing lower level model of the cosmos. This may mean that its rules are in flux, and are flexible; the shape that these rules take depends on who controls their reality. As noted previously, the rules of the cosmic game are themselves shaped through play, as the players strive to externalize themselves and their reality through playing, and as the rules congeal and shape the play and its players. The game is not, then, a rigid mold or template that is set within the cosmic gap; rather, like all of the cosmos, it is an evolving organic form.

We have argued that when holistic higher order beings enter the game, they descend and their encompassment is necessarily diminished. But what of their antagonists? These, outside the game, often are lower order beings who are highly successful in play, regularly defeating their higher order opponents, just as Pārvatī beats Śiva. They are the trickiest and most successful players, and these lower order beings move up through the game at their opponents' expense. They expand their being through the spaciousness structured into the game. Indeed, cheating seems to depend precisely on the loosening of cosmic density and the opening of empty dimensions of space and time, as we can see from an unusual Sanskrit verse that actually spells out the nature of these tricky moves:

> With a hundred winks
> the god who bears the crescent moon
> silences *her* smiling, witty friends
> as he slides his men across the board,
> counting wrongly,
> skipping squares
> to trick the goddess in the deep
> and crooked games he plays to win
> a tight embrace.[158]

As in other cases we have seen, the stakes are explicitly erotic—the loser will owe a long embrace; to achieve victory, Śiva deliberately attempts to trick the goddess, in ways that make sense in terms of the structural metaphysics of this game, as described above. Thus, cheating may involve moving one's tokens *too far* (a loosening of spatial density); counting pieces *wrongly* (a loosening of temporal density); and overshooting, that is, *skipping* spaces (again, a loosening of spatial density). All such moves, conspicuous and predictable as they may be, depend on the lack of dense connectivity that constitutes higher cosmic levels. Lower order beings are more at home, as it were, on lower cosmic levels, and, therefore, they are able to congeal reality (in this instance, the rules) in their favor, thereby also reifying the cosmos outside the game. More precisely, the lower order tricksters who triumph through the game are, in themselves, *less defined* than their divine antagonists; these tricksters, unlike Śiva and Pārvatī, can play both sides of the game, thereby superseding its logic of increasingly rigid separation. They erase defined boundaries out of delight and can therefore master this game, which, no less than any other externalization, is shaped through play. Such lower order beings often seem to be moving toward closing the gaps in being—an upward direction never available to the god through the game. We will explore a graphic example of this process in section 12. Here, one should bear in mind that in this ludic world, the most defined or the most solid is always the most empty.

The transformation of the androgyne form into Śiva and Pārvatī playing dice is both the downward movement of the cosmos (its fragmentation) and its externalization (the separation of other from self). The extreme density of internal cosmic connectivity, indexed by the androgyne, is forced to loosen radi-

158. *Karpūracarita-bhāṇa* 2:
s*merāḥ kākṣa-śatair nivārya nibhṛtaṃ cāturya-dhuryāḥ sakhīḥ*
sāriṃ sārayato mṛṣā gaṇayataḥ sthānāny atikrāmataḥ/
kaṇṭhāśleṣa-paṇe durodara-vidhau candrârdha-cūḍā-maṇer
devīṃ vañcayato jayanti gahana-cchadma-kramāḥ kelayaḥ//

cally within the game. We emphasize that this extreme density of internalization is fluid, not solid; soft, not hard. The relevance of these distinctions will become evident later. We note here that the substance of simultaneity (if one can speak of this), the simultaneity of total knowledge that characterizes high levels of holism and encompassment, requires both the density and the fluidity that enable the cosmic being to be everything and know everything at once. The analogies of dense solidity and hardness evoke more the separate positioning of things next to one another and, therefore, their distinctiveness, regardless of how very close they may be to one another. The dice-game model of the cosmos aggressively rends this density. As emptiness opens within the cosmic Self, through time and in space, the simultaneity of total knowledge vanishes; god, entering his model of the cosmos, is diminished, his future momentarily uncertain.

As a model of the cosmos, the dice game allows no juncture of reconnection for the higher order fusion and union of the androgyne. The externalization of the cosmos is also the congealing of its divided parts. Self and other, male and female, time and space—all become hardened forms of reality. The dense fluidity of being that characterizes a lack of identity in the higher-order cosmos disappears. Instead, the playful fluidity of being drains into the gaps between congealing forms of reality. At these lower levels, the transformative potentialities of this playful fluidity of being exist in the interaction between forms; between beings that often clash at their borders; across the gaps (the tears within tears) that have come to separate them from one another. Much of the struggle that beings like Śiva and Pārvatī wage in order to reunite with one another entails overcoming their own boundedness and limitation of form so they can flow again into one another.

Within the dice game, the initial division of the androgyne into separate genders does not revert toward their fusion. Śaiva cosmology is permeated by eroticism on levels lower than that of the androgyne.[159] The sexual attraction and union of Śiva and Pārvatī should, in principle, move the cosmos toward higher levels of holism and encompassment. But a full and active eroticism is absent from the androgyne, since sexuality comes into play with the separation of genders, with the division of self and other. In the myth, therefore, just as the androgyne divides into Śiva and Pārvatī, one might expect that these two figures could potentially join in fruitful, sexual union, flowing together, reintegrating the cosmos and moving it once more toward holism. We should note, however, that sexual union necessarily joins the externalities of beings endowed with congealed borders. No matter how intense their efforts to destroy these boundaries of being, to fill the emptiness between them with their unity, these efforts are ultimately futile. We will argue later that the movement

159. See O'Flaherty 1973.

and momentum toward reintegration must come from within, just as the deepest innerness initially generates fragmentation and separation.

Moreover, the option of sexual union is obviated by the dice game. Indeed, Nārada offers the pleasures of dice as an alternative to those of lovemaking. The ruptures that form through the game (including that of gender) are profoundly antierotic, and the congealing into difference turns destructive. Pārvatī, separating from Śiva, turns to him not in erotic passion but, rather, with the rage of dice play and conflict. The game model ensures that, once divided from one another, the pair will be driven further apart, not reunited. As the cosmos descends and externalizes, its porousness expands. This process has direct ramifications for the kind of offspring that Śiva and Pārvatī engender. Always lacking fullness, they are partial beings, exemplars of the dangerous directions in which the externalizing, congealing cosmos moves.

The rupture of the androgyne externalizes separate, engendered selves, male and female. Indian bodies, Indian selves, are conceptualized as mixtures of female and male attributes. These characteristics begin to achieve some self-attribution in the figure of the androgyne; but the more externalized, engendered body and self that follow from the androgyne's rupture move further toward the separation of distinctively engendered selves in unisexual bodies. Each congealing gender searches for the boundaries of its own identity. In Śaiva mythology, this quest is more pronounced for Śiva than for Pārvatī, although it undoubtedly affects them both.

Nonetheless, there are hierarchical differences between the genders in Śaiva cosmology. The higher cosmic encompassment is conceived of primarily as male. As maleness is externalized on a lower level of cosmos, through the destructive rupture of the androgyne, self-knowledge is lost and the borders of the male self become unclear. Perhaps Śiva is pushed to panic about who he is. In this cosmology, however, the female belongs "naturally," one may say, to a lower level of encompassment along the vertical axis, and the immediate consequences of the androgyne's rupture affect Pārvatī's sense of self less than Śiva's. This seems evident in the *Kedārakhaṇḍa* myth as the dice game ends. On the other hand, the deepest innerness of holism may have more affinity to the female: "insideness" is the capacity to be a container and to be contained. These are more likely to be female attributes of being (note, though, that we are speaking of affinities, not of essence; in processual terms, the female movement is ever deeper inward). Thus the game also ruptures the holism of encompassing cosmic height (which becomes male) through that of deep innerness (which becomes female). In this light, the *liṅga* itself looks like an extrusion or materialization of containing femaleness, the *yoni*—as, indeed, all its iconic representations in India suggest.[160]

160. One can also understand now why shedding the seed is often considered destructive; the creation of children is an act of still greater extrusion, a move away from innerness. *Liṅga* icons do not penetrate the *yoni* but, rather, extend outward from it.

At the close of the game, Śiva cannot believe what has befallen him.

> This time Pārvatī won and demanded that Śiva hand over what he had staked [his crescent moon, necklace, two earrings, and apparently much more]. Śiva merely smiled and said something true: "I wasn't really beaten by you, dearest; look at things from the right perspective. No living being can overcome me. You shouldn't talk like this. Play dice as much as you want—I will always win."
>
> Pārvatī replied: "I did beat you. There is nothing surprising in that. . . . There is simply no doubt about it—you have lost. You just don't realize it." Still, he refused to pay up: "You speak out of egoism; please reconsider." Pārvatī laughed: "It is quite true—there is no one who can beat the great god—except me. I have won at this immaculate game."

As the game ends, the players leave its strange loop. Outside the game once more, Śiva completely disbelieves his loss. Returning to the universe that is identified with his being, he tells Pārvatī to look at things from "the right perspective"—as the cosmic encompassment of total knowledge, Śiva cannot lose. Yet who has shaped reality? Pārvatī is vehemently adamant that Śiva has lost. This argument is pivotal to the epistemological status of the dice game within the holistic, hierarchical cosmos.

The protagonists take the perspectives of opposing realities—Pārvatī's is from within the spacious game model of the cosmos, and Śiva's is from that of the dense cosmos that encompasses the game. Humankind's perspective (one of dissociated, partial beings) is closer to Pārvatī's. Indeed, it is important for our existence that she win. There are two stakes in the dice game: externalization/creation and reabsorption, victory and defeat.

> If the goddess wins, that means creation; if Śiva wins, that means the opposite of creation.[161]

In other words, if Pārvatī wins, lower levels of the cosmos, including our own, externalize and come into existence. If Śiva wins, they do not, since everything returns to the homogeneous, dense connectivity of the innermost level of cosmic encompassment.

In the *Kedārakhaṇḍa* myth, from Śiva's perspective, the game has no special status—indeed, no special locus—that nullifies the dense cosmic processes of his total knowledge. From Pārvatī's perspective, the reality of the spacious game, with its plastic, bending rules, *is* the cosmos. From the perspective of the game, Śiva's encompassment of the universe is nullified, once

161. *Skandapurāṇa* 4.88.5–12; see section 8.

he enters into its model of a diminished cosmos—the empty rip within his own being that opens between Pārvatī and himself. From the perspective of the cosmos outside the game, Śiva cannot be diminished. Yet the existence of the game is this very hole in his inner being. His loss within the game is precisely his loss of holism, the opening of this gap within himself and his descent into it. His loss follows inevitably from his reluctant entry into the game (he is virtually coerced by Pārvatī). As Pārvatī's attendant, Vijayā, says to her at a later point:

> It was wrong to play dice with him [Śiva]. Haven't you heard that dicing is full of flaws?

These flaws are not of a moral character (as has often been claimed for various Indian mythic and epic gamblers, including Yudhiṣṭhira) but, rather, reflect the opening of a cosmic glitch, the spaciousness of uncertainty—of time, space, self, and gender—that activates the universe. The direction this activation takes depends on whether the cosmic whole enters into a part of itself from which holism as an outcome is eliminated.

The dice, we have said, are modular detonators—they are, themselves, tiny models of connectivity within the divisive field of the game. The dice homologize qualities of microcosm and macrocosm and are therefore able only to generate connections in their interaction with other parts—for example, with the selves and genders of the players. True, these connections are forged within, and in tension with, the parameters of the game. These parameters insist initially on the rupture of continuities among any and all players, and on the clearcut division between winner and loser. Nonetheless, as the dice take apart the cosmos, ripping its holes wider and lower, these detonators are also re-forming the world through the connections they generate in fashioning an outcome for the game. So, when the cosmic whole enters the game as a player, the play of the dice would seem to flow against the epistemological status of the game. One might expect cosmic encompassment to pass from loser to winner, from Śiva to Pārvatī, as she incorporates and assimilates those parts of him that he has wagered and lost. Yet this is not the case in Śaiva cosmology.

Śiva's loss is Pārvatī's gain, but Śiva's loss of cosmic encompassment does not endow Pārvatī with this quality of holism. She does not come to encompass the cosmos, perhaps, in part, because this transfer of qualities is one of externalities, of exterior properties of Śiva that are added to Pārvatī's own exterior. Although these properties increase her holism, they cannot bring it to fulfillment. The transfer of qualities from Śiva to Pārvatī offers an exterior origin of being, while the essential source of being is deeply internal. As we argue later, the way toward the full reintegration of the cosmos begins within, from the inside of being, as did its initial fragmentation. Śiva's loss, one may say, is the gain of the phenomenal world; but it also raises questions about his fragmented, engendered being—about who he is, and about his search for a male identity. Even though Pārvatī (because she is always a "part" in this cosmology) has a better sense of her self, of who she is, she too emerges none too pleased from the game, despite her triumph.

The cosmic dice games of Śiva and Pārvatī are frequently interrupted, leaving a rupture that ramifies conflict as the players lose their footing on the slippery slope of the game board. Or, these games end in argument, with the completion of a round, as in the *Kedārakhaṇḍa* myth. Then the movement toward internalization and reintegration takes more tortuous and circuitous routes. In the *Kedārakhaṇḍa*, Nārada, the original instigator of the androgyne's externalization into the game, breaks in as conflict between the newly isolated genders begins to escalate:

> "You are speaking nonsense," he said to the goddess; "you are talking about the supreme lord of the universe and its inner being, invincible, formless, formed and beyond form. How could you beat him? You do not know Śiva, since you are only a woman."
>
> This infuriated Pārvatī. "Shut up," she screamed, "your fickle and unstable nature makes you talk like this. Śiva was born through my grace, born and set securely in his place."
>
> Nārada fell silent, but Bhṛṅgin spoke up: "You should not talk so much. Our lord is not given to mutation, but you are yoked to a feminine state. You came to Śiva after giving in to desire . . . "

Both Nārada and Bhṛṅgin—the skeletal hypermale, imbalanced involute being who represents Śiva's descent and search for the borders of his own identity—are telling Pārvatī that as a woman, she cannot know the truth of Śiva, and that properly she is his devotee and servant. This is a straightforward restatement of Śiva's holistic encompassment of his hierarchical cosmos, and of Pārvatī's lower place in this ordering. She responds to it with fury:

> I have Śiva as my inner being, and Śiva always abides in me. How can you [Bhṛṅgin], through the power of language, articulate the notion of separate existence between the two Śivas [i.e., between him and me]?"

She curses Bhṛṅgin to be without flesh—to lose those soft tissues given the body by the female, and to be reduced entirely to bones, to male qualities,[162]

162. O'Flaherty 1980:316.

full of emptiness between the hardnesses of their congealed parts—and she challenges Śiva (who does not respond) to negate her power.

Pārvatī is now the autonomous, active female principle; and she takes back from Bhṛṅgin, a male analogous in formation to Śiva, those female qualities that constitute the male as a full being. Indeed, in other texts, Bhṛṅgin's extreme maleness so imbalances him that he would be unable to stand upright if Śiva had not given him a bony, third leg. Bhṛṅgin exemplifies the externalized, outer limits of male identity, of what it is to be wholly male but only male, teetering and tottering within his own self, within his inner emptiness, utterly antagonistic to the female, and without desire to reunite with her. Once more, the consequences of the game drive toward the antierotic, the denial of the viability of the joining of genders. The conflicts generated by the game produce the absolute rupture of continuity within gender, an outcome that is the extreme opposite of the androgyne.

> Pārvatī, still angry, swiftly removed with her hand the snake Vāsuki that Śiva wore around his neck, along with many other ornaments of his—the crescent moon, the elephant's hide, the serpents, Kambala and Aśvatara, and finally, tricking him with words, his loincloth. Bhṛṅgin and the other servants averted their eyes in shame. Śiva, too, was ashamed, and spoke in hostile tones to Pārvatī: "All the sages, along with Brahmā and Viṣṇu, are laughing at this joke. What have you done? You were born in a good family. If you know for a fact that you beat me, then at least give me back my loincloth."
>
> But she merely laughed. "Why do you need a loincloth? When you went into the Pine Forest, beguiling the wives of the sages, pretending to beg for alms, you were clothed only in space. You were such a pure, rarefied sage. Those sages worshiped you, and they made your loincloth fall, so you might as well let it go. After all, I won it at dice."
>
> Śiva was so enraged that he opened his third eye and directed it at Pārvatī. Still she went on smiling: "Why are you so intent on staring at me? I am not Death [Yama], or Desire [Kama], or Dakṣa's sacrifice, or the Triple City, or Andhaka [all of whom Śiva destroyed]. Why bother with this blazing gaze? It is all for nothing that you are becoming Virūpâkṣa—'Ugly Eyes'—in front of me."
>
> As she went on in this vein, Śiva began to think about going away to some deserted place, where a man could be happy by himself—free, devoid of attachments, his thoughts under control, beyond desire and passion, aware of ultimate truths; in short, both happy and wise. So he left her and went to the Siddha wilderness. . . . Pārvatī, for her part, went into the women's quarters, in a foul mood.

There, she spoke to her attendant, Vijayā, in terms reminiscent of the first movement of the Vedic cosmic Self: *"I just wanted to play with him for fun, for the sake of the game, in order to play with the causes of his emerging into activity (udbhava-vṛtti-hetubhiḥ)."* Vijayā's advice to Pārvatī is to pursue Śiva:

Go quickly, before he is too far away, and appease him. If you don't you will be sorry later.

Given the homology of game and cosmos, the outcome of the contest shakes and upsets cosmic reality. Śiva cannot resist as Pārvatī strips him naked of attributes of self, of godhead, and adds them to her own. Indeed, she exposes and mocks his genitals and the impotence of his masculinity, as she previously had stripped Bhṛṅgin of his flesh. She easily deflects his fury, and even his terrifying third eye loses its potency. Śiva acknowledges that Pārvatī's knowledge, gained within the game, is superior to his ("If you know for a fact that you beat me. . . ."). Emerging from the game, he is diminished, a lesser version of the self that entered the contest. The destructive reverberations of the game drive the pair further apart from each other. Pārvatī remains at the zenith of Kailāsa but is unhappy, isolating herself within her female self, in the women's quarters. Śiva walks alone into the empty, unbounded wilderness, a location that complements the loss of his sense of self. Bhṛṅgin, the still lesser Śiva who has been petrified into sterile maleness because of his hostility to the female, totters without his flesh. The dice game has externalized, congealed, and separated genders, destroying the likelihood of their fruitful union and driving the porous cosmos toward the Andhaka outcome.

We have seen how ludic modeling is involved intimately in the creation of the gaps in god, in the self-division of the cosmic whole, its externalization and descent. The fluidity and flexibility of play have powerful affinities to the dense fluidity of higher levels of cosmic integration, and, therefore, to the special capacity to act on the latter. We have suggested that all beings with gendered selves—that recognize self and other—exist as gaps in god, as the spaciousness of being in time and space, and, therefore, as beings characterized by absence and a lack of completion. The dice games of Śiva and Pārvatī (and other ludic forms in which they engage) almost always unravel cosmic order by dividing and diminishing it. It is on this basis that phenomenal shapes (always partaking of the emptiness and absence of the gaps in which they are formed) coalesce, congeal, and harden. The engendered self and other are such shapes. In this respect, conscious self-identity entails absence and the quest for the other, in a search for self-fulfillment. We have also mentioned Bhṛṅgin, the outer limit of Śiva's most externalized descent into hardened maleness. Along this way, there is still the rogue figure of Śiva's tragic offspring, Andhaka.

But there is also the issue of what may be called the way back toward cosmic holism, and how, or for that matter whether, it can be accomplished. If the playful impulse is fluid and top-down, dissolving the cosmos from deep within itself, are there parallel processes that begin with congealed, separated forms and drive the cosmos inward, toward holism? We will argue that there are three processes of this sort that complement the ludic in different ways. One is violence, which, like play, attacks form. Violence usually begins with congealed, phenomenal shapes and rends them so as to destroy their unique form, including their existence. Violence breaks down form, thereby attacking the existence of gaps within god. Violence includes sacrifice, which is often directed from lower to higher cosmic levels, in a quest for transcendence and greater holism by a closing or a narrowing of the tears within the cosmos. Put otherwise, higher order beings play in order to descend; and lower order beings commit violence in order to ascend. However, for example, god, who performs violence, ascends higher than can a demon, for god is the greater encompassment to begin with. Violence, we should add, is rarely, if ever, fully successful in accomplishing the holistic joining together of parts, because it begins as an external assault, an attack on form, from the outside, that attempts to destroy the boundaries that separate and define forms. Because of its external, processual character, violence usually leaves behind a product of itself, a part that, however small, remains a basis for division.

A second process that drives toward holism is the erotic, the joining together of genders that have separated, externalized, and congealed. The erotic seeks holistic fulfillment by driving externality within, thereby fluidly fusing the exterior and interior. This rarely succeeds fully in Śaiva cosmology, perhaps because, like violence, the erotic acquires its force externally, in the gaps between beings, between genders. Beginning from exteriors, the erotic does not succeed in fully erasing these gaps. Moreover, as mentioned earlier, no offspring of Śiva and Pārvatī is ever created through conventional sexual union.[163] All are generated by one or the other of the couple, and all, therefore, are flawed in some way; each lacks some significant aspect of being. The difficulty of balanced reproduction through offspring is related directly to the difficulties of reintegrating the Śaiva cosmos following the rupture of gender. Eroticism and the ludic have an intimate, contrary relationship. Indeed, play as erotic fun, as foreplay, as the beginning of intercourse and the realization of holism, turns into ludic absence, fragmentation, and the overelaboration of parts that are sterile versions of their whole. Play, one may say, often short-circuits and destroys the erotic drive toward holism. Some versions of the creation of Andhaka take this route.

The third process that drives toward holism is *tapas*, which we discuss in chapter 3. In Śaiva cosmology, *tapas* potentially has the greatest capacity to accomplish holism because it begins from within, from the interior of being, melting down its internal divisions and relating to its homogeneity as the microcosmic homology of the macrocosmos. This process has tremendous attrac-

163. See Handelman 1987.

tion for the other gender. But then, *tapas* often is short-circuited, in turn, by eroticism, as in the *Kedārakhaṇḍa* myth. If play thus short-circuits the erotic, and the erotic short-circuits *tapas*, violence may be said to short-circuit itself—by always leaving some form of external residue (Andhaka's bones).

From the human perspective, the most attractive of these three processes that drive toward holism is the erotic. Obviously, despite the flawed cosmic offspring of Śiva and Pārvatī, for human beings the erotic is crucial for societal reproduction and continuity. But the erotic is also a sort of compromise between violence and *tapas*. Violence strives for holism through the clash of others that smash one another's hard external borders. *Tapas* is completely internal to being, melting down differences into the soft, undifferentiated flow of a liquid togetherness. The erotic combines elements of violence (otherness, externality) and *tapas* (selfhood, interiority) in joining the apparent hard exteriority of the male to the soft interiority of the female. Yet the erotic also thrives on *māyā*—the transformative power of phenomenal realities in which no thing is as it seems, or in which one thing conceals another. So, Śiva's *liṅga* is the exemplar of vital maleness and hardness. Yet in southern India the soft, liquid seed within the *liṅga* is thought of as female: "The sign of maleness is really the locus of female qualities in a man."[164]

The *Kedārakhaṇḍa* myth shifts from the division of the holistic androgyne to the controlled violence of the dice game and the consequent separation of Śiva and Pārvatī. Eroticism then, in the sequel to the game, draws them tentatively back together. But this apparent movement toward reunification or reintegration is not entirely successful:

> Pārvatī took the form of a tribal woman [an untouchable Śabarī], dark and lovely, with bright red lips, a splendid neck, a curvaceous body staggering under the weight of two magnificent breasts, her waist thin but hips and thighs fleshy and golden, with bangles on her arms and peacock feathers in her hair. Carrying a bow in her hands, a quiver on her back, she seemed to be reviving Desire, while the very bees and peacocks in that wilderness were overpowered by love.

Pārvatī has beaten Śiva at dice, shaming him and taking from him many of his external attributes. The female and male have separated and congealed in space and time, through the medium of the dice game and its aftermath. In this respect the game is profoundly antierotic. The diminished Śiva walks off by himself, far into the wilderness, to do *tapas*. Śiva is more male than he was, since his female self, Pārvatī, has left him. Pārvatī, the winner, expands to include his attributes and also remains within the inner centricity and the hierar-

164. Egnor 1978:69.

chical apicity of Kailāsa, the cosmic mountain. Yet to seek him out, she transforms herself into a female beauty, elaborating her womanly attributes, but disguising herself as a woman of very low status. The epitome of the expansive fullness of the female, in her separation from the male, she complements the diminishment into extreme maleness of Bhṛṅgin, and, indeed, of Śiva himself.

What is Pārvatī disguising? Perhaps she is hiding the partial encompassment that she acquired in the dice game. This superiority is antierotic because it has produced gender separation. So in hiding her advantage, she also disguises her antieroticism. To do this she becomes a supremely attractive female. Disguised as a lowly woman, she is seductive to Śiva but of no apparent threat to his encompassing superiority. Indeed, she basically accepts his superiority, as demanded:

> She went to where Śiva was sitting, deep in meditation on the Self, his eyes closed—he who is one and many, without limit, fashioned only from his own understanding. Confused by the humming of the bees, he woke up and saw her, and wanted her. As he reached for her hand, she vanished. Now Śiva, destroyer of Desire, was overcome, in his turn, by the pain of separation; he who knows no delusion was overwhelmed by delusion. He called to her, "Who are you, and to whom do you belong? Why are you wandering in this wilderness?"
>
> She said, "I am looking for a husband who is omniscient, who fulfills all needs, who is free and without mutations, the lord of the worlds."
>
> Said Śiva, "That's me! I'm the right husband for you."

The Śabarī seduces Śiva from his *tapas*. He forgets about his meditation on Self. He wants nothing else but to join erotically with her. His externalization and descent are again evident as he is taken over by delusion, for he cannot see Pārvatī, through the Śabarī disguise. She mocks his omnipotence, saying that she seeks an omniscient husband. He insists that he is that—but, taken in by a disguise, clearly he is not. He continues to pursue her, accepts her criticism of his behavior toward Pārvatī and her mockery of his detachment. He becomes the erotic counterpart of that Śiva whose true vision and total knowledge were occluded by the dice game. Here, his perception and knowledge are clouded by the erotic. The erotic seems now a continuation of the game, in which Pārvatī again gets what she desires by trickery. Śiva tries to break away from her again, leaving for another part of the cosmos, "where even Yogis cannot go." Yet he is eventually enticed back to reign in state with Pārvatī—this time as separate engendered beings, not as the androgyne.

Both the antierotic, controlled violence of the dice game, and the erotic disguise that emerges from the game's separation of gender, work against cosmic unification and holism. The myth begins with a focus on the high degree of inner integration of the cosmic being, the internal joining of the androgyne. The dice game rips this innerness apart into externality, into separate genders that first clash with each other and then depart from one another. Their separation stresses the congealing evolution and descent of the cosmos. Śiva goes into *tapas*, the most powerful mode of cosmic reintegration, generated entirely through the melting innerness of being. Then Pārvatī's erotic disguise—itself a play on the valuing of the externality of being over its innerness—pulls Śiva out of his *tapas*, awakening an erotic longing in him; but this longing leads to a lesser mode of union, the sexual joining of externalities, as Śiva and Pārvatī reign over the cosmos together as separate genders in a more spacious universe. This is the solution most often sought by human beings in their lives—whatever the desires of the god, which more likely point in the direction of dense innerness, total knowledge, and the encompassing whole.

11
Excursus: When Viṣṇu Plays Dice

The metaphysical specificity of Śiva's game of dice, and the deep resonances with the latter game that we can discover in the *Mahābhārata* and earlier (Upaniṣadic) texts, become still more clear when we look at other forms of the dice game—in particular, the game as played by Śiva's major rival, the great god Viṣṇu. Many stories, from different strata of the tradition, speak of Viṣṇu as being fond of the dice.[165] In some cases, these tales seem to have emerged through contact with the Śaiva materials, where dicing is so central, as we have seen; but in every instance, the Vaiṣṇava reframing of the game carries with it a consistent transformation of metaphysical assumptions. Viṣṇu, we should recall, is Māyāvin—a Trickster—and it is in this guise that he participates in the game of dice. For purposes of comparison, we will look briefly at one medieval description of Viṣṇu's dicing, from the Telugu *Viṣṇu-māyā-nāṭakamu,* by Cintalapūḍi Yĕllanāryuḍu (2.11).[166] We limit our discussion to the scene of the dice-game proper, which sets up the basic problem addressed by the narrative as a whole.

Viṣṇu and his wife Lakṣmī wanted to play dice, and they pronounced their initial wagers: she staked the gem upon her head, and he—the *kaustabha* jewel on his chest. Each of them was hopeful of, and intent upon, winning [*jayāśā-buddhi*] as they began to play. The deities in heaven, watching, had their own favorites:

165. See, e.g., the Tamil folk epic *Aṇṇaṉmārkatai*: Beck 1993, 2:433, 596.

166. We wish to thank Velcheru Narayana Rao for reading this text with us.

Bhūdevī, the Earth, wanted her husband Viṣṇu to win, whereas the wives of the gods were rooting for Lakṣmī; Sarasvatī, goddess of wisdom, wanted both of them to win.

Whenever Lakṣmī lost one of her pieces, she would go into a pout; she was angry when she was unable to bring her scattered pieces to the stage of "ripening," when the player reaches his goal. For his part, Viṣṇu simply laughed when the count failed to add up. After a while, he said: "The game is tied; let's start again." But Lakṣmī insisted that, in fact, she was winning: her pieces were ahead of his. Viṣṇu disagreed. Now Lakṣmī became even more angry, and more insistent. As they went on, it was clear that he was about to lose; it was his turn to throw, and he wanted to win this time, but instead, the throw went against him. So, tricky as he is, Viṣṇu smiled and said to himself: "Let's see how she will be if she loses a game." He used his skill at illusion [*māyā*]: now, when she threw the dice, everything turned upside down. The numbers were different than before, and she began losing. She was upset; her face paled, her body became lusterless; boiling in anger, she threw the dice ever more quickly, but each time the same number turned up on all four sides.

Finally, Lakṣmī realized that this was Viṣṇu's *māyā*. Smiling harshly, she said to him: "Is it right to deceive me like this? Do you want to give my gem to your other wife [*Bhūdevī*]? You can have it—you don't have to win it by cheating in this game. Who needs it, anyway? You want to show off the skills you like to show to fools. Your magic is ephemeral, like words written on water, like snow, like bubbles or mirages—all unreal. *My māyā*, on the other hand, is different—it is better than yours, and wholly real. You can lord it over all the worlds only because I am there beside you. Just watch: I will reabsorb into myself all your riches and splendor. Let's see what happens to your fake *māyā* then." And, unmoved by the pleas of Sarasvatī, Lakṣmī swallowed up all the beauty of Viṣṇu's world. His city, Vaikuṇṭha, went blank, empty, dead, as Lakṣmī went away.

But Viṣṇu was not discouraged for long. To humble his wife, he created, out of himself, a duplicate Lakṣmī, who restored the splendor of his world.

The text moves slowly toward the poignant moment when the "real" (and now strangely superfluous) Lakṣmī, who has exiled herself from heaven, confronts her newly created double—and is forced to acknowledge her husband's ultimate superiority. In this sense, Viṣṇu can be said to have won at the game of dice.

How does this happen? Śiva, as we have seen, never truly achieves this conclusion; he is apparently far more dependent on Pārvatī than Viṣṇu is on Lakṣmī. The entire crisis engendered by the game (as we might expect, on the basis of the Śaiva versions) is resolved here by an extraordinary act of creation by the male divinity, who, at the moment of explosion, surprisingly extricates himself from the rule-bound situation within play. This is something quite new to our experience of the dice, although in other respects, Viṣṇu's game is clearly continuous with Śiva's: Once again, we find the male pitted in bitter rivalry against his own female part, in a game with high stakes, which, sooner or later, breaks down in conflict. Moreover, the issue of trickiness, or cheating, is, once again, central, an explicit subject for argument between the two tricky players. In this case, the issue assumes an ironic ontic cast, the overt question being which of the two *māyās*—his illusion or hers, the male or female—is "real."

In a way, it is this question of trickiness that most clearly differentiates Viṣṇu's game from Śiva's. When Śiva enters into the game, he is, it seems, entirely bound by it; his self-knowledge diminishes through the play, and the sleight of hand (or cheating) that he naturally demonstrates is also, basically, internal to the game, an inherent feature of its "rules" and structure. In Viṣṇu's game, by way of contrast, the argument about rules, and cheating, actually destroys the game, as if there were a level of play that somehow remained outside the setting of the dice, and encompassed the latter. The game falls apart when Viṣṇu acts in a way that Lakṣmī perceives as outside the frame. Unlike Śiva, Viṣṇu appears to be able to move in and out of the game relatively freely. Put differently, what we are seeing here is a differentiated typology of illusion, hierarchically ordered. Thus, there is, to begin with, the illusion that belongs to the game itself, that is proper to it: this is that form of deceit that the text seems to refer to as "ripening," and that involves forms of verbal insistence, whatever the actual state of the pieces on the board. (The Telugu verb *pikku*, used in this context, connotes both this "insistence" by the player that he or she is winning, and the player's propensity to "cheat" or to "deceive".) Lakṣmī can win only in this mode, where one shapes reality by insisting that it conform to one's own wishes or perceptions. Such a "ripening" really means that the game itself is evolving into its fullest form, developing its own reality, which includes insistent trickiness. At the moment of transition, however, we suddenly find another level of illusion brought into play:

"Let's see," says the god, "how *she* will be if she loses a game." He then proceeds to turn the play upside down, as if acting from a place outside it, with powers capable of effecting what is going on inside. This level of trickiness jumbles the game entirely, so that it is, in effect, no longer possible to tell winners from losers. This is the level of Viṣṇu's *māyā*, an encompassing force that envelops a remarkably centered and stable divinity, and serves him as needed. Finally, because of the operation of this latter level, we reach a point where Lakṣmī withdraws *her māyā*, thereby impoverishing the world of her husband, though only temporarily. The text moves toward improvising a mode in which the two primary, rival forms of illusion, his and hers, can be confronted and put to an empirical test.

"His" constitutes the winning move. In a sense, there are no real rules for Viṣṇu in his play. He completely controls the as-if, constructed character of the game—in effect, he enters into a game within a game when he is ready to manipulate the results completely (all four sides of the dice turn up with the same count). This game within a game is a parody of the usual play; and while it moves into breakdown and crisis, as in the Śaiva game, and thereby detaches the female part of the godhead from the male part, Viṣṇu is under no compulsion to go away, or to perform *tapas*, in order to reconstitute his shattered wholeness. He remains basically balanced and stable in himself, and is capable of re-creating the lost female part on his own, apparently without any act or process of transformative internalization.

All of this contrasts nicely with the devolutionary course of Śiva's game, and with Śiva's own, seemingly inexorable devolution within it. The intradivine process described there follows a different logic from that implicit in the Vaiṣṇava game. Śiva is taken in by his own *māyā*, becoming subject to the game and its course, and the fragmentation that the game produces within this god can only be addressed by a radical change in direction, usually from a situation of extreme internal isolation. In Śiva's case, one can hardly speak of control; the trickiness that is part of the game leaves Śiva himself tricked, unable to meet the goddess in her autonomy and clarity. The only stability here is that of the ongoing game itself, while any attempt to stabilize Śiva, inside or outside the game, throws everything else off center. Viṣṇu's game shows us a god whose surface manifestations may well deceive us (and those around him), although beneath these masks, a relatively more solid and continuous innerness can still be found. The lurking question that then arises, as we watch him playing at dice, is a deep one, perhaps capable of being formulated as follows: Does this god really control ultimate reality, or is he, perhaps, deluding himself?

12
Unfettered, the Trickster Who Plays with God

Śiva, drawn into the dice game, is taken apart during the game—engendered, stripped naked, diminished, objectified, overwhelmed by time. The process turns him, as it were, inside out, thereby creating discontinuities in his being, empty spaces, black holes, whereas once—before the game—there was continuous, dense simultaneity of self and the cosmos. As this happens, as the god becomes spacious and emptied out, questions naturally arise: What is left of his innerness? Is this divinity still, in some sense, filled with existential residues? Or has he become no more than an empty shell?

A set of stories addresses these questions explicitly, while, at the same time offering us a surprising alternative image of wholeness, defined this time as male. They speak of Trickster-like gamblers who take on the god—actually forcing him to play—and who, like the goddess, always beat him at dice. Lowly characters in themselves, these unruly gamblers move toward higher level orders of existence by playing dice with God, and defeating him. They are impudent, supremely confident, unstable, unpredictable (thus reminiscent of ritual clowns);[167] above all, they are perfectly at home in the shifting and fluid world of the game—indeed, they are in a sense analogues of the game itself, or human embodiments of its inherent trickiness and flux. Emerging from below—unlike the god, who enters the mode of play from his higher order level of wholeness—they act as solvents on any form of solid or static being, including the rules of the game they play. This is their peculiar power: While Śiva devolves into rigid and limited forms, the Tricksters use the medium of the game to dissolve all objective obstacles to self-completion and expansion upward. Gifted, as it were, with a congenital fluidity of being or perception, they always produce wholeness for themselves, in the created cosmos, at the expense of the god.

We will follow one of these stories in some detail, noting its thematic continuities with others of this type, and its relationship to the fundamental issues raised by the game of dice. The prototype is, perhaps, the tale of Ṭhinṭhākarāla in *Kathā-sarit-sāgara* (18.71–186). But the text we will use is the *Niraṅkuśopākhyānamu* of Rudrakavi, a sixteenth-century Telugu poet probably associated with the Quṭubshāhi court in Golconda.[168] Rudrakavi appears to belong to the generation after the golden age of Telugu poetry, at the Vijayanagara court, under Kṛṣṇadevarāya (1509–1529);[169] his playful and eloquent poem should, no doubt, be seen in the context of his immediate predecessors' powerful statements on human identity, its origins and limits, and its links to the divine.[170] For our purposes, too, the question of the hero's humanity, vis-à-vis his divine opponent, is central and expressive: How is it that a lowly gambler, dissolute and unreformed, can bend the recalcitrant deity to his will?

The story is framed by a question that a king, Dharmaśīla, poses to the sage Pulaha: A desire for sensual pleasure is the most serious of all addictions; is there anyone subject to it who yet remains *outside* the domain of evil (*pāpabāhyuḍu*)? To this, the sage replies, at first, with an abstraction:

167. Handelman 1981; Shulman 1985:200–10.

168. On the questions of dating and a possible relationship to the famous Malkibharāma (Ibrahim Quṭubshāh, patron of Telugu poets), see Vasumati, n.d.:116–21. Tradition insists that Rudrakavi was of the goldsmith caste. We wish to thank Velcheru Narayana Rao for reading this text with us and commenting on it.

169. This despite the later attempt to identify him as one of Kṛṣṇadevarāya's eight court poets.

170. See Shulman 1995.

> Desire exists not in words but in the mind; neither speech nor external guise give any indication about one's capability to achieve release. Some energetic (or aggressive, or active, or foolish) men are obsessed with women, in thought, words, and deeds, yet they reach a goal [*sadgati*] which even the wise cannot attain. They are born with this ability as a result of former lives.

The story of Nirañkuśa—"Unfettered"—will exemplify this perspective; we will follow Rudrakavi's narration closely, including the asides, comments, and explanations he occasionally offers in relation to the strange events he describes.

> Unfettered was born in a Brahmin family in Māṇikyapura. He was married to a proper wife, and properly educated in the ancient texts; but he preferred the study of erotics to the Vedas, and the company of courtesans to that of his wife. With the courtesans he would play dice endlessly, with great skill. His mind was always focused on women, wherever he went. He depleted his wealth in a life of dissipation; despite his mother's attempt to direct his heart back to his wife, he persisted in his obsession until he was utterly impoverished—when the Madam unceremoniously threw him out.
>
> Thus humiliated and distressed, Unfettered headed for the forest, where he came upon a ruined Śiva temple, its wooden doorways rotted away, birds nesting in the eaves, bees filling the sanctum with their noise. He went inside and, in harmony with the divine structure of the cosmos [*daiva-ghaṭana*], addressed the god [in the form of a *liṅga*]: "You are famous for your omniscience, but that may be just like the wood-apple eaten by the elephant.[171] You may lack an inside altogether [*lona loṭ'ai*]: what you have is only an attractive surface. Will you play a game of dice with me, to test this question? I should warn you, though, that playing with me—the best of gamblers—is not at all like joking around with Pārvatī, or like strolling through the gardens on Kailāsa, or climbing through the sky, or dancing after defeating the demons in battle. I've played with experts from all over the world, but I've never seen anyone like you, who just touches the dice and turns away from the game. These are not just empty words: I have a dancer [*nartaki*] on my side, who can defeat anyone at all."

How lucidly Unfettered articulates the latent questions about this game! There is the notion that Śiva is omniscient (*sarvajña*)—but perhaps this is all show and, in reality, the god is empty inside. There is a way to test this—the game of dice—but Unfettered already knows that this is dangerous for Śiva, a mode quite unlike his other amusements and preoccupations (like playing with Pārvatī, dancing the dance of destruction, and so on). And this tricky gambler knows, in advance, that he will win; he speaks and plays from a position of apparent

171. The folk belief is that the elephant swallows the wood apple whole and digests its inner core without disturbing the shape or skin of the fruit, which reemerges, still intact, in the feces.

harmony with the divine energies (*daiva*) that govern the cosmos; these energies will "dance" dependably for him in the game.[172] The image of subtle, flowing movement is beautifully appropriate to his inner state. Nirañkuśa, too, has already undergone a certain process. His initial losses in wealth and status (to lower opponents) leave him in the paradoxically happy state of having nothing; like the Ṛg Vedic gambler discussed earlier,[173] he has held back nothing. We could describe him as devoid of surface, utterly unencumbered with externalities, full only of himself—the opposite of the god who devolves downward in play, thereby becoming heavy with attributes, partial disguises, and frozen or fragmented forms. All such guises, including the *liṅga* in the ruined temple, are exteriors—it is no wonder that no one comes to worship in the abandoned shrine. Faced with this reality, Unfettered brings to bear an unerring sense of what the god must be—that is, hollow, trapped in a congealed surface. Still, the god *is* present, and thus the question of Śiva's knowledge remains alive, eliciting even more extreme rhetorical challenges:

> But what would they wager for? Unfettered listed the possibilities—the god's bull Nandin, or his matted hair, or his trident, or the moon he wears on his crest, or his Silver Mountain. . . . But in the end he decided to make things simple: they would wager a whore for a whore. Having announced this, Unfettered awaited the god's response; but Śiva remained silent. "If you're thinking it's best not to answer, since if you play you will certainly lose, then you can be sure I won't let you slip away," declared Unfettered. "Besides, this omniscience of yours is inappropriate. Throw it away. Compete with me—you can't be a great warrior and a crybaby at the same time."
>
> Still Śiva said nothing. "If you are determined not to talk," said Unfettered, "then I have thought of a solution. I will play for you, making your moves in all honesty. Don't you know that this game is the real cause of your knowledge, Oh lover of Pārvatī?"[174] And he spread the board before the god, who is like a bee that sips from the lotus blossoms that are Pārvatī's breasts. He began to play, with determination, very rapidly, always looking ahead to the next move, following the dice wherever they led him, quickly doubling, calling out the throws—doubles! twelve! ten! eight! double three! two [which, by sleight of hand, is four]—and sometimes shouting, "You're lying!" or, "I'm lying!," to make things fair.[175] In this way, intent on winning for each side, Unfettered played with great skill—and, through the power of fate [*daivagati*], he beat the god.

172. There is an intriguing and powerful continuity between this theme and the image of the *apsaras* dancer who brings luck and success at the dice game, described in *Atharvaveda* 4.38; cf. Bloomfield 1897/1964:149–50 and his commentary (412–14).

173. See n. 45.

174. *nī vidyakū brāleyâdri-sutā-jīvita-nāyaka nĕttambu kāraṇamb' ĕṟūguduvā* (p. 51).

175. *dhṛti pĕmp' ŏndãga sārĕ sārĕ payi sārĕm jūcucun sārĕ vo-/*
vu taṟim bovucu joḍugaṭṭu taṟi ṟivvul mīṟa joḍiñcucun/

This is as close as we get to a technical description of the game. There is no question of unfairness; Unfettered is equally committed to both sides (*ubhaya-pakṣa-jayâpekṣa-rūḍha-cittūḍ'ai*). This impartiality does not, however, preclude "trickiness," even "cheating" or "sleight of hand"—since, as we know by now, this is the natural mode of play, inherent to the game as an aspect of its very structure. By the same token, each player must, it seems, accuse the other of "lying" (an ambiguous verbal form nicely allows Unfettered again to play both parts). And of course, given his internal identification with the flux of the cosmos (*daiva*), our hero wins. There is never really any question about this, anyway. More poignant is the fact that he, the lowly human gambler, has to speak and play for a god who is silent, petrified, lost inside the stone (and yet wholly and sensually obsessed with his own female persona, if we take the epithets and metaphors seriously). If omniscience can be said somehow to characterize this dense existence, it remains a useless and inert form of knowledge that Śiva can be urged to surrender—perhaps, as Unfettered says, in the interest of achieving some other form of self-knowledge through the medium of the game. There is, indeed, no other way. As we saw earlier, once the game begins, the god's perception is occluded, his wholeness impaired; and, given this vector of devolution, he will surely lose the game and be asked to pay.

Now Unfettered looked at the god and said: "Give me the girl, without hesitation, skilled gambler that you are. When we made the wager, I didn't specify which whore I had in mind. Now let me tell you. I want the most beautiful woman in the universe, the one soldiers die for and people sacrifice for and sages give up their *tapas* for—Rambhā, the courtesan of the gods. Did you hear what I said? People who know the right ways don't have to be asked to make good on their wagers. Is it right to sit there silently, without paying? I'll complain to the elders."

Unfettered now took his red upper cloth and tied it tightly around the *liṅga*.[176] And he continued his complaint against the god: "I could hardly claim that fairness is one of your qualities—didn't you take a devotee's wife for yourself? And you don't have the courage to give up anything—you own a whole Silver Mountain, but still you beg for alms! As for fame, you are famous for being Nambi's

---

jata bārā padi dacci ittiga dugā cevañca tīvañca bŏñk-/
iti nā nartakiy añcun āḍĕn ubhayāngī-karamb' epāragan.

The third line consists of borrowed terms for throws specific to the dice game (*bārā* = 12; *dacci* = 8; *tīvañca* = 4; *dugā* = 2). *pŏṅkiti,* an elided verbal form, is ambiguous: either "you are lying" or "I am lying." *nā nartaki* is unclear, perhaps another technical term—related to the "dancer" that Unbounded has previously claimed to have on his side?

176. This is called *pŏgaḍa-daṇḍa*—a neck clasp used as a form of punishment (e.g., for failure to pay tax).

pimp.[177] Your heroic nature became evident when Arjuna overcame you. Could you be a lord? You served as Bāṇa's gatekeeper. But none of this is really your fault; I blame the gods who keep insisting that you know everything. Actually, your whole lifestyle is pathetic; you only get by because you were lucky enough to happen upon that wife of yours. But for her, could one say anything about you? Unlike the god of love, I am not disturbed in the least by your owl-like gaze. So either bring me the woman at once, or slink away without pride."

He pulled the edges of the cloth even more tightly together, strangling the god. Śiva then appeared before him—perhaps because he accepted his defeat at the hands of someone who spoke the truth; or because he respected his aggressive devotion, a reflection of the fact that Unfettered was more of a god than he was;[178] or possibly because Unfettered was really an idiot, and this brought out the god's compassion. In any case, the vision of Śiva overwhelmed the impudent gambler, who began to shake with fear. Śiva calmed him: "Don't be afraid, I lost, you won. You defeated me with song and play. If I don't pay, won't people say I'm a eunuch?" Still, Unfettered prayed only to be allowed to achieve release at the god's feet.

Śiva found this amusing. "You've suddenly started speaking words that injure truth. Did you play for the ecstasies of release, or for a woman? You promised not to lie in the course of the game, so why start now? I will give you exactly what I owe. Anyway, release is not such a great thing. It will come to you naturally in the course of time, if you go on thinking about me. Meanwhile, take this remarkable woman and have a good time." And Śiva summoned Indra and ordered him to send Rambhā to earth, to satisfy the Brahmin.

There is a question of being true, of speaking the truth, and of accepting the real effects that proceed from the causal forcefulness of the truth. The game has produced its standard result, which Śiva himself affirms. Unbounded's vituperation, and the coercive strangling of the *liṅga*, finally squeeze the god out of his stony state. Though the epiphany is then too much for the gambler, the god is determined to go through with his part of the bargain. Release, he announces, is a trivial matter, which hardly requires further effort; Unfettered would do better to stick with the whore he bargained for. The poet, no more restrained in his language than his hero, boldly describes the true balance of forces: Śiva's omniscience is quite unfounded, and his successful human opponent in the dice game is, perhaps, superior—more divine, more whole—than he is.

Unfettered thus gets the girl. Once again, the god has been diminished, insulted, taken apart. But the underlying theme of the dice game—the question

177. Śiva acquired this reputation when he sought to conciliate Nampi Ārūraṉ's first wife Paravai on behalf of this devotee. See Shulman 1990:xxxiii–xxxiv.

178. *atyadhikuṇḍu devuḍ' anun añjali-dauṣṭyamu jūci mĕcci* (54).

of objectification, or rocky congealment—seeks yet another expression in the sequel to this game:

Rambhā came to Unfettered, and they made love joyfully and long, reaching heights that were, each time, entirely fresh, unknown before. So impassioned was this loving that Rambhā remained on earth with Unfettered, whom she preferred by far to all her usual, immortal lovers. When Indra learned from Nārada about this choice of hers, he cursed Rambhā to become a stone, of terrifying shape, in the Pallava kingdom. She pleaded for compassion, and Indra relented a little and announced that her curse would end when the rock would fall, in pieces, to the earth. Then he sent her away.

Rambhā went straight to Nirankuśa and, weeping and sighing, told him what had happened. He was not disturbed in the least: "In thought, word, and deed, I have made you the only woman for me, as Desire is my witness. My only mistake was in being somewhat stubborn. I've never seen you cry except for tears of pleasure. Why are you making such a fuss about this curse? I thought there was some real problem! Just go and become a rock at the edge of this city, and I will take care of all the rest." She smiled a little dryly: "Can't you let me in on your plan?" "Woman," he replied, "words are one thing, deeds another. Just leave it to me."

So, at his command, Rambhā became a rock—as tall as a hundred palmyra trees, hard and wide as a mountain. People shuddered at this sight. One day, impelled by divine forces [*daiva*], King Śatrundama mounted his horse and rode to the rock, despite the advice of all his ministers. There he was possessed by an ugly demon [*brahmarākṣasa*] who inhabited a fig tree. This king, who had never been unbalanced even in his dreams, was now shaken to the foundations: he babbled madly, wandered off by himself, laughed uncontrollably, stared wildly, uttered lies and nonsense, ran barefoot over the earth. Before, he had remained unperturbed even in the presence of beautiful women; now he was disturbed in every way. The ministers covered him up somehow or other and bustled him back to the palace; they brought exorcists who chanted *mantras*, but the king remained in the demon's grip.

Unfettered heard about this and realized that this was his opportunity to release Rambhā from her curse. He went to the court, bowed to the king and the great lords, and praised Śatrundama. "I have a divine game in me" [*nāk' ŏka daivalīla kalad'*], Unfettered said—and then, speaking as if possessed, sighing, weeping, his body shaking, he cried out that the demon would leave the body of the king only if the great rock were pulverized and sifted through a winnowing fan. The ministers were confounded but, in desperation, decided to try this plan. "The joke has come true: hit the ass and the teeth fall out![179]" they said. At their command, people from all the villages in the kingdom came with whatever implements they could find and pulverized the stone. Rambhā emerged, beautiful as ever, from the stone powder.

179. A Sanskrit proverb: *pṛṣṭha-tāḍanād danta-patanam.*

> Unfettered embraced her and, flicking away her tears with his fingernails, said: "For my sake you underwent this suffering, suppressing your unearthly beauty in a rock." Rambhā replied: "I achieved *real* immortality only when you became my friend, through the auspicious ripening of my deeds. I will never forget you, and I'll be back from time to time, either openly or in secret. The joining of body to body is no great achievement; the connection that matters is when heart meets heart." With this she went back to heaven, where Indra was amazed to see her, and very angry, assuming that his curse had failed to take effect. She explained to him what had happened—how Unfettered had liberated her from the curse—and now Indra himself came, driven by curiosity, to meet this clever Brahmin who had beaten Śiva at the game of dice. He offered Unfettered a boon, and the latter asked, first, that King Śatrundama be cured and, second, that Rambhā come and stay with him. Indra readily granted the first but insisted that the second was impossible: Divine women simply shouldn't stay on earth, but could only visit there occasionally. He promised that Rambhā would return, and that Unfettered could love her as before; in the meantime, he could live happily, as a king, surrounded by his wife, parents, and children. And so it was: Unfettered flourished, devoted to Śiva, always at one with truth, a credit to the Twice-Born castes, intent upon the three goals of human life [desire, profit, and the right action], proficient in the four Vedas, as handsome as the god with five flower arrows [Desire], familiar with the six philosophical disciplines, brilliant as the Master of the Seven Horses [the Sun], endowed with all eight forms of sensual delight and with the nine kinds of hidden treasure, his fame filling all ten directions of the cosmos.[180]

Perhaps instinctively, the poet concludes his narrative with the kind of playful counting wisdom traditionally associated with the successful dice player.[181] To the end—which is no end—Unfettered remains everything his name implies, a free and fluid being, inimical to boundaries, unintimidated by hierarchical authority, labile, dynamic, and resistant to all forms of objectification. He is unencumbered and undefined, his lowliness being a strange, recursive looping back (or down) to deep innerness, inimical to anything that is merely surface. It is for this reason that Rambhā's curse is of so little consequence to him: he knows that he can dissolve the rock she has become, as he corrodes and destroys all solid masses, all reified concepts or rules. For him, even Indra's curse is only an opportunity for further play. In this respect, Unfettered is, in human terms, the antithesis of any stable identity or embodiments of authority, such as we find in Śatrundama, the hapless king. The latter, understand-

180. The ten are the four quarters, the four intermediate points, the center, and the zenith.

181. Recall Nala's acquisition of the "heart of the dice" (*akṣa-hṛdaya*), the facility with numbers that allows him his final victory in the game. See Shulman 1994; also Grierson 1904. But is Nala's gift the ability to calculate rapidly and correctly, or the ability to *create* and shape reality as he knows it? In the latter case, he would belong in the same series as Unfettered. See our further discussion in section 13.

ably, from this perspective, is literally demented when he comes into contact with extreme objectification—that is, the rocky Rambhā. There is surely a sense in which this king's experience is seen as paradigmatic for human minds in general, with their dangerous propensity to delimit, regulate, and categorize in rigid ways, thereby making others, and the living parts of their own selves, into lifeless objects. Such a perceptual stance, it seems, is actually a form of madness.

To this drama of deadly self-objectification, Unfettered brings a reckless readiness to play, which includes a kind of wily quick-wittedness in any rule-governed domain. In the game of dice, as in love, he is never truly fettered by the rules. No doubt, this is the reason he is also so successful in his loving: more than any other figure we will meet, including—above all—Śiva and his wife, Unfettered approaches the goal of an erotic holism, the reintegration of the divided and exclusively defined male and female parts of the being. For Śiva and Pārvatī, as we shall see, marriage remains burdened by frustrating externality, a doomed attempt to merge two separate innernesses via two congealed exteriors. Not so for the tricky gambler, who, as Rambhā so eloquently attests, has somehow managed to bring about the true connection between hearts.

Not for nothing is Unfettered said to be more god than god. When Śiva enters the dice game, usually under the magnetic impetus of the female, he shrinks into petrified states of reduced existence. Here, by way of contrast, the male successfully resists all such diminution, and it is the female who undergoes the severe loss of rocky condensation—apparently because of the gods' envy of her good fortune in the domain just described. Indra, king of the gods, is trapped in his admittedly divine identity, and characteristically insists on the necessary separation of psychocosmic realms. Superhuman courtesans such as Rambhā "simply shouldn't stay on earth." His curse is thus, in a real sense, the desperate but natural projection onto Rambhā of the circumscribed and frozen state of being in which Indra normally finds himself, at great internal cost. He puts a curse on her, so that she might be as cold, contained, and fixed in place as he is.[182]

Here, stoniness has the quality of frozen density, in contrast to the fiery density of the godhead before it enters into play; and it is the labile, uneven, human trickster, a slippery *subject*, who finds a way to deobjectify his lost lover. The stone is pulverized and even winnowed—stoniness itself being reduced to a soft and powdery dust—and, in a moment of considerable emotional power, the captive woman emerges, full of movement, from what had once been

182. It would be interesting to explore how often the curses in Hindu stories externalize an ongoing internal struggle within the curser.

rock.[183] The other stories from this series offer expressive variations on this theme. Thus, in the Tamil text *Mataṉakāmarājaṉ katai,* the gifted gambler plays with (and for) Viṣṇu in his temple, and, naturally, wins; when the stone image of the god remains silent, refusing to pay, the trickster takes hold of the image of Viṣṇu's wife Lakṣmī and proceeds to walk away. This forces Viṣṇu to speak up at last, and he promises to pay his debt the next morning.[184] Observe how the stony goddess is actually uprooted, forced into movement, kidnapped by the master of the dice.[185] In the parallel tale of Ṭhinṭhākarāla, from the *Kathāsaritsāgara*, the divine courtesan, frozen into a stone image (*śālabhañjikā*) in a temple, sees her trickster-lover and even feels him brush against her; in despair, she begins to weep.[186] Could anything capture the real nature of the existential predicament more precisely than this picture of the weeping stone? Not surprisingly, this moment leads directly to the destruction of the temple and the girl's release.

In all these stories, the key to the hero's triumph lies in his creative ability to bend the rules to his purpose. In a deeper sense, the rules hardly exist for him as such; he refuses to allow them to solidify into static or constraining forms, just as he dissolves other objectified realities that stand in his way. In this respect, he is far better suited to the deceptive and constantly shifting game than his divine opponent, who, by entering this arena, has already become caught up in the self-impoverishment of bounded existence—for example, by congealing into the rocky forms one finds in his shrine. The contours of the temple icon are clear-cut, conventionally defined. For that very reason, "the gods themselves are helplessly terrified of anyone who is deeply flawed, off balance [*viṣama*], and quite indifferent to the desirable or undesirable outcome [of the game]."[187] Imbalance suggests movement, internal dynamism, and a kind of freedom. It means making rules into a malleable medium of potential transition in one's state: thus, convention dictates that a move in the dice game is acceptable if the opponent fails to contest it; by this logic, Ṭhinṭhākarāla, the trickster-hero of the *Kathāsaritsāgara* story, forces the iconic images of his divine opponents to play with him, and to lose. Śiva—in the guise of Mahākāla,

183. Compare the famous example of Ahalyā, cursed by her husband to become a rock, and revived at the touch of Rāma's feet: *Rāmāyaṇa* 1.48–49; cf. the discussion in Narayana Rao, Shulman, and Subrahmanyam 1992:165–67.

184. *Mataṉakāmarājaṉ katai* 8 (1975:156–69).

185. Later in the story, the 11 towers of the Viśvanātha temple in Benares have to be demolished and rebuilt in order to free the celestial courtesan from her petrified state.

186. *Kathāsaritsāgara* 18.174–75.

187. Ibid., 18.95.

Death or Time—counters with another useful rule: A player can always state, *before* the dice are thrown, that he opts out of the game (*ito 'haṃ nirgato dyūtāt*, 18.90). For a moment, the trickster is stymied, unable to coerce the god into play. Then he prays to him, depicting Śiva verbally in a humiliating, naked form, sitting with his head between his knees, as his attributes and possessions—the crescent moon, his bull, his elephant's skin—have all been lost to the goddess at the game of dice (18:99). This act of visionary blackmail, all too true—in effect, another, unexpected move in the game—bears fruit: the god produces the voluptuous girl.

This is the standard outcome, but there are others. Veñkaṭeśvara, the lord of Tirupati, played dice with a north Indian Yogi named Haṭhirāmji; as usual, the god lost. That is why the Haṭhirāmji mutt at Tirupati is situated 100 meters higher up the hill than the god's own temple.[188] A variant of this pattern, from the world of Tamil Śaiva hagiography, shows us Mūrkkanāyaðār, "the fool," one of the 63 exemplary devotees of Śiva (*nāyaṉmār*). A gifted dice player, this man was obsessed with feeding other worshipers of the god. When he exhausted his own resources, he took to playing dice in order to be able to buy food for the devotees. He would entice his opponents by letting them win the first round (*muṟ-cūtu*), then defeat them, without fail, in subsequent rounds (*piṟ-cūtu*). If they refused to pay, he would stab them with his dagger.[189] The trickster's perfect attunement to, or harmonic resonance with, the dice can also, it seems, provide ecstasies other than the erotic.

13
One More Game

To speak in terms of "attunement" or "resonance" may, however, be somewhat misleading. Basically, the trickster's gift has to do more with an internal fluidity that eludes and dissolves all forms of external concretization. This option, however, is *never* available to the god, for whom the very entry into play is already both constricting and potentially destructive. Only lower level characters who move upward, like Unfettered, can bring to bear the kind of elasticity that allows for anything like a real victory in this game. Notice that a victory of this sort is utterly distinct from the contrived results of the Rājasūya-type dice games, which control the outcome by manipulating the *bandhu* inter-

188. Field notes, Haṭhirāmjimutt, Tirupati, May 12, 1993. See also, P. M. Muniswamy Chetty 60–63: initially the Yogi played for the silent, impassive deity; later, the god started coming every day to play, of his own volition.

189. *Pĕriya Purāṇam* 3623–34.

connections, homologies, and parallelisms that pervade the ritually conjoined levels of reality—and which also manage to keep the center out of play. Dice cubes marked with the conventional, numbered dots may well present us with images of a cosmos in perfect order and sequential process, its texture continuous and harmoniously integrated—the secure and symmetrical world that the ritual seeks to bring into being. Something of this hope attaches to the famous case of Nala and the knowledge he acquires, the so-called *akṣa-hṛdaya* ("heart of dice");[190] but we may be closer to this "heart" of the matter if we conceive of Nala's newfound knowledge not as a technical expertise in counting magic, or even as a hard-won facility in calculating a series of complicated moves with many dice or tokens, but, rather, as a creative ability to bring external reality into line with his own precise, internal imagination of it. In this sense, Nala really belongs with the tricksters, who are more god than God.

The point, of course, for our purposes, is that God himself (perhaps also herself) is considerably less than God—from the moment he/she begins to play. The game disrupts his inner consistency, opening up holes and spaces in his being, rendering him porous, hollow, and continuously hungry. We have tried to explicate the logic of this process as observed, first, in the *Kedārakhaṇḍa* version of the game. In lieu of summary, let us turn here to one more version of Śiva's game with Pārvatī—this time, not *chaupar* or its south Indian equivalents, but the Tulu game known as *cĕnnĕ* (a version of mancala, as we have seen):[191]

> Īśvara Dĕvere (Śiva) and Pārvatī Devi decided to play *cĕnnĕ*, so Pārvatī went up to the seventh floor and brought down the golden and silver beads needed to play the game. They set up the board and began to play. Īśvara Dĕvere lost the first house in the first game, and when they played a second game, he lost the second house. When they played the third game, he lost a third house, and when they played a fourth game, he lost a fourth house. They played a fifth game and a sixth game and a seventh game, and he lost them all. After he had lost the ninth game, Isvara said, "I'm hungry and thirsty. My head's spinning and I feel giddy. Quick, Pārvatī, go inside and bring me milk and water."
>
> Pārvatī got up to get the milk and water for him. As she crossed the threshold of the room, she tripped and banged her head on the top of the door. "Alas! Alas! Why has the threshold obstructed me and the upper part of the door hit me?" Then she thought to herself, "These obstructions may be a sign of some inauspicious act which is to befall me."
>
> Bringing the milk and water, Pārvatī returned to the *cĕnnĕ* table. As she sat down, she noticed that the *cĕnnĕ* board had been turned around so that the win-

190. See the discussion in Shulman 1994.

191. See our discussion in section 5 of this chapter. The following text is reproduced from Claus 1986:290–93.

ning side now faced Īśvara. Pārvatī became furious and kicked the board over. Seeing what she had done, Īśvara became angry and, grabbing her by her braid, he slapped her. Jumping in anger, Īśvara said, "I'm going to shoot birds." Then he cursed Pārvatī by saying, "I hope your silk sari is eaten by white ants!" He stormed out of the house, taking with him his golden knife, silver snuff box, and silver lime box.

As soon as he left the house, Pārvatī began to menstruate. For three days she remained outside, and on the fourth day she made preparations for her bath. She crushed soap nuts, and she called the Maḍivāla [washerman] boy to bring her *maḍi* [ritually pure] clothes. When he brought them, she said, "Keep them on the plank on the porch."

Then she brought him water to wash his hands, and she gave him a large rice meal. When he was through eating, Pārvatī said, "Take betel leaves and areca nut as you want." He chewed, and then she brought him a cup of oil with a spoon, and she poured heaps of oil onto his head. Then she took a measuring pot and she filled it with rupees and gave it to him.

"Now I'm leaving, elder sister," said the Maḍivāla.

"Yes, you may go," said Pārvatī.

As soon as he left, Pārvatī thought to herself, "Now I think I'll have a look at my good silk sari in that trunk." When she opened the trunk, she found that it had been ruined by ants! "Alas! Alas!" she cried, putting the sari back into the trunk.

Pārvatī quickly pounded some charcoal and added water to it to prepare a paste. She smeared the paste on her face to make herself black. Then she changed her sari, put on a *muṭṭale* cap of a Kāḍu Korpālu [Untouchable], and took a curved knife. Then Pārvatī went to the forest and sat down at the base of a tree. Using her curved knife like a comb, she began to pick the lice from her hair. While she was doing this, along came Īśvara Dĕvere.

He stopped by her and said, "What are you doing here, Kāḍu Korpālu?"

"Oh, nothing, Dĕvere! I'm just sitting here and picking lice from my hair," replied the Korpālu.

"Don't stop what you are doing because of me," said Īśvara. "I've got some fine areca nut, so sweet that the bats have chewed its outer husk, and I have the choicest of betel leaves. Let's chew together!"

"Oh, no, I don't want to, Lord!" said the Korpālu shyly. "I have my own areca nut that I collected from fallen nuts, and I have some wilted leaves that have already turned yellow. What's mine I will chew!"

But Īśvara was insistent: "What you have, you keep for later. Let it remain with you. Let's chew the tender leaves that I have and let me hold your hand!"

"Oh, alas, my Lord! What kind of a way is that to speak to a Kāḍu Korpālu?" she said.

"What difference does it make if you are a Kāḍu Korpālu? You're a human being, aren't you? I'm a human being, aren't I? Our blood is the same, isn't it?" answered Īśvara.

"What you are saying is not right," she said. "You are a Dĕvere and I am a Kāḍu Korpālu."

Then Īśvara and the girl remained in the forest together for two days and three nights. On the third day, Īśvara said, "I'm going now, Kāḍu Korpālu."

"If you are going, then go, but just one thing. If I get pregnant, who will pay for my expenses?"

"I will provide for your needs. Here, I have a golden knife, a silver case for lime, and a silver snuff box. I also have a golden ring with my seal. Take these things. Use them for your expenses if you get pregnant!" said Īśvara. "Now I am going back to my palace, Kāḍu Korpālu." Īśvara ran back home by one path and Pārvatī ran home by another path.

When she returned to the house, Pārvatī quickly took a bath, put on *kumkum*, the red dot on her forehead, and combed her hair. Before she even had a chance to put on her sari, Īśvara arrived home. He sat down on the swinging plank, and Pārvatī brought him milk in a dish and water in a bowl. As she gave him the water she said, "I have a feeling that you had sex with someone."

"No, I didn't," said Īśvara.

"Didn't you have sex with a Kāḍu Korpālu? When you left here, you took your golden knife, your silver box for lime, and the silver snuff box. Didn't you give those things to the Kāḍu Korpālu?"

"I didn't give them to her," said Īśvara. "Don't say things like that about me. I didn't do it!"

"Don't lie to me! The Kāḍu Korpālu came here and gave those things to me!"

"Where did you see her?" asked Īśvara.

"She came here and gave them to me," repeated Pārvatī.

"Didn't white ants eat your silk sari?" asked Īśvara.

"No, even though you gave a *vara* [curse] as you were leaving, nothing happened," answered Pārvatī.

"While I was gone, what did you do? What happened here?"

"Nothing happened here!" said Pārvatī. "I didn't hold the hand of a Maḍivāla nor did I eat the *ĕñjāḷu* [leftover food] of a Maḍivāla."

Then Īśvara drank the water and the milk she had offered him and said, "You have no defects. You were born from truth. Let us be on good terms together."

Clearly, this Tulu story, from a remote and culturally distinctive part of south India, runs parallel, for the most part, to the Sanskrit myth of Śiva's dice game that we have cited at such length. Śiva plays with Pārvatī, and loses to her; an argument develops, and the game explodes; the two players are separated from one another, only to come together again in an erotic context, itself laden with tensions, masquerading, and further division. A certain advantage remains with Pārvatī throughout. Indeed, Śiva's consciousness, so to speak, is conspicuously deficient: his spiraling losses in the game are, if anything, intensified by his utter failure to recognize his own disguised wife in the forest, and by his subsequent loss to her of the surviving pieces of his former life that he has brought with him—the knife, snuff box, lime box, and signet ring (the latter a particularly powerful statement of his identity, which he is prepared to give up). Essentially, whatever he once had is transferred to her, although she has her own loss as well—the silk sari devoured by white ants. The latter theme is suggestive of the darker side of *her* process—technically winning at the game, she nevertheless strikes her head against the threshold, is then stripped of her external covering, rendered impure (first, through menstruation; later, through an Untouchable disguise), and, as such, exiled from her home.

For all that, Pārvatī appears to represent, in this story, an image of relative fullness, in contrast to the sense of emptiness that plagues the god. Recall, too, that this is the inner logic of the game itself: *cĕnnĕ* is a game of concave holes that are waiting to be filled by seeds or tokens. It is, then, meaningful that the spatial center of the story—the palace of this divine couple—is emptied out as a result of play. But it might be more accurate to think in terms of surface, as opposed to depth, as the more powerful axis of development in this rich tale. Śiva, in this light, is driven toward the surface, toward states of increasing superficiality and arid externality. He cannot penetrate his wife's disguise, cannot see her for who she is; he is wholly taken in by the surface that presents itself to him, in his ever-more-reduced and porous state. For Pārvatī, the black skin she simulates is never more than a useful disguise; she is aware of herself throughout, and purifies herself successfully, in the total absence of her husband, with the help of a seductive, but ultimately innocent, encounter with the Washerman. She strikes her head on the threshold, but such borders and surfaces can only impede her, never fully arresting her movement. If the game could be said to have made her an Untouchable, in one sense or another, she nevertheless continues to possess the wit and the means to overcome this state, and even to achieve satiety and the satisfaction of exposing Śiva's failures and lies.[192] Her innerness, we might say, survives more or less intact, and in a state of fullness, whereas *his* escapes through gaping holes and interstices to the impoverished surface. It is there, exiled in the external, that Śiva remains trapped. He offers her the signs and tokens of his exteriority—but he himself still cannot see.

No wonder, then, that this god is habitually described as hungry. In our story, he demands milk and water—initially as a ruse to remove Pārvatī from the arena, so that he can turn the board around; but the myth ends with another offering of liquids, which he internalizes, while, at the same time, acknowledging her superiority, her truthfulness, and his defeat.

> You have no defects. You were born from truth. Let us be on good terms together.

192. On the motif of the markers of identity—here, the snuff box, etc.—left by the lover in the hands of his disguised or duplicitous beloved, see Doniger (in press).

These are his words, which we might translate simply as: "You have won." He ends up by accepting liquid from her, as if proclaiming both his own emptiness and the terrible elusiveness of any truly fluid innerness for male gods.

Eating and chewing are also central elements of the erotic encounter in the forest: "Let's chew together," says the god, to which the Untouchable Korpālu replies, "What's mine I will chew!" Both statements are accurate reflections of existential realities and needs. In general, we could say that this god hungers for himself—that is, he yearns to reinternalize all those parts of himself that have slipped out of him into the world (and into his partner). If he could but eat up those lost pieces, he might be whole again. This hunger—for food, for love, for sex, for knowledge—is, finally, a desperate fantasy of fullness. From the viewpoint of the world—that is, of our own existence, as scattered pieces of this godhead, negatives to the positive realities of his prior wholeness—this makes his presence and his attention into a literally consuming force. It may also explain why we, as partial beings, are capable of devouring, or internalizing, him.

But from *his* point of view, the process is almost hopeless. He is caught on a hook embedded so deep that even the most powerful moves toward reconstitution will also inevitably become stuck on it. Once the outward movement of self-objectification begins, once the fragments of continuous innerness splinter and escape, the god expends himself in the pursuit of shadows; and every step back, every act of deexternalization, or reinternalization, is susceptible to a reversal, a diversion, or a seductive countermove. No solution on the level of externalities can really work—hence even the erotic recombination of the separated male and female parts, as in our story, produces more of a truce than a true reunion. "Let us be on good terms together": this is Śiva's perhaps quixotic wish, plaintive and appealing. It might even work, for a while—until the next round of dice.

II

The Andhaka Outcome

Nothing is ever stable in itself for even a passing moment; everything grows and wanes. . . . If we want to speak of a lessening of constituent features, that is female; if we wish to speak of their externalization, that is male.[1]

I am a token in this battle, a life-and-death game of dice between two players, Śiva and the goddess. Whoever wins gets me.

[Pārvatī to Andhaka's envoy][2]

1
Withered Clown

There is a dependable witness to Śiva's game of dice, a witness whose presence eloquently speaks to the nature of the process implicit in the game. This is Bhṛṅgin—fleshless, bloodless, an eery composite of dessicated bones. Bhṛṅgin is the skeleton at all of Śiva's feasts. We have seen him, first, at Elephanta, where he watches the dice game that sets the whole mythic scenario in motion; but he is also present there with Śiva as he dances, and in the Rāvaṇa panel, at the end of the pilgrim's circumambulation. Even more to the point, Bhṛṅgin appears in his earlier form—as Andhaka, Śiva's doomed child—in the panel that represents the artistic culmination of the entire series in the

1. *Mahābhāṣya* of Patañjali 1, p. 246 (on Pāṇini, 1.2.64); see the discussion in Deshpande 1992:37.

2. *Vāmanapurāṇa* 40.51, reading *padātiḥ* for *patākā*, in the first *pada*, with several manuscripts.

Elephanta cave. Andhaka's transformation into Bhṛṅgin completes and concludes one central developmental strand that emerges from the game, and also opens up a second major course or sequence. To state the matter in a crudely linear dimension, perhaps foreign to its logic: when Śiva plays dice, at once engendering and isolating himself (as male) in the game, he moves toward a moment when he will be forced to impale his blind son Andhaka on his trident, thereby producing the parodic masculine, misformed Bhṛṅgin, in a world of destructive sexual isolation and existential impoverishment. At the same time, given the Andhaka outcome, an alternative path toward reconstituting the self-fragmenting godhead becomes available and active.

The dice game opens up spaces inside god—spaces of uncertainty, of tentative selfhood, of devolution outward. Andhaka is one such space, dark, menacing, unformed. Once externalized by the god, with Pārvatī's help, this dark gap in the texture of reality objectifies itself, congeals, petrifies—although it remains pregnant with dangerous energies of desire. The Andhaka story is about the god's relationship to this potentially destructive and uncertain part of himself, viewed in the context of an internal split in the godhead, along lines of gender and the general problems consequent upon Śiva's self-externalizing drive. In important ways, this story shows us what it really means to call god a male, taking this label seriously, and nonmetaphorically. If Śiva can be referred to by the pronoun "he"—as the texts repeatedly do, as we do in their wake—then, sooner or later, "he" must deal with "his" aborted Andhaka-self.

Note that these two—Śiva and Andhaka/Bhṛṅgin—are, in any case, remarkably alike. Bhṛṅgin's emaciated body looks like a caricature of the yogic Śiva, at the higher reaches of self-transformation, via the internalizing mode we refer to as *tapas*.[3] It is entirely appropriate that this ghoulish figure should be assimilated to the ranks of Śiva's terrifying, usually deformed or misformed followers (the Śaiva *gaṇas*); all of them show us that side of this god that is off balance, hideous, saturated with death. In addition, Bhṛṅgin has a third, bony leg, a gift from Śiva that allows this pathetic skeleton somehow to stand erect; here, too, the servant and follower mimics or caricatures his ithyphallic lord.

The story told to explain this feature claims that Bhṛṅgin was unwilling to worship Śiva in any but his (the god's) entirely masculine persona; and that when Śiva appeared to him as the androgyne, this fanatical devotee became a bee or beetle (*bhṛṅga*) that burrowed straight through the middle of the androgynous body, thus circumambulating only the male half, on the right. The goddess, very angry, put a curse on him to make him lose his flesh and blood (i.e., the female parts of the body), and he was reduced to a ghoulish skeleton,

3. We discuss this term at length in chapter III.

barely able to stand; Śiva then helped him by granting him a third leg, growing out of the space between the other two.[4] Already, we see here the undying animosity that reigns between Bhṛṅgin and everything feminine. There are, however, other attempts to understand his emaciated state—for example, by deriving it from his anxieties about Śiva's contrary nature:

"Śiva lives by begging, so how
can he get rich?
Once Pārvatī took half his body
in a game of dice.
Now Gaṅgā stands guard on his head
lest she steal the other half
in her rage.
O Lord, where will it all lead?"

Withered Bhṛṅgin ponders this,
his heart in pain.[5]

One hears the consistent note of suspicion about Pārvatī's intentions vis-à-vis this god; observe, also, the stable link between Bhṛṅgin and the game of dice. This game is always on his mind, in a manner related to more general concerns about the uncertainties and dangers that surround his god:

"He's nobody's servant.
Doesn't farm the land.
Won't buy or sell.
Inherited nothing from his ancestors.
Can't count on relatives for help,
or, for that matter,
on anyone else.
All he likes—
to the point of madness—
is dice and women.
He won't stop playing.
So, naturally, our Lord
has come to this.
And what will happen to me?"

4. Krishna Sastri 1974:165 (and see plate 105); Gopinatha Rao 1914–16:2,1,322–23; *Tirucĕṅkoṭṭumāṉmiyam*, 22–26. And cf. O'Flaherty 1980:316–17.

5. *Saduktikarṇâmṛta* 155 (anonymous).

Though he wears himself down
with such worries, Bhṛṅgin
can still protect you.[6]

God is imperiled by some threat from within, which takes the form of a "mad" obsession with women and the dice; Bhṛṅgin worries about this double enemy, to the point of shriveling his body to near extinction. If Śiva succumbs, so to speak, what hope is there for his servant? In these verses, this panic-stricken worrywart assumes a somewhat ludicrous guise. Some texts actually seem to characterize Bhṛṅgin as a kind of Vidūṣaka, or clown, at Śiva's unruly court, thereby both enhancing his parodic role and establishing a still deeper relation between his story and the dominant mode of divine play.[7] But if we wish to understand Bhṛṅgin more fully, including this link to the theme of playing, we will have to look in detail at the ancient story of his prior, unreconstructed demonic form.

2
Mistress of Play

The *Mahābhārata* refers quite often to Śiva as the slayer of Andhaka, but never tells the story (see figure 13). There seem to be no earlier references. Iconographic depictions become frequent by the middle of the first millennium; these include the astounding carvings at Elephanta and Ellora that we discuss later in this chapter. By far, the most complete Purāṇic version is that of *Śivapurāṇa*, which is relatively late (presumably several centuries later than the cave panels); we will follow this version closely in the next section. There are earlier accounts in the *Harivaṃsa* and the *Matsya*, *Kūrma*, and *Vāmana Purāṇas,* sometimes including Andhaka's transformation into Bhṛṅgin. In addition, the ninth-century Kashmiri poet Ratnâkara composed a long lyrical narrative (*kāvya*) on this myth, the *Haravijaya* ("Śiva's victory")—unquestionably, one of the richest of surviving accounts, replete with powerful insights into Andhaka's relations with other Śaiva (and early Tantric) materials. Later, the south Indian tradition absorbed, localized, and extended the Andhaka myth in highly original ways.

6. *Saduktikarṇâmṛta* 154 (Bhavânanda).

7. Nannĕcoḍa refers to Bhṛṅgirīṭa as *parihāsa-peśalâlāpa-hāsyâlāpa-vyākulita-hāsya-rasa-rasāyaṇa-pūrita-sthāna-mandiruṇḍai* (3.2)—"positioned to effect the alchemy of comic flavor, stirred up by jokes and witticisms and amusing words."

FIGURE 13. Śiva kills the demon Andhaka. Elephanta, Cave 1.

The common core of all these tellings includes the following archaic elements: Andhaka was an embodiment of demonic darkness, often described as blind; he was the son (sometimes an adopted son) of the famous demon Hiraṇyakaśipu (traditional enemy of Viṣṇu in his Man-Lion form), or of that demon's brother, Hiraṇyâkṣa. He performed *tapas*, won great power, and tried to direct this power toward fulfilling his lust for Pārvatī, Śiva's wife. Śiva fought against him, impaled him on his trident, and burned away his flesh and blood.[8]

8. *Kūrmapurāṇa* 1.15.121–218; *Harivaṃśa*, app. 29C; *Vāmanapurāṇa* 40, 44; *Varāhapurāṇa* 27; *Matsyapurāṇa* 179, 252; and cf. *Liṅgapurāṇa* 1.93; *Padmapurāṇa* 5.43.7–96; *Skandapurāṇa* 5.2.51.

This is, then, a myth of the god's attack on another demonic enemy, who is linked with blindness or darkness, and with desire for the female part of the divine. Around this core, various additional elements have become integrated into the later tellings, which usually insist that Andhaka was Śiva's own son, born when Pārvatī covered her husband's eyes. In the course of Andhaka's war against the gods, the latter are often said to have fled and to have disguised themselves as women. Moreover, a critical stage in the final battle requires yet another form of female presence: when Andhaka was impaled by Śiva, his blood dripped to the earth, and from each drop, new Andhaka clones emerged; to prevent this continued generation, the Seven Mothers joined the fight, and their leader, the gruesome Cāmuṇḍā, held a bowl beneath the wounded demon to catch his blood (see figures 14 and 15). Out of this moment of total conflict

FIGURE 14. Śiva slays Andhaka. Ellora, Cave 15.

FIGURE 15. Detail of Śiva slaying Andhaka: Cāmuṇḍā catches Andhaka's blood. Ellora, Cave 15.

comes a movement of transfiguration; Andhaka's consciousness expands to recognize Śiva as god, and Śiva renames him Bhṛṅgin and makes him leader of his ghouls (*gaṇapati*). Many texts also connect the slaying of Andhaka with Śiva's violent dance.

We will attempt to work through the various strands elaborated by both textual and iconographic representations of this myth; our primary text will be the full *Śivapurāṇa* version, supplemented by the Kashmiri *kāvya* and by the other Purāṇic accounts. We will also examine the Tamil vision of Andhaka in Arcot, in relation to another localized figure who replicates some of the Andhaka themes; and we will conclude with the expressive sequel to the Andhaka story—that is, the myth of Andhaka's son Āḍi, another outgrowth of the game of dice. Indeed, the dice game and its implicit metaphysics should always be kept in mind as the wider context of this story; Andhaka/Bhṛṅgin, as already stated, seems to be an unavoidable by-product of this game. Just to establish this stable association with the generalized context of playing, and to give something of the characteristic flavor of the medieval variants, we will start with the following rather simple, late, and truncated version of the story.

The demon king Hiraṇyakaśipu, who was killed by Viṣṇu, had two sons—the pious Prahlāda, who refused the kingdom, and Andhaka, who ruled after his father's death. Andhaka tortured his body, fasting for thousands of years, his inner being at peace, without anger, desire, pride or envy. At length, when Brahmā offered him a boon, he asked to be free from old age and from dying.

Brahmā granted this boon, although no one born fails to die; and he also promised him that his kingdom would be as fruitful as the graveyard, and as filled with thorns and cruelty.

Now Andhaka wanted to fight the gods, to take revenge for his father's death. At first, the demons routed the army of the gods. Śiva appeared, eager to help them—by summoning up the goddess from the fire. He said to her, "Every female in the world bears your form. I will give you troops of Mothers, emaciated by hunger, to devour the demons. Because your very essence is play [*keli*], you will be known as Kelīśvarī, Mistress of Play. Whoever worships you in this form will be victorious in battle."

The Goddess and the Mothers set off to do battle with Andhaka; but his demon-soldiers, holding fast to their masculine nature [*pauruṣe sve vyavasthitāḥ*], refused to strike back at these women. Nārada arrived and told Andhaka that they were not really women at all, and that the goddess had materialized out of the fire to kill him. As they were talking, a dreadful cry resounded through the world—the cry of the demon warriors as they were being eaten, or half-eaten, by the voracious Mothers. Andhaka could do nothing to save them, so he released a weapon of darkness that covered the universe in black; only he, the demon king, could see. He struck down the Yoginī warriors, but new ones constantly arose. In despair, he sought out his guru, Śukra, and Śukra went to do *tapas*, offering his flesh into the fire, at the shrine of the Golden Lord [Hāṭakeśvara, in Gujarat]. There, the Mistress of Play appeared before him and asked him not to destroy his own body. He, in turn, begged her to offer Andhaka the same succor she had previously given Śiva. Kelīśvarī, Mistress of Play, taught Śukra the science that is called Deathless, by which dead demons could be revived.

At Śukra's urging, Andhaka, too, worshiped this goddess as well as the other Mothers, according to their proper rank and order [*yathājyeṣṭhaṃ yathākramam*]. The devoured demons were now revived. But Andhaka was still angry at Śiva. He sent a messenger to tell Śiva to leave the gods alone, and to stay put on his

> mountain, Kailāsa; otherwise, Andhaka would destroy him. Enraged, Śiva came to fight. They hurled weapons at each other, then fought hand to hand. Śiva struck Andhaka through the heart with the Kaubera weapon and impaled him on his trident. Thus impaled, whirling around like a wheel, Andhaka understood his situation and began to sing Śiva's praises; he begged Śiva to finish him off quickly. But Śiva said, "I never intended to kill you. You will become one of my troops [*gaṇas*], released from your demonic form of being." Because Andhaka was still buzzing loudly like a black bee [*bhṛṅga*], he received the name Bhṛṅgirīṭa.[9]

The ultimate transfiguration of the impaled demon is a stable element in the story; Śiva's antagonist, apparently close to him on various levels, becomes his faithful follower in the end. The intimate relations between these two figures seem to find expression, in the present case, in their parallel connection to the goddess Kelīśvarī, the impartial Mistress of Play. She initially sides with Śiva, then transfers her energies to Andhaka at his teacher Śukra's request. It is very striking that this goddess, clearly the emotional and metaphysical centerpiece of this version, occupies a space somewhere between the two warring camps; she is, we might even say, the strange medium of connectivity that binds Andhaka to Śiva, a fiery and playful presence that structures their agonistic meeting. Indeed, as such, she apparently embodies the play impulse as such, which belongs to nobody but is molded by the desires and needs of the antagonistic players.

This goddess holds in her hands the keys to life and death (hence, also, the keys to time). She knows a science that is named Deathless, through which slain demons can be revived. She pleads with Śukra not to destroy his body. In general, the vast destructiveness unleashed in the story moves toward reversing itself through her intervention. Andhaka will be transformed, not slain. At the same time, as part of the same process, there is a persistent theme of transformation in another direction altogether—that is, the constitution of sexual identity; the gods' army turns into a militant female force (although there remains some question, according to Nārada, about the real gender of these warriors). Faced with Andhaka, males are feminized. A strangely parallel polarization has taken place: Women appear as emaciated, devouring mothers, while two of the main male figures—Śukra and Andhaka—become emaciated, fleshless, in the course of their violent *tapas*. Bhṛṅgin, we recall, maintains his skeletal male state within Śiva's domain, *after* his transfiguration.

So, Andhaka presents a challenge to be met by devouring divine females, while he himself is a violently decomposed male, and is, in this sense, close to his ultimate enemy, Śiva. It is this process of decomposition, in association with

9. *Skandapurāṇa* 6.149–51.

a form of apparent sexual inversion and polarization, that we seek to understand. But there is more. This version of the story emerges out of the shrine of the goddess Kelīśvarī at Hāṭakeśvara, in the village of Vaḍnagar in central Gujarat; there is a suggestion of Tantric worship at this shrine of the Circle of Mothers, "according to their proper rank and order"; and it is surely not by chance that the innermost quality of the goddess Kelīśvarī herself, called into manifestation because of Andhaka's threat to the gods, is, as her name reveals, related to the notion of play.

What kind of game is the goddess playing?

3
Birth, Body, Transformation

In many of the medieval versions of the story, it is the playfulness of the goddess that causes Andhaka to be born in the first place. (Another extension of this theme is that Andhaka embarks on his conflict with the gods only after he finds the goddess playing with Śiva.[10]) When Ratnâkara offers a synoptic narrative of Andhaka's birth, in the sixth canto of *Haravijaya* (6.188–189), he begins precisely with this point (here, Spring is speaking to Śiva, who apparently needs to be reminded of the entire sequence):

> You were happily resting, once,
> on Himâlaya, when Pārvatī stole up
> from behind. She was smiling
> gently at her own joke as she quickly
> covered your eyes with her soft hands
> and as quickly released them.
> But all at once a male
> was there, born, eyeless, from You,
> the Ancient Male,
>
> like a seed germinating in the darkness
> that the Black Mistress of Night
> breathes out
> to kill.[11]

10. *Padmapurāṇa* 5.43.7–96.
11. See the discussion of this verse by Smith 1985:144–45.

It all starts as a joke (*parihāsa*), a graceful and playful act carried out by the smiling goddess. It takes but a second—indeed, the Sanskrit phrase (*kara-paṅkaja-sthagita-mukta-cakṣuṣaḥ*) suggests a virtual simultaneity, the eyes of the god both hidden and released. For a moment almost too fleeting to record or to notice, just barely on this side of the border between time and timelessness, the god cannot see; his vision is blocked by his partner, which is to say that his sight is forced inward, away from the external world usually illuminated by Śiva's eyes. This is not, however, a true turning inward (such as we find when the god begins his *tapas*) but, rather, an act of occlusion and self-diminution, as if the god were being squeezed into an inner gap, a dark space opening up within him—very much as in the game of dice. And suddenly, as a result of this internal slippage, and again in apparent repetition of what happens in the game, we find an active presence externalized and polarized along lines of gender: a blind male (*puruṣa*) emerges from the god who is identified as the Primeval Male, and who is brought into relation with a destructive female entity, the Dark Night of cosmic dissolution (*kṣaya-kāla-kāla-rajanī*).

Andhaka is, then, the seed nurtured in a feminine darkness, produced when the god falls through, or into, an empty space within himself as his female part playfully occludes his vision. His birth is accompanied by a form of gender isolation that will accelerate and intensify, in increasingly dangerous directions, in the course of his career. He clearly constitutes a threat—to the godhead, its wholeness, its potential for seeing itself and others. This seed will grow to fruition under conditions of increasing porousness within this god, in his externalizing mode—that is to say, under conditions in which Śiva is made to confront a self, in play.

Let us see now how the *Śivapurāṇa* tells the story, from this same point of departure.

Once Śiva, eager to amuse himself [*vihartukāma*], came to Kāśī [Benares] and made it his capital; he set a dreadful Bhairava form of himself as its guardian at the border. Then he gave himself over to playing with Pārvatī on the eastern slopes of Mount Mandara. As they played, Pārvatī, in jest, closed Śiva's eyes with her two hands, delicate as golden lotuses. At once, a vast darkness engulfed the world.

The hands of the goddess were drenched in fluid born of passion [*madâmbhaḥ*]. This fluid, heated by contact with the god's body and by the fiery eye on his forehead, became a drop [*bindu*] that grew to an embryo (*garbha*), that turned into something not human—something blind and fearsome, angry, ungrateful, deformed, black, covered with matted hair and also beautiful body hairs. It made a lot of noise, singing and laughing and dancing and weeping, licking with its tongue.

Śiva said to the goddess: "Why are you frightened of this creature? You did this by covering my eyes." She smiled and released his eyes, and the world was lit by a great light, which made the creature look even more horrible. She asked

> her husband, "Who is this deformed being that has appeared right in front of us? Why was he created, and by whom? Whose son is he?" Śiva, the gamester [*līlākara*], said to the playful goddess: "This is Andhaka [from *andha*, "blind"], born of my sweat when you closed my eyes. You created him, and you and your friends should care for him." Out of compassion, Pārvatī accepted this task.

As we can expect, the context is one of continuous play. Śiva finds a terrestrial home (in Kāśī) because he needs a place where he can play—and he protects this place with a frightening part of his own being. The goddess joins him in his games, during which she produces the misshapen Andhaka, in the manner we have already discussed. A hideous blackness pours out of the god—or perhaps it would be more precise to say, again, that he pours into some part of his own internal emptiness, which, heated, swelling, expanding rapidly from a seedlike drop of fluid to something more grand, frightens the goddess into asking its name and the nature of her relation to it. She asks from a position of obvious alienation, feeling no responsibility or kinship—Andhaka, produced via her instrumentality, is not truly hers, not even like her in any real way. He is far more like the god—indeed, in some sense he *is* the god in his occluded and diminished mode.

It is crucial to observe that this birth story unrolls in stages, at least two of which can be distinctly defined. There is the initial act of blinding, forcing the god into his inner gap, which is initially unformed, black, terrifying in its boundarylessness. But this is rapidly succeeded by a kind of expansive crystallization into some perceptible misform, a concrete or congealed being that is noisy, active, full of feeling (Andhaka sings, laughs, dances, weeps). Such a process of consolidation—condensing black space into a shaped and substantial entity with visible contours—intensifies the threat to higher order beings (Śiva in his more holistic mode, or conjoined to the goddess); indeed, in a certain sense, this process is paradigmatic for what the Indian texts think of as demonic (*āsurī-bhāva*).[12] *Asura*s like Andhaka move from dark spaciousness to more crystallized and bounded forms; in this, they are very like the gods. Perhaps even more pressing, however, is the sense in which the process Andhaka exemplifies in being born is also paradigmatic for creation, in the sense of externalization, generally. The entire world, seen from this van-

12. In general, we would probably do better to avoid this Western term in speaking of Hindu myths. *Asura*s are "demonic" only in inhabiting different levels of a single, fragmented universe; usually, they have some direct relation to notions of holistic being and the threat of an undifferentiated or unshaped field of force. They also, however, tend to exemplify stasis or blockage in what should be a fluid and self-transforming cosmos. The Vedic texts tell us the *asura*s used to sacrifice into their own mouths—a precise image of a closed and frozen system.

tage point, is but the hardening contours of certain gaps—ultimately intradivine gaps in the process of being externalized—that congeal or cool into recognizable and semiautonomous beings. It is this, above all, that is meant when Hindus speak of *māyā*, the "artifice," or even "illusion," of perceived reality.

The true nature of the threat implicit in this process is clarified—also in terms of the perceptions and emotions of the newborn, malformed child himself—in the next episode of the text:

> It was the cold season: Golden-Eyes (Hiraṇyâkṣa), the king of the demons, egged on by his wife, performed *tapas* in order to attain a son. [He was jealous of his elder brother Hiraṇyakaśipu, who had five sons.] Śiva, pleased by his worship, appeared and offered him the son born out of his own [Śiva's] self—that is, Andhaka. Hiraṇyâkṣa now happily conquered the gods and hid the whole earth in the underworld. Viṣṇu, in the form of the great Boar, split open the surface of the earth, entered the underworld, and cut off Hiraṇyâkṣa's head; he then crowned Andhaka king of the demons and brought the earth back up on his tusk.[13]
>
> Andhaka, the youthful king, was playing with his step-brothers when they, blinded with passion [*madândhāḥ*], teased him cruelly: "Our father was a fool when he adopted you, ugly as you are, blind and quarrelsome. There is simply no way you could have inherited our kingdom." This cut home. At night, Andhaka went away to a desolate place to perform *tapas*; he stood on one leg, fasting, his arms raised above his head, for ten thousand years. Every day for a year he cut off pieces of his own flesh, covered with blood, with a sharp knife and offered them into the fire. Finally there was nothing left but sinews and bones; all his blood was gone, and he was about to throw his corpse-like body into the fire when the gods intervened. Brahmā promised him that he could choose whatever he liked as a boon. He asked that his cruel brothers become his servants, that he be given a divine eye, that the gods pay him tribute, and that he be immune to death at the hands of any living creature, including Viṣṇu and Śiva, who is everything. Brahmā said: "No living creature has yet been born, or will ever be born, who will not be swallowed up by Death. And in any case, good males like you should not desire to live too long. So name some cause of your eventual destruction."
>
> Andhaka replied: "There are three kinds of women—the best, the middling, and the least. There is one from their midst, a true jewel of a woman, who will always be like my mother. She is unapproachable [*agamyā*] by body, speech, or mind, unattainable in the world of men. When I desire her, out of my demonic nature, then, and only then, will I be subject to destruction."
>
> Brahmā was amazed at this, but, meditating on Śiva, he quickly received his orders. Accordingly, he announced to Andhaka that he would have whatever it was that he wanted: "Rise up, achieve your desire, go to war with heroes." But

13. There now follows an interlude, during which Viṣṇu, as the Man-Lion, kills Hiraṇyakaśipu.

> Andhaka needed something more: how could he fight without a body? So Brahmā touched him, and his flesh was restored. Happy, able now to see, Andhaka went to his city, where his brothers conferred the kingdom upon him.

Andhaka, prematurely heir to his adoptive father's kingdom, is sensitive, ashamed of his misshapen ugliness and blindness. Out of this shame, he is driven toward *tapas*, which, in his case, takes the striking form of actual self-mutilation. This inchoate, half-formed being is incapable of the internalizing self-regeneration that *tapas* properly entails; instead, he lops off bloody chunks of his own body, to the point where he is reduced to a bony skeleton. This is the first mention, in this linear and sequential narrative of the Andhaka myth, of a tendency that we know to be basic to this figure, in both of his major forms—as the spurned demon-son of the god, whom he will threaten; and as his eventual transform Bhṛṅgin, skeletal witness to the game of dice. In both cases, the reduction to bones (and perhaps sinews, but without flesh or blood) is clearly a statement of isolated and hypertrophied masculinity. Generally, in India, the female is felt to provide the softer components of the body, while the male supplies the rudimentary skeleton.[14] Andhaka/Bhṛṅgin is thus a powerful illustration of gender isolation—that is, of that direction in the internal devolution of the godhead that follows the separation of male and female parts, in accordance with the fragmenting logic of the dice game. The gaps that have opened up in the god congeal along rigid and impoverished lines, in which the male is wholly cut off from the female, and driven, in this reduced state, to ever-greater degrees of impoverished self-definition in relation to the lost or absent other. As we saw, there is a sense in which this process of increasing rigidity and stiffness, the static blockage of movement, is characteristic of such demonic beings generally.

To state this in different terms: what Andhaka reveals to us, already at the very beginning of his career, is a near-total exteriority—a dense male self with no real inside, unless we are willing to include the empty spaces between his bones (somehow similar to the gaps in the porous deity that make Andhaka possible in the first place). In this latter sense, Andhaka is, again perhaps, all too much like his father. In another, more perspicuous sense, both father and son illustrate contrasting states of extreme density, which demarcate a certain metaphysical range. Śiva's holistic being, before the dice game, might be described as dense insofar as total and simultaneous connectivity rules therein. But Andhaka's congealed hardness is of the order of diminution; it encompasses nothing but itself, and even perceives itself as flawed and lack-

14. One thus finds an anomalous figure such as Bhagīratha, born without bones, as the result of the coupling of two women: *Padmapurāṇa*, *svargakhaṇḍa* 16.11–15.

ing. This is why Andhaka must ask Brahmā to restore him to a more adequate bodily form. What is more, the sense of absence, and its specific focus, are beautifully articulated by this demon's vision of his own eventual destruction. In effect, he can survive—by his own admission—only so long as he fails to pursue the missing feminine person whom he dimly recognizes as being like his mother. This feminine self is also somehow connected to a notion of the center, of what comprises the central (innermost) point of reference; this point is seen as unattainable, although we can already guess that Andhaka will be utterly unable not to seek it. Once again, he reminds us of his father. The unattainable female from the middle of the series of all possible females is the dependable source of Andhaka's self-destruction. As always, the boon won from *tapas* is very precisely conceived and formulated, always including, in the fine print at the end, its own antithesis. Futile, residual maleness is an option within god, or within god's emerging self, predicated on the destructive attempt to reconstitute a feminine innerness from the outside. Seen in this light, it actually matters very little that the lost female is Andhaka's mother (more precisely—and here the language of the text is careful and clear—she is an as-if mother of this crude male). This story is less concerned with incest, even broadly defined, than with understanding the composition of sexual identity per se.

The remainder of the story works out these premises in a consistent series of variations on the theme of doomed exteriority, and the inevitable polarization of gender that it entails. Andhaka and Śiva must confront each other in terms of their complementary need for the goddess, which is also an attempt by god to reconsolidate himself, closing off the dangerous internal rifts and spaces in which that self can tenuously survive:

> Andhaka now conquered the entire universe, took thousands of beautiful women for himself, spent tens of thousands of years playing with them, drinking, enjoying himself. He did not know what could give him happiness. His mind was blinded by passion, and by evil company. He was ruining the Vedic way of life, applying evil logic, oblivious to the Brahmins, the gods, the gurus. Wholly ruled by divine fate [*daiva*], his life was a ruin.
>
> After millions of years, he went to Mount Mandara [his birthplace]; intoxicated by its beauty, he built a city there. One day his ministers saw an enchanting woman on the mountain and reported back to him: "There is a cave with a sage in it, his body covered with snakes and ash; he has four arms, an elephant's skin around his waist, a sword, a trident, a rosary, a bow and arrows. His eyes are closed in meditation. Not far from him stands a monkey-faced guard, and there is also an aged, white bull. Near him is a woman, young and charming, adorned with coral, jewels, and gold. *Only a man who has seen her can be said to have eyes*. She is the wife of that sage, but she is worthy of you."

Andhaka, shaken by desire, sent his ministers to fetch the girl. They said to the sage, "Whose son are you, and why are you sitting here? To whom does that woman belong? She really ought to go to the demon king. How do all these things fit together—your ash-smeared body, covered with snakes and skulls; Lady Ganges in your matted hair; the crescent moon; bones taken from a corpse; and, above all, erotic union with a woman? Give her to us. Why perform *tapas* with a woman? It just isn't right. Lay down your weapons, and go on with your meditation. If you disobey us, you will be liberated from this body!"

Śiva, acting in a worldly mode, thought of Andhaka as a man of limited intelligence. So he smiled and said, "What if I were Śiva? What would you gain from me? Why talk with such false tones? I don't remember any father or mother; ugly [or formless, *virūpa*] as I am, I am performing a vow, the Pāśupata vow, never accomplished before. It is well known that none of this has any real roots in me, but it is very difficult for me to abandon anything—for example, my beautiful, patient wife, the embodiment of perfection of a kind that pervades everything [*sarvagatasya siddhi*]. Anyway, you demon, you may take whatever you think suits you." And Śiva was silent.

When the ministers reported back to Andhaka, he, penetrated by lust and drunk on the boon he had received long ago, came to fight, as a moth moves toward a burning lamp. At first, Vīraka, Pārvatī's son, who was on guard at the entrance to the cave, defeated him; soon other demons joined the fight, and were also routed. As ghouls began to dance amid the bloody heaps of flesh and marrow, Śiva turned to Pārvatī and said, "My dear, I have performed this dreadful Pāśupata vow; but the power derived from it has now been lost—because of my daily and nightly contact with you. That is why something immortal is being attacked by something mortal. So I am going to create a frightful wilderness where I will perform an even more dreadful form of *tapas*, without fear. As for you, you will be without sorrow." So he went away to perform his vow for a thousand years, something no other god could achieve.

Pārvatī waited for him, in that cave, alone, frightened, devoted, sad, guarded by her son Vīraka. Andhaka returned and fought with Vīraka for 505 days and nights. In fear, the goddess thought of the other gods, and they—Brahmā, Viṣṇu, the snakes and Siddhas and others—became women and hid in her cave. After all, it is forbidden to enter the inner chambers of a royal palace; that is why the gods assumed thousands of female forms before they could enter that cave. As Vīraka returned to the fray, many fearsome goddesses joined them—Brāhmī, Gaurī, Nārāyaṇī, Baiḍaujasī [Indrāṇī], Vaiśvānarī, Nairṛti, Yāmyā, and hundreds of others. The demons turned pale, thinking only of flight or death. Gaurī fought a miraculous battle there, helped by these females and Vīraka.

True to his inner drives, Andhaka always produces stark sexual polarization. A reduced and disarticulated male himself, he faces, in the first instance, a series of violent female warriors, who successfully defeat the demonic forces. They come into play only after the usual complement of male deities, unable to survive the magnetic distortions emanating from Andhaka's attack on the missing woman, are themselves emasculated and feminized, to the point of hiding behind the goddess in her cave. Śiva is absent at this point: There remain, on the field of conflict, only Andhaka, the goddess, the womanly gods, and the horrific female deities. It is as if Andhaka could produce in the male only two possible responses to his threat: faced with this lopsided, innerless masculinity, maleness must collapse into a no-less-lopsided femininity, pusillanimous or ferocious (in a way, it makes little difference). There is no middle ground at all. This, we are told by the text as well as by many other *purāṇic* versions of the story, is the origin of the Devouring Mothers (Mātṛkās), the death-ridden form of female divinity that haunts the human world, and that we find bound up with Andhaka and his battles in the carvings at Ellora (especially in Cave 14).

The *Śivapurāṇa* version innovates in its colorful dialogues—between Andhaka's ministers and the meditating god, and between Śiva and Pārvatī. The demonic vision is, of course, correct, though skewed, in its perception of Śiva as burdened by contradictory attributes, especially the presence of a woman in his yogic sphere. There is a question about what precisely one sees when the goddess comes near: Is it a matter of enticing feminine beauty, an entirely sexualized focus of desire, or is it, rather, something related to the less diminished form of being that the unbalanced male remembers in his isolation? In any case, there is a certain poignancy in the text's statement—addressed to the demon named Blind—that "only a man who has seen her [the goddess] can be said to have eyes." It is also very striking that the law of polarization affects Śiva, the devolved godhead, as well. He has lost the fruits of his vow (as he tells his wife), because of his continuous contact with her; and the only remedy is for him to remove himself to a still more remote, and entirely masculine, domain. We may be reminded here of Śiva's flight to the wilderness after the game of dice breaks down.

And it is from this point of farthest movement *away* from the goddess that Śiva returns to complete the cycle of separation and reabsorption with his unhappy son:

> Andhaka was lining up his soldiers in array when Śiva returned—a thousand years had passed—like the radiance of a thousand suns at the end of an eon. He, the great god, was angry. Now the women fought even harder, and Pārvatī bowed to him; he embraced her and entered the cave. The women were dismissed, while Vīraka remained at his post at the entrance.
>
> Andhaka could see neither Śiva nor Gaurī now, so he sent a messenger to say: "You should have nothing to do with a woman. Let her go. You are no sage, you are my enemy, and I will send you to the realm of Death." Śiva replied, burning with sadness: "Fight with me if you have the strength to do so. The weak

cannot even maintain their body; let them do what they must, and I, too, will do what I have to."

A great battle began. The demon Vighasa swallowed the gods, but Śiva made him disgorge them. When Śukra, the guru of the gods, revived the slain demons, Śiva swallowed him. Andhaka then created endless demons out of his own body. Śiva impaled him on his trident, while Viṣṇu, using Yoga, took on a female form and hungrily drank the falling drops of blood. Andhaka fought on alone, his blood all dry, striking with his palms, knees, feet, nails, and head, remembering his identity as a warrior.

At last, pacified and extinguished [*śānta*], he was pierced through the heart by Śiva's trident; he dangled there in the sky like a pillar [or like Śiva, the Pillar: *sthāṇu-sadṛśa*). Half his body was burned dry by the sun, and half drenched in rain; still, he did not die, though his form was like snowflakes in the face of the cruel sun. Śiva, satisfied and compassionate, praised by Andhaka, made him the chief of his troops. Then Śiva went back into his cave to play again, joyfully, with Pārvatī.[15]

How alike these two enemies are at the end—as at the beginning—and how true to form! Andhaka dangles in the sky like a pillar, albeit a *broken* pillar—still an iconic reminder of the ithyphallic presence, replete with desire, which normally characterizes his impaler. Both of them, after all, are intent on uniting with the same goddess. As we can now expect, this final act of impalement comes with a transformed awareness, which will allow the desiccated and bony Andhaka to become Śiva's *gaṇapati* as the reformed (and still skeletal) Bhṛṅgin. The drift toward bloodless exteriority, which marks the early stage of Andhaka's career, remains consistent to the end. But the reality that Andhaka comprises is ultimately subsumed, the congealed gap burned away and closed, the threat to the godhead extinguished. A residue of rejected maleness survives as Bhṛṅgin: this is the true Andhaka outcome, the internal movement from lustful Andhaka to the misogynist and isolated Bhṛṅgin, cut off from the female by hatred so intense that it precludes any return to a more complete state. Still, the blind aspect of externalized divinity gives way to a moment of blazing illumination, like a thousand suns at the end of the eon. This is also an angry moment, in which the god, who has slipped into one of his own black spaces, and then acquired a certain fragmented selfhood, consumes this unwelcome self in fury (often, though not in our text, the fury of the dance). Andhaka is reincorporated, drawn inward (just as Śiva sucks the dangerous demonic guru Śukra into himself as the penultimate act of this battle), in a mode of heated fusion. Immediately thereafter, this same god, now presumably enhanced, perhaps projected back onto a level of greater wholeness, is said to enter another black inner space—the cave—where he can resume his game.

15. *Śivapurāṇa, Rudrasaṃhitā* 5.42–49.

4
Andhaka at Ellora

To move outward from the god, via his inner gaps, is, in this world of Śiva's stories, *always* an act of destruction. Indeed, if we review and simplify the process that we have just followed in detail, we can see how destructive energy intensifies and builds toward a violent culmination. One begins with a rent in the fabric of reality, through which diminished pieces of the god slip out into dark and amorphous domains of being. These blind pieces of a divine self consolidate themselves, congeal, objectify. They acquire a sex that is increasingly opposed to, and separated from, its complement. This is a movement downward and outward in terms of the divine totality, and it brings about a shift in perception. In his Andhaka persona, Śiva can no longer see himself at all. His blindness is iconic. From his vantage point, the entire cosmos can only be unrelieved darkness, a vast gap hardening into bone or stone. There is something intolerable, for the godhead, in this blindness, which is, however, also a mode of knowledge, especially self-knowledge, structured around occlusion; to know himself, the god has to shrink into limited and divided parts of himself, blocked-off areas of blindness. This fractured and occluded state is also dynamic: Seeking to reconstitute itself—to see—the Andhaka fragment is destructively sucked back into the whole. If we take this as the basic sequence, then a certain self-limiting cycle is completed.

Now, look at Andhaka in Cave 15 at Ellora—perhaps the most terrifying sculptured panel in Indian art (see figures 14–16).[16] One feels the closing of the circle. A divine space is violently collapsing inward. Śiva, driving upward, with unimaginable power, toward the demon, is held and circumscribed by the elephant's flayed skin, which also extends to include Andhaka. This skin describes a limit, a perceptual and existential horizon within which the poignant drama of the god's battle with his son must reach its climax. The demon, in a pose of worship, facing his destroyer, is remarkably human, as if we ourselves were truly Andhaka—dark gaps in the inner texture of god, frozen into solid form. By the same token, *we* are the natural, gaunt, and lonely witnesses to the god's game of dice.

To complete the closure, the goddess reaches out with a bowl to catch her son's blood (Śiva, too, extends a bowl for this same purpose). Her movement, counterclockwise, creates the lower half of the circle. But how tragic is this gesture of the mother, spread-eagled beneath her dying son, heroically intent on preventing any liquid part of him from escaping back into the world, thereby externalizing himself in further destructive cycles of regeneration. She shows us a centripetal movement of reabsorption, pulling her son inward in the face

16. See Kulke 1970:56, n. 62.

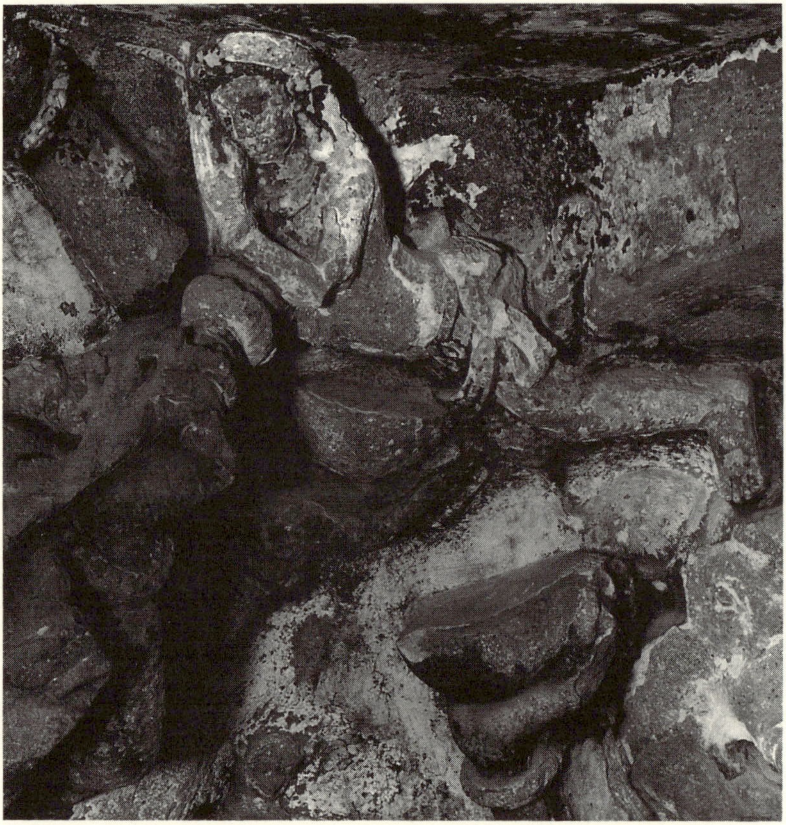

FIGURE 16. Detail of Śiva slaying Andhaka: the demon, impaled, faces his destroyer. Ellora, Cave 15.

of his father's centrifugal attack. If she fails—if a single drop falls outside the circle—the cycle will repeat itself entropically forever: Andhaka, or Andhakas, will congeal again into blind, objectified being, hyperdifferentiated (as pure males) vis-à-vis the encompassing godhead.[17] So, the entire desperate, highly energized effort is aimed at sealing the existential gap. Śiva, slightly elevated above the horrific mother Cāmuṇḍā, with one foot raised, as in the dance, is destroying a malformed, misconceived, tentatively human part of himself. Successful, he gives himself fully to the dance (the contiguous panel to the right).

17. Andhaka is thus continuous with Vedic speculations about hyperdifferentiated creation, *pṛthak*; see Smith 1989:50–69; 1.7 at n. 100.

This is how Ratnâkara sings of this moment:

> Viscous blood poured
> from Andhaka's breast
> into the skull the Goddess held,
> and as she, Cāmuṇḍā, sipped it,
> her body kept ripening into redness
> even as *he* was changing in himself,
> while with her fingers she was rapidly
> crushing his clones, the seeds sprouting
> out of his male power
> in a constant stream.
>
> His blood was boiling
> in the trident's flames,
> and then, all at once,
> he was all ashes.
> The gods and demons stared
> in wonder. Nothing was left
> of that demon's form except
> light penetrating the body
> of the god who bears the crescent moon.[18]

At the final moment of reabsorption, the darkness and emptiness that had become a living, threatening demon are converted into light. The once-open space has closed. This transition from blackness to brilliant light takes place against a backdrop of violent reds—the boiling blood, dripping into Cāmuṇḍā's bowl; the red drops that keep producing further replicas of Andhaka, rapidly germinating outgrowths of his still vital masculine seed; and the concomitant internal ripening within the dread goddess, whose body turns red as she sips this gory potion. Initially (in the verse from *Haravijaya* (6.189) cited at the beginning of section 3), Andhaka was a blind seed "germinating in the darkness / that the Black Mistress of Night / breathes out / to kill"; now his seed has

18. *tad-vakṣaḥ-kaṭakād asṛn-nipatitaṃ sândraṃ kapālôdare*
pītvā tat-pariṇāma-pāṭalam ivâtamraṃ vapur bibhratī/
cāmuṇḍâṅguli-koṭi-bhāga-malanāt tad-vīrya-bījâṅkurān
acchinnâkhila-saṃtatīn sarabhasaṃ cakre praticchandakān//
triśikha-dahana-jvālātāpa-kvathad-bahulâsṛjaḥ
sapadi vapuṣas tasyâśeṣāt kṛtād atha bhasmasāt/
stimita-nayana-vrātair dṛṣṭaṃ surâsura-maṇḍalaiḥ
śaśidhara-kalā-mauler jyotiḥ śarīram athâviśat// (50.88–89)

multiplied to devastating dimensions as a white-red army of self-replications attempts to escape the god's tightening grasp. The act of reinternalization—as the goddess literally drinks up the proliferating demonic beings—is seen as producing a transformation in both her inner state and in Andhaka's; both are changing, maturing, ripening together (the key term here is *pariṇāma*, "transforming"), through fiery redness, as if the entire process described by this myth were aimed, from the start, at this point of heated fulfillment and fusion. A black tear inside the god first congeals and petrifies, achieves awareness and tenuous self-definition, and then is melted down again in the red-hot reconnection of this abortive self with its more encompassing, higher order self, the active divinity who welds together these dangerous rifts within his prior density.

And this divinity then breaks into his dance, as if energized by this act of fusion. The progression we see in Cave 15 is also present in the much earlier Cave 29 (at Dhumar Lena, shown in figure 17). Here, the slaying of Andhaka, which is depicted directly opposite the panel showing Rāvaṇa's attack on Kailāsa, leads us (in the *pradakṣinā* circumambulation) directly to the dancing Śiva—an ungainly panel juxtaposed with the Yogic Lakulīśa. Precisely the same sequence unfolds at Elephanta: following the *pradakṣiṇā* around the central *liṅga* shrine, one moves from the impalement of Andhaka to the dance, and then to the lonely Yogin. This seems to be a coherent subseries within the overarching thematic concerns of the sculptors and the narrators of these Śaiva myths. Following the logic implicit in this visual organization of the materials, we would argue that Śiva is impelled—from the moment he enters the game—toward the Andhaka outcome, or toward the violent reinternalization of this piece of his being; the destructive energy then reaches its climax in the god's wild dance. From this extremity of destruction, there is, in essence, one way back to a less traumatic level of wholeness—that is the way of *tapas*, in which the Yogi turns inward toward an integration that includes marriage and erotic union. This part of the story is told in chapter III.

Here, we may, however, observe the forcefulness and logic of the Ellora panels, from a slightly wider perspective—resuming our earlier discussion in the previous chapter. The basic building blocks are remarkably constant, even if the particular configurations vary. In every case, the dice game appears to provide a key to the organization of these icononarrative materials. Take Cave 14, Rāvaṇa-ki-Khai, which was apparently originally a Durgā shrine with images of the violent goddess on either side (Durgā to the north; Mahiṣāsuramardinī to the south) as one enters. (See figure 18.) To the left, a series of Vaiṣṇava panels extends the length of the wall; facing them on the right is a parallel series of Śaiva scenes, beginning, at the far right, with the game of dice (see figure 19). So here the game is either the first or the final tableau, depending on the direction of circumambulation; in either case, it frames and contextualizes

FIGURE 17. Śiva slays Andhaka. Ellora, Cave 29 (Dhumar Lena).

the Śiva panels. Moving past it inward, into the cave, we pass the dancing Śiva (see figure 20), with an eery skeleton peering out from between his legs—another testimony to the destructive aspect of this dance, and to the strange intimacy that links this god with skeletal figures such as the barren Bhṛṅgin. Then there is Rāvaṇa shaking Kailāsa—driving the goddess and the god back together (see figure 21)—and, finally, Andhaka—a rough and unhappy rendition that still, as at Elephanta, magnetizes much of the free-floating energy in the cave. Here, everyone has his place: Śiva, almost impassive, is pulling the impaled demon inexorably back toward himself (see figure 22); Andhaka, his hands folded in worship, faces extinction without flinching, as his blood flows, with precision, into the bowl extended by the god; and the goddess waits in

Ellora, Cave 14

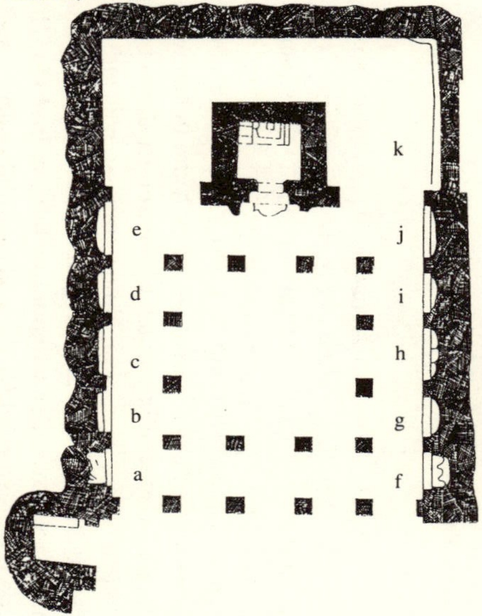

Key to sculpture panels

a Mahiṣāsura Mardinī
b Gaja Lakṣmī
c Varāha
d Viṣṇu with Śrīdevī Bhūdevī
e Viṣṇu with Lakṣmī
f Mahiṣāsura Mardini
g Śiva and Pārvatī playing dice
h Naṭarāja
i Rāvaṇa shaking Kailāsa
j Slaying of Andhaka
k Sapta Mātṛkās with Kāla Bhairava

Ellora, Cave 15

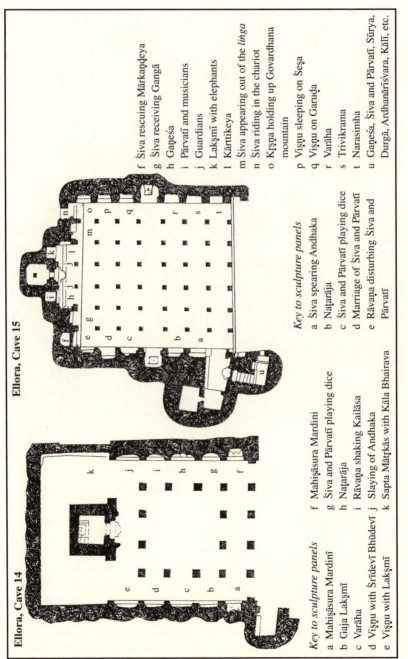

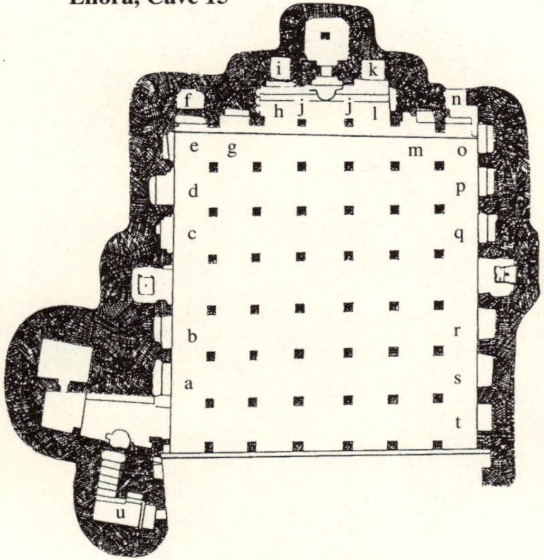

Key to sculpture panels

a Śiva spearing Andhaka
b Naṭarāja
c Śiva and Pārvatī playing dice
d Marriage of Śiva and Pārvatī
e Rāvaṇa disturbing Śiva and Pārvatī
f Śiva rescuing Mārkaṇḍeya
g Śiva receiving Gaṅgā
h Gaṇeśa
i Pārvatī and musicians
j Guardians
k Lakṣmī with elephants
l Kārttikeya
m Śiva appearing out of the *liṅga*
n Śiva riding in the chariot
o Kṛṣṇa holding up Govardhana mountain
p Viṣṇu sleeping on Śeṣa
q Viṣṇu on Garuḍa
r Varāha
s Trivikrama
t Narasimha
u Gaṇeśa, Śiva and Pārvatī, Sūrya, Durgā, Ardhanārīśvara, Kālī, etc.

FIGURE 18. Layout of Ellora, Caves 14 and 15. Drawing by George Michell.

seeming isolation in the lower right, sealing off this lower egress from the divine circle. Still further into the cave—indeed, largely hidden by the goddess's sanctum—is a melancholy group of the Seven Mothers together with Death himself as Kāla Bhairava. As we know, this group is intimately linked to the Andhaka myth, hence also joined to it in iconic continuity in this setting. Structurally, we might associate these mothers with the violent Cāmuṇḍā of the Andhaka panels; yet each of them holds an infant on her lap, thus calling up potential energies of nurture. Thus on one edge of the cave, we have the dice game, taking the world apart; and on the other margin of the Śaiva series, there is a suggestion of maternal care, in the presence of death, holding the

FIGURE 19. Śiva and Pārvatī playing dice. Ellora, Cave 15 (Rāvaṇa-ki Khai).

world briefly together. The centrifugal force of the dice game, a drive outward from the center, is met by centripetal, internalizing forces at the other limit of the frame.

Cave 21, representing perhaps the height of the classical style at Ellora, expands the frame symmetrically. This is a *liṅga* shrine, with two major panels on either side: The game of dice is on the right (see figure 23); Rāvaṇa shaking Kailāsa, on the left. The countervailing force of these panels is conspicuous at first glance: The dice game, as always, is centrifugal, driving the two players, Śiva and Pārvatī, apart; Rāvaṇa, pushing at the great mountain from below (see figure 24), drives this pair together in centripetal need or desire. The dice game unfolds into externalizing and, eventually, destructive

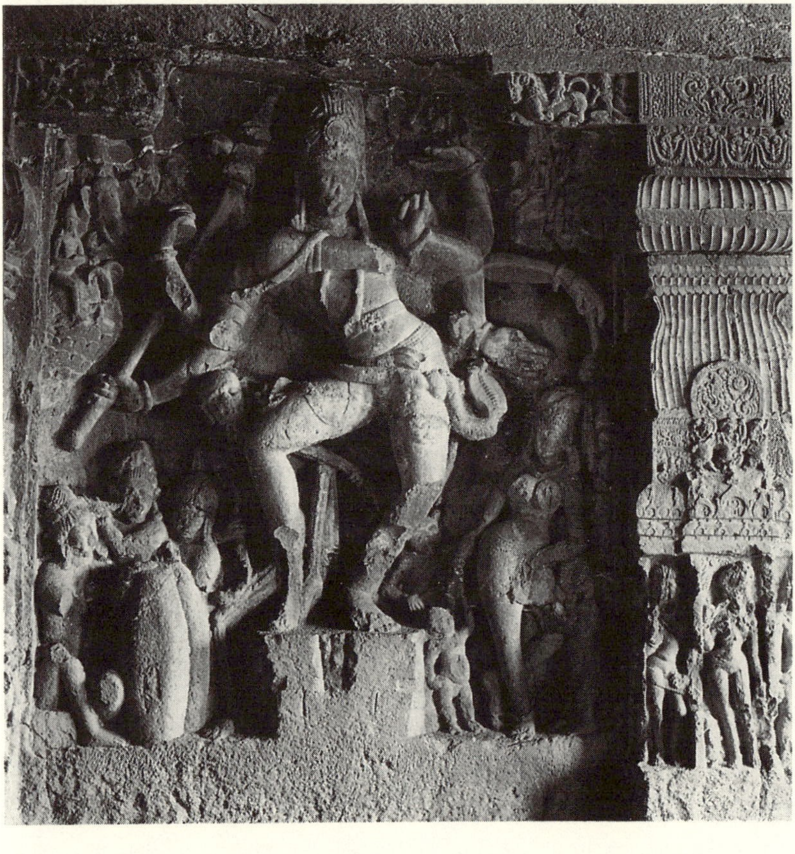

FIGURE 20. Śiva dancing. Ellora, Cave 14.

FIGURE 21. Rāvaṇa shakes Mount Kailāsa. Ellora, Cave 14.

modes; Rāvaṇa seems to embody an external threat (unlike Andhaka, he is never said to have been born out of Śiva) that produces movement toward a fusion and reinternalization of the separated pieces of god. Andhaka himself is absent from this cave, but his story survives here, resonant and menacing, in the enormous panel of the Seven Mothers who are together with Gaṇesa, Kāla, and Kālī, along the right-hand wall (see figure 25). To the right of the dice game, we also find the standard sequel to the slaying of Andhaka—Śiva dancing his wild dance. Directly across from the deathly mothers, on the left-hand wall—the side of the centripetal reunion—we find, logically enough, the long panel depicting Pārvatī's *tapas* and marriage.

FIGURE 22. Andhaka impaled. Ellora, Cave 14.

At Dhumar Lena (Cave 29), as at its model, Elephanta, the primary components of the entire series are all present, in an intelligible sequence, irradiating and enfolding the *liṅga* shrine that stands alone in the interior. This cave has several potential points of access. If the original entrance was on the south, then one begins the circumambulation with the dice game (on the left)—precisely as at Elephanta. Standing here, looking directly at the two players (see figure 26), one can also see Andhaka—the inevitable product of their game—out of the corner of one's eye. In this Andhaka panel, alive with primitive violence, the demon-victim remains outside the god's elephant skin, though he is turned back toward it, toward the god moving upward to impale him (see figure 17). Here, it is Śiva alone who holds up a bowl to catch Andhaka's drops of blood, thereby completing the act of containment and internalizing closure. Śiva is intent, focused, frightening in the sureness of his destructive movement; the goddess sits, somewhat remote and detached, with one hand on her breast, shielded, from a rain of demonic blood—the blood of her dying son—only by the open bowl the god holds over her head, directly beneath the contorted demon.

Across from Andhaka, we see the Rāvaṇa panel, vertical, centripetal, perfectly centered. If one entered the cave first from the west, one would begin *pradakṣiṇā* with Andhaka—here framing the whole sequence—and conclude,

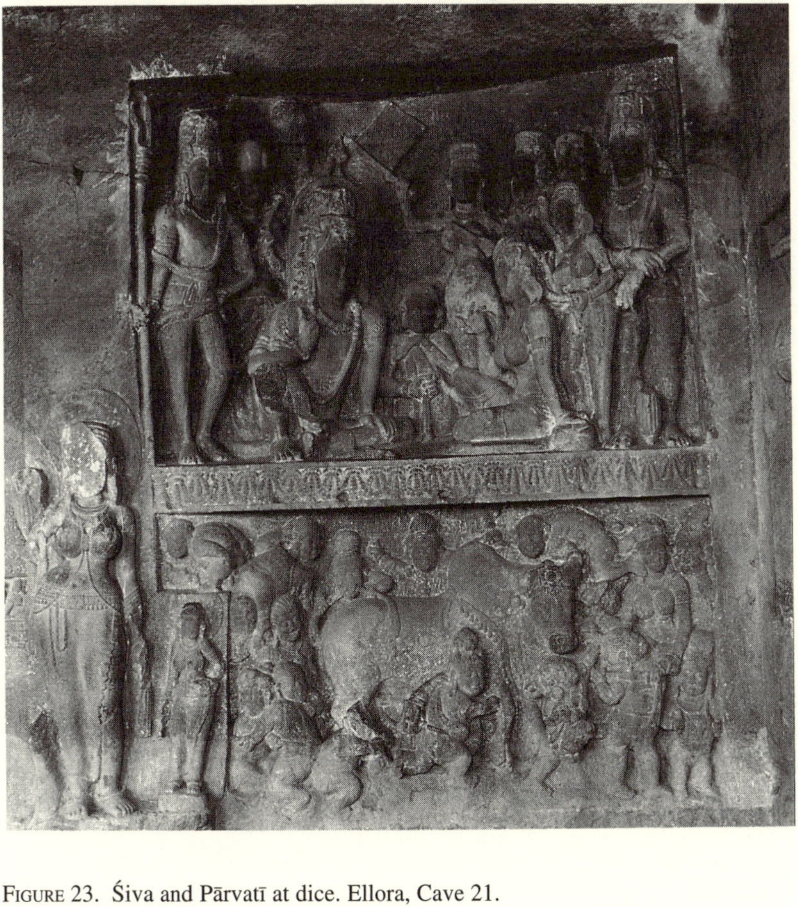

FIGURE 23. Śiva and Pārvatī at dice. Ellora, Cave 21.

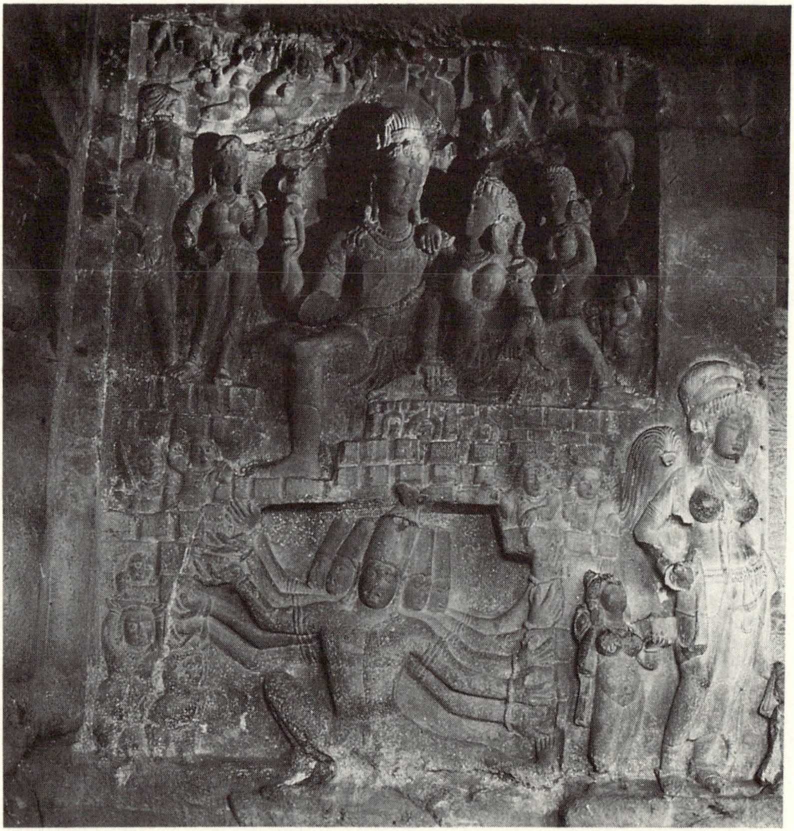

FIGURE 24. Rāvaṇa shakes Mount Kailāsa. Ellora, Cave 21.

as at Elephanta, with Rāvaṇa. Once again, Bhṛṅgin is present in this scene, hovering over the god as the latter fondles Pārvatī's breast—his nonchalant response to the demonic threat. Proceeding through the cave, one passes the dancing Śiva, who faces Lakulīśa; then, on the other side of the *liṅga* shrine, we have the marriage scene exactly opposite the game of dice. Marriage temporarily reunites what the dice game has severed, or is again about to sever.[19] Similar sequencing can easily be observed at different points in the Kailāsanātha

19. The dice game and the marriage are also juxtaposed in Cave 15, following the two great panels of Andhaka and the dance (with an empty niche between these).

temple at Ellora—the great masterpiece of the Ellora carvers, a complex symphony in stone.

Let us now sum up the fundamental intuitions that seem to pervade all of these series of panels, seen in relation to the textual sources we have quoted for these myths. They posit certain recurring perceptions: that god moves into and out of himself, or upward and downward—from the density of being that reigns at the highest level to the porous spaciousness that opens up inside him in the lower range; that god can, in some sense, fall into or through these very gaps in himself, and that he can get lost in their blackness; that slippage of this kind is, finally, the major form his *presence* takes (for us); that these holes or

FIGURE 25. The Seven Mothers and Death. Ellora, Cave 21.

spaces tend to congeal at their edges, thereby constituting our world; that the Śaiva cosmos thus created is, like the godhead, or like the psychic innerness of any living being, a pastiche of solidity and empty spaces, textured rather like Swiss cheese. Further, that, for Śiva, this process is the only way to achieve selfhood and self-knowledge, which are tenuous, perhaps unwelcome, and partly occluded or blind; that the way back from this descent into selfhood is through processes of internalization that melt down the congealed contours and recombine lost parts; that all this is play, uncertain but far from random, initiated by the female persona within god and always requiring her elusive separation from the male persona, who is driven to pursue her from within his own

FIGURE 26. Śiva and Pārvatī at dice. Ellora, Cave 29.

being; that outer movement in this game is, finally, destructive, while inward movement is erotic and integrating, though never finally so.

What this series offers us is not a story, which might be able to reach an end, but a map of sensed and structured potentialities that inform a highly specific vision. Still, there is something missing, a singular element relating to the notion of transition among levels and a more precise characterization of the higher order point of departure. We can approach this problem by turning to a set of medieval regional variants of the tradition, from northern Tamilnadu, which, as it happens, lays a particular claim to Andhaka and his story.

5
Andhaka of Arcot

Śiva killed Andhaka at Tirukkovalūr in South Arcot District, some 150 miles southwest of Madras. The shrine at Kovalūr is therefore one of the eight "heroic sites" (*vīraṭṭāṉam*) of Tamil Śaivism, an ancient list that binds together and localizes, in the Tamil country, eight major mythic tales.[20] There is a late-medieval Tamil *purāṇa* from Kovalūr, by an anonymous author (who certainly lived later than the sixteenth-century author of *Iṟaivācanallūrpurāṇam*, from whom he borrows). Here is the way this Tamil poet tells the story:

One day on Mount Kailāsa, Pārvatī asked Śiva what lights were capable of removing darkness from the world. He answered: "The sun, moon, and fire—and these are my three eyes." She wasn't sure about this, wanted to know for certain, so she covered his eyes, including the eye, in the middle of his forehead, that had made Desire lose his body. Now the god's body seemed to be on fire; the burnt ash smeared on it was like the ashes left over from that flame, and the massive fog of darkness was like smoke pouring from it.[21] All living beings, beginning with the gods, became inactive and confused, prostrated by the darkness; the sun and moon wandered about ineffectively. Was it day or night?[22] Śiva himself became blue-black [*nīlam*], as did the mountain.

20. On this series, see Shulman 1980:81–82, and 1990:xlix–l.

21. *tiruvurut taḻal poṉṟaṉav attiruvuruviṟ/*
pŏru vĕṇṇīr aḻaṟ pŏṭiy ĕṉa tikaḻntaṉa pŏṭi meṟ/
paravi mūṭiya karum pukaiy ĕṉapparaviyatāl/
viri tuṇaṅkaṟuṟ paṭalaṅkaḷ kalantav avvitame//

22. *curar mutal uyirkaḷ ĕllām toḻiliṉṟi naṭaiyum iṉṟi/*
viraviyav iruḷāl vāṭi mĕlint' uṭal kiṭattalāṉum/
paritiyum matiyum ĕṅkum parantu niṉṟ' ulavalāṉum/
iruḷ paṭum ikkālattaiy irav' ĕṅko pakal ĕṅkeṉo/

Thousands of years of the gods passed like this; living beings were terribly weakened in their bodies, and suffered greatly. Filled with mercy without end, Śiva addressed the goddess: "You have played a good game, that has resulted in the death of multitudes of good lives.[23] Thousands of divine years have gone by. Where is your compassion?" Now Umā had a change of heart and removed her hands from Śiva's eyes. Out of the great mass of darkness that had spread like radiant poison, or like the deeds that living beings do, like a towering black mountain, like the mercy of the god whose neck is stained dark—out of this blackness there emerged a demon, by Śiva's command. Formed from darkness, he was called Andhaka. He was like Dhūmaketu, the comet who brings ruin to the world; or like harsh acts; or like a mind that does not contemplate the five syllables of Śiva's mantra.

For a long time this demon stood in fire, meditating on Śiva, with burning anger and hatred for his family.[24] At length, Śiva appeared and offered him a boon. Andhaka asked that he never be weakened or destroyed by any living being of the two classes [*irutiṇaiyuyirāṉ*—i.e., animate/inanimate? male/female?]. Śiva granted this and disappeared.

Now the gods offered tribute to Andhaka, and he plundered their world. They complained to Brahmā, and he went with them to Viṣṇu, who said: "I know why you have come. No one can destroy Andhaka except the lord of Kovalūr. The right thing is for us to go worship his feet." So the gods went to Kovalūr and prayed to Śiva, and he appeared to them in the *liṅga*, told them not to be afraid, sent them home and prepared for war.

With his troops—Mahākāla, Nandin, Guha, Vināyaka, Kuṇḍodara, Śastā, Nikumbha, Daṇḍapāṇi, Bhairava, Vīrabhadra, Vakramukha, Sunāsi—the great god went to war against Andhaka. Who can describe the playfulness that our father displayed in fighting the demon formed of darkness? With love and desire [*ārvam*], Śiva impaled Andhaka on the tip of his trident. He began to dance, in joy, after piercing the demon with his hero's laugh. Andhaka squirmed and danced with him, like pole dancers balanced on a tall pole.[25] In his sorrow, he worshiped Śiva: "Forgive my evil, committed out of simplicity and ignorance. Master me, give me mercy. Is there any substantial reason for your wrath? You are the only refuge for those who follow a bad way, sharp with suffering, acting out of the misery of ignorance."

Śiva felt compassion [*nayantu*] and removed the demon's sorrow. "Before, you were chained; now all your being has been burned away on the trident's tip." Andhaka fell at the god's feet and asked to worship at this place (Kovalūr) in pure love and to have knowledge of Śiva [*civañāṉam*]. Śiva, delighted, made him lord of his hosts—a boon that could not be achieved even by fasting for

23. *naṟ ṟiruviḷaiyāṭṭ' uṟṟāy nalluyirttŏkuti vīya.*

24. *kŏtitta ciṉa maṟattinŏṭuṅ kulavayiram ĕṉa vaḷarntu.*

25. *kaḻāyar mīp putuk kāmp'eṟi cuḻa'ṉaṭañ cĕy aṅkam polum.* The prose version appended to this text says: "like someone impaled on a stake" (*kaḻuveṟṟappaṭṭavaṉaip pol*).

> many years in a cave in the wilderness. Then the god hid himself again in the *liṅga*. Śiva was named there: Conquerer of Karma. That city is a Vīraṭṭam—a place of heroism.[26]

What has this south Indian reworking of the Andhaka materials added to the story (apart from giving it a concrete and familiar locale)? We will look first at the demon's birth. Pārvatī is playing, but she is also curious, impelled toward an empirical test of what Śiva tells her. She covers his eyes, and his fiery body seems to be emitting smoke, vast clouds of it that pervade the universe, killing multitudes of living beings. This blackness, still rooted in the god, has a certain ambiguity about it: It is akin to a deluge of poison, or to a dark mountain, but also to the pervasive, undifferentiated mercy (*aruḷ*) of this same god. At this early stage, that is all there is—a foggy, coagulating mass of darkness emerging like smoke from Śiva's glowing form, but also seemingly expressing the absence of his normal illuminating gaze. An inner transition in the goddess is necessary for the next stage to unfold; she is moved to compassion by her husband's words, and removes her hands from his eyes. Now light and vision are restored to the cosmos, and, simultaneously, by the god's own command—note that voluntaristic element, new to the myth—the darkness hardens into a defined, demonic shape. In the universe of Tamil Śaivism, all forms seem to reflect the radiant vision and intentionality of the god.

But let us linger for a moment with the primary image—at first glance, seemingly figurative and expressive—of Andhaka's birth from a smoking fire. Perhaps the Tamil poet is offering us a way to go deeper into the tantalizing issue of ontic levels and their meaning. What if Śiva's higher order existence is truly a kind of fire, as the text asserts, and as so many devotional and *purāṇic* contexts confirm? We have spoken of the godhead as dense with being, a mode of total interconnectivity, timelessness, simultaneity—before the game of dice begins. We can now add a further attribute: the density of divine wholeness is a fiery, heated state, radiant, fluid, and internal; in chromatic translation, it becomes red, which may also be described in terms of ripening (as we shall see later in relation to *tapas*). It has the unbroken connectivity of fire—already in Vedic India the primary medium of connection among domains—although it is capable of being obscured or occluded in part, which is to say that discontinuities do emerge in god. Black, blind spaces punctuate the red-hot texture of totality, forcing this deity to cool and congeal in an outward movement of self-generation. This is the usual progression within the game of dice, but a parallel process produces Andhaka and, indeed, most demonic entities in a cosmos crystallizing out of the godhead's internal gaps. We might think of these

26. *Tirukkovalūrppurāṇam* 2.8–93.

gaps, for now, as black spots within a dense and subtle flame; and there are occasions when the poets go further, and describe the god's fiery being itself as paradoxically dark, like the black sun of the Veda.[27]

The Arcot Andhaka, like his father, has an affinity with fire; he stands within a blazing flame for thousands of years, and his own innerness is also aflame—with hatred. This internal burning seems to replace the earlier theme, in versions we studied previously, of Andhaka's self-mutilation to the point of a skeletal residue. At Kovalūr, the stress is not on Andhaka's physical emaciation, or even on his hypertrophied masculinity, divorced from female components of the identity. Rather, one sees a creature whose power is fueled by animosity, a black internal state that has to be burned away by the god in his active and violent mode. At the same time, this final act of destruction, which leaves the victim teetering at the tip of the trident like an uneasy pole dancer, is rich with love and desire. Śiva, we might conclude, loves this alienated, smoky self that has emerged out of playfulness, blocking, and the god's own creative glance. For his part, Andhaka achieves the great feat of rupturing planes of reality, transforming his being, very much after the fashion of the impaled sacrificial victims motivated by a cathartic devotionalism widespread in South India.[28] By the same token, it is this reformed devotee—paradigmatic in pursuing the most direct path to the Śaiva goal—who has to struggle to balance himself, like the dancer wavering on his stilts. This unbalanced meeting in confrontation is highly characteristic, for this milieu, of any transition toward the divine.

Andhaka is given the initial boon of invulnerability to beings of the two classes—perhaps animate and inanimate, but also possibly male and female. Śiva, who eventually destroys him, is thus, by definition, outside this categorization. The Tamil myth is not interested in the standard sequence that reduces the godhead to an ever more extreme and external, continually impoverished masculinity. Here, the godhead resists this impoverishment. In its local guise at Kovalūr, divinity becomes active—dancing joyfully, replete with love—when made to confront the detritus of its own temporary obstruction. This detritus is a form of hate, consolidated under the renewed gaze of its father, then burned away by this same father's violent act of love. There is no question of a lost female persona, or of rivalry for the goddess and mother, or even of the Andhaka outcome we have come to expect under the rubric of Bhṛṅgin. The god removes his own blockage and, at the same time, presumably remains porous with the spaciousness and fluid energies that the devotees identify as *aruḷ*, a flooding form of love.

27. See Syrkin 1965.

28. See Shulman 1989.

More generally and abstractly, we have a god composed, as it were, of fluid fire, a dense inner being that is, nonetheless, subject to discontinuities in the guise of black spaces; through these spaces, the god devolves outward into time and bounded form, in a process of cooling and congealing. Externalization is the mode in which these discontinuities exist and have an effect: Śaiva mythology is, primarily, about them, their consequences and meaning, and how to repair them. We ourselves exist only in these gaps, as, in a certain sense, does the god himself, insofar as he may be said to have a self. "He" has no control over these black spaces, which are loci of uncertainty; it is thus logical that "he" is often said to be ruled by his devotees, subject to their whims and needs. At the same time, the level of dense fire is always somehow present; prototypical demons such as Andhaka transform themselves by being consumed within it; there is also a sense in which this order pervades, in soft and subtle radiation, all other levels of the cosmos. One conspicuous concretization of this presence is the major focus of Śaiva ritual, the stone *liṅga* so often said to be, in origin and essence, a pillar of flame.[29]

The density of stone is thus, for our purposes, a transposition—all too easily misconstrued—of the more delicate and pervasive density of fire. We can illustrate this point by turning briefly to another version of the Andhaka myth, from northern Tamilnadu—in this case, from the city of Kāñci; the links between the Kāñci and Kovalūr texts are transparent, although the former also innovates in an unexpected direction.

Andhaka, the son of Hiraṇyâkṣa, worshiped Śiva and won a boon. All the gods, Viṣṇu and the others, turned their backs and fled from him; in terror, they took the form of women, their breasts so heavy that their fragile waists were in danger of breaking under the load. Circling the world in search of refuge, they at last came to the Silver Mountain, Kailāsa, where they hid under the protection of the goddess Umā, mother-in-law of Vaḷḷi.

After some time, Śiva went to the Forest of Pines to test the truth of the sages there, and to take away their confusion. Meanwhile, Andhaka heard that the gods were hiding on Kailāsa in the form of women; furious, he went there to attack them. Viṣṇu was able to create innumerable women through the grace of the goddess; they went into battle with Andhaka and defeated him, and he fled in disgrace.

When the wives of the sages in the Forest of Pines heard Śiva's drum and his flute, they hurried to him with alms, just like the *ācuṇam* bird that is so sensitive to music that any sudden loud noise will make it drop dead. They could not take

29. On the fiery *liṅga* of Sthāṇu, see Shulman 1986. The *liṅgôdbhava* myth, another attempt to describe the first descent of the godhead in this form, speaks of Śiva's self-revelation in the *liṅga* of fire (at Tiruvaṇṇāmalai/Aruṇâcala).

their eyes off him—his luminous smile, bright mouth, broad arms and chest, the thighs that Pārvatī massages until her hands turn red—and as they stared at him, their saris came undone. His body took over their entire innerness [*uḷḷam*]; modesty and other feminine virtues disappeared; they were as if drunk on toddy, singing and dancing. In the fierce heat of their desire, the sandal paste dried on their bodies, their pearl necklaces were charred to ashes, their garlands turned black. If they tried to hold up their slipping saris with their hands, they found themselves unable to offer him the alms they had brought. So they spoke to him, as they twisted and turned in desperation: "We wish to give you great wealth (or: the alms of our breasts, *taṉappiccai*); take them and go. Since we have become naked as Jains in our passion, just who do these saris belong to? Are they ours or yours? Our mounds of Venus and your waist [*alkul*] seem so similar—let's put them together and compare, to achieve certainty. We gave you the alms you were seeking; now if you refuse to give us the one little thing we want, won't that be disgraceful? If you refuse us, do you think we'll let you go without a battle? If you are thinking of running away in panic, forget it. Come and unite with us."

Their husbands, the sages, saw them lose their control and tried to curse the god, but the curses failed to reach him. They began a cruel sacrifice; out of the fire emerged the demon Muyalakað, a tiger, a snake, a deer, a ghostly *bhūta*, a flame, and an ax, all of them projected at the god; but he simply took hold of them and began to dance. The sages were weary and afraid, and he gave them understanding. They turned to him in worship and asked him to grant release, the supreme pleasure.

He said: "If that is what you want, go to Kāñci and live there. Whether you are without attachment or chained by attachment, even if you are pigs or vultures or dogs, snakes or worms, even trees or grass, if you die in Kāñci, you will certainly reach my feet." These 48,000 sages were then reborn, in the four social classes, in Kāñci, where they spent their days worshiping the *liṅga*. For everyone who lives in Kāñci is a sage; every rock there is a *liṅga*; each drop of water is the Ganges; every word uttered is a mantra; every act is a form of serving Śiva. The lord of death can hardly enter that town.

Now Śiva could return to Kailāsa with Pārvatī. The gods, still in women's form, were happy to have him back. Andhaka decided to try again to capture the divine 'women' who had seen him run away. At the gods' request, Śiva sent Bhairava, his own violent form, and Bhairava caught the hard-hearted demon on his trident and danced in joy. True knowledge graciously arose in Andhaka and, as he lay there pierced by the trident, he sang the god's praise. Bhairava said to him, "My son, what is your wish?" Andhaka replied: "Just one thing—release." "Then," said Bhairava, "let us go together to Kāñci.' Bhairava took the impaled demon and made him bathe in the Śivagaṅgā at the Kampam shrine in Kāñci, thereby releasing him from existential bondage. As for Andhaka, he disappeared into the *liṅga* there that bore his name, and became one [*ŏrumai pĕṟṟāṉ*].[30]

30. *Kāñcippurāṇam* of Civañāðayokikaḷ, *Antakêcappaṭalam*.

This version begins with the standard polarization: The male gods turn into women and hide from the hypermasculine demon. The ending, too, is very close to the earlier accounts. A final reabsorption and reidentification closes the gap between the two antagonists, although here this merger takes place in the *liṅga* at Kāñci—seen, apparently, as an ultimate form of the fiery and active god. Both Bhairava and Andhaka melt into this all-embracing, all-destroying density of divine being, a petrified flame. Andhaka is, thus, Śiva, first in part, then wholly so.

In between these two edges of the story, however, we find, this time, not the tale of Andhaka's desire for the goddess (in fact, he seeks someone else, the feminized gods), but a lively version of the most convoluted of all Śaiva myths—that of Śiva's seductive entry into the Dāruvana, the Forest of Pines. To do justice to this story, we would have to write another book. For present purposes, it must suffice to note how the polarized eroticism, with its inevitable reversals in sexual identity, is echoed here. The wives of the sages respond to the god with brazen passion, partly couched in paronomastic doubling, as if language itself had to split in two in order to accommodate the intensity of this experience (a figurative male sense coupled with a literal female mode?). But this doubling within language is, in effect, a form of expansive expressivity, a fiery connection of isolated or separated levels that burns away the harsh external surfaces of speech. Śiva has taken over the women's inner spaces, which are now heated, melting down the barriers that normally control action and perception. One result of this liquid process among the women is a certain loss of overt and conventional feminine qualities (such as modesty and shyness). Falling in love makes women more masculine in this cultural perspective—in effect, dissolving the surface features of sexual identity—even as it usually emasculates the male, who is reduced to supine helplessness. The women thus hopefully suggest to Śiva that their saris could be his.

More deeply, it would seem that the general liquefaction described here reflects an ontic state of heightened innerness and holism. It is this state that renders Śiva immune to the sages' attacks, and that eventually melts down even their resistance. At first, these sages, with all the rage of jealous exclusion, far from love and its melting borders, curse the god whom they perceive as a rival. They are, perhaps, experiencing, in their own right, Śiva's primary trauma, the elision of the female; they thus act from a place of relative rigidity and destructive objectification, the polar opposite of their wives' transition toward internal fluidity. To their credit, these same sages ultimately turn out to be capable of transformation through the apparently fluid medium of understanding.

Many classical Sanskrit versions of the story end with the god's castration (or self-castration, with the collusion of the sages); this helps to explain his presence among *us*, in the world, in the aniconic form of the fiery stone *liṅga*. One might have expected this sexual transformation to turn up here as well, under Andhaka's magnetic sway; but Tamil versions of the Dāruvana myth almost invariably replace the castration with Śiva's violent dance, in the course of which the god subsumes the sages' curses and the various weapons they try to use against him.[31] And so at Kāñci, too, the Forest of Pines becomes a venue for the god's dance of destruction and incorporation, still in the context of the myth of Andhaka, and in line with more ancient versions of Andhaka's story, which conclude with the dance.

The South Indian tradition likes to distinguish between various dances ascribed to Śiva (sometimes there is a list of five or six, parceled out among several shrines);[32] and classical iconological manuals also make a distinction between the more destructive *tāṇḍava* dances and the graceful (*lāsya*) styles.[33] One could argue about which category is being exemplified by the dance panels at Elephanta and Ellora.[34] Be that as it may, the logic of the myth clearly combines the Andhaka outcome with Śiva's dance, in a context of vast destruction—so vast that, in effect, the god has done away with *everything external to himself*. The dance is the moment when the direction of the cosmic process shifts dramatically—when externalization per se becomes reversed. There is simply nothing at all out there any more. The world as seen from, or through, Śiva's dance is one which is being, or has already been, sucked back into the infinite density of the whole. This is, then, a moment of ultimate centripetality, as we see so clearly from iconic depictions of the dance. It is from this point on that the god is forced, as it were, into *tapas* and Yoga—that is, into self-internalizing processes of melting and combining. Where else can he go? Not by chance, the dancing Śiva at Elephanta is posed precisely across from—leading into—the lonely Yogin.

This juxtaposition, perfectly analogous to the development of the Andhaka myth at Kāñci in terms of Śiva's dance in the Forest of Pines, is also consistently displayed in iconographic sources throughout the southern part of the subcontinent. At the Madhukeśvara shrine in Mukhalingam, in northern Andhra, for example, we find a brilliant vision of Andhaka's death: Śiva, ithyphallic and wild, with staring eyes, has rammed through the demon's horizontal body with his trident, while a spectral goddess (one of the Mātṛkās?) gloats at his feet; the more pacific form of the goddess is seated further afield. "She turns back her head and looks at her lord in wonder and admiration and the latter touches her chin with his right hand."[35] The entire scene is beautifully con-

31. On this point, see O'Flaherty 1980:139–40.

32. See Dorai Rangaswamy 1958, 1:440–42.

33. O'Flaherty 1980:130–33.

34. See, e.g., Collins 1988:53–57; also, Berkson 1983:12–13.

35. Masthanaiah 1978:78; see plate 35.

tained by the rounded medallion of the *caitya* arch, in line with the general sense of closure and inward movement that we now associate with Andhaka's demise. Immediately atop this scene, we find Śiva dancing, again in the presence of the goddess.[36] Perhaps we can now understand why South Indian paintings of the dance—whether by Mysore-school or Tanjavur artists—so regularly make Bhṛṅgin a conspicuous witness to Naṭarāja's dance in the company of his consort, Śivakāmiyammai (the goddess at Cidambaram).[37] Recall, too, the skeletal figure lurking between the dancer's legs at Ellora in Cave 14, and the spectral witness of Śiva's dance at Elephanta. This bag of bones is all that is left of a world that was once outside the god.

The Arcot Andhaka has shed some light on the fiery composition of the Śaiva godhead, and on the way Andhaka's destruction ignites the god's doomsday dance. Before we draw the threads together, we need to explore further the notion of sex reversal, which so regularly occurs in Andhaka's vicinity; perhaps we will be able to deduce something new about the way sexual identity is conceptualized in this Hindu cosmology. To flee from Andhaka, the gods hide themselves in a female form;[38] sometimes they also engage him in combat out of this same state of assumed female identity, as in the Kāñci text we just studied. We know that Andhaka/Bhṛṅgin is trapped in a unilateral masculine mode, all bones and holes, and that, as such, he works on all engendered beings in his vicinity. He seems magnetically to draw all maleness to himself, leaving only femininity behind or around him. Andhaka violently polarizes gender into mutually exclusive and antagonistic types. We also know, at least in part, why this should be so: We are dealing with an ultimate form of fragmentation and externalizing objectification, destructive in every way.

Another striking exemplification of these dynamics comes from a different site in Arcot, some 30 miles southeast of Andhaka's battleground with Śiva at Kovalūr. Here, in the village of Kūvākkam (Ulundurpet taluk), we find a strange analogue to Andhaka in the folk deity Aravāð/Kūttāṇṭavar, recently studied by Alf Hiltebeitel in a remarkable essay.[39] There is every reason to regard these two figures as articulating and recapitulating a shared thematic range focused on the problem of having a gender—and of being god. Kūttāṇṭavar is a dancer, worshiped also by dancing castrati. Identified with Irāvat of the Sanskrit epic,

36. Apparently in close proximity to this scene, one finds a detailed carving of Śiva's game of dice: *ibid.*, 79.

37. E.g., Sivaramamurti 1974, figs. 145, 148, 149. We wish to thank Anna Dallapiccola for this reference and for helpful remarks on Bhṛṅgin in relation to Śiva's dance in South Indian painting.

38. See also, *Upatecakāṇṭam* of Ñāðavarotayar 73.1–3 (2168–70).

39. Hiltebeitel 1995.

this deity is said, in the Tamil *Mahābhārata* tradition, to have offered up his flesh and blood to Kālī in a pre-battle act of self-sacrifice on the Pāṇḍavas' behalf; then, fighting on (in residual skeletal form?), he is slain on the eighth day of the war, by the demon Alambuṣa.[40] In Villiputtūrār's fourteenth-century version of the epic, Aravāð cuts off his limbs one by one, in an order sanctioned by Śākta ritual—much like Andhaka's violent self-mutilation, an offering up by the male of his softer, feminine parts—but Aravāð's head survives, "like a radiant lamp," to witness the ongoing war.[41] The oral folk tradition in Arcot adds an eloquent mytheme to these classical statements: Aravāð is reluctant to die unmarried, so Kṛṣṇa takes the enchanting feminine form of Mohinī to provide him with a bride.[42]

At Kūvākkam, and elsewhere in Arcot, this god is worshiped in a colorful set of rituals linked closely to Draupadī and her Tamil cult. Among other features of this ritual series, a dramatic meditation on maleness is clearly prominent: Aravāð/Kūttāṇṭavar is classed as a heroic male (*vīraṉ*) whose iconography and narrative bear out this identity; like Andhaka and Bhṛṅgin, this figure is a disarticulated aggregate of bones and head, lacking flesh and blood. (Like Andhaka, he has cut away these softer parts of his own body, in an act of worship; but where Andhaka performs his self-mutilating *tapas* for Śiva, Aravāð is focused on the violent and predatory goddess.) Any intimate connection between Aravāð and another male seems to require the latter to reverse his sex: Kṛṣṇa, drawn to him in compassion, becomes Mohinī (and is imitated in this respect by the Tamil villagers, who tie the *tāli* marriage necklace around their necks in order to marry this god and then cut the *tāli*s and break bangles in mourning for him, after his ritual dying). Far more extreme, but clearly continuous with this vision, is the act of self-emasculation by the Alis, who choose to worship Kūttāṇṭavar as his devoted wives or widows; after literally dismembering themselves on the full-moon night of Cittirai in the hot season, they may dance in procession with pots containing the severed penises on their heads.[43]

During the festival, these Alis histrionically mourn for Aravāð, for whom they have sacrificed their masculinity; no doubt, their mourning also embraces this abandoned aspect of themselves. Aravāð himself remains, as Hiltebeitel remarks, a "perfect male being."[44] The striking fact, consistent with our analysis of the Andhaka materials, is that this "perfect" (singular) male demands so

40. *Pāratavĕṇpā* of Pĕruntevaðār 413–53, 601–3; see Hiltebeitel 1995.

41. Villiputtūrār 5.355–61, 6.262–67.

42. Hiltebeitel 1995, including summaries of the earlier literature; see also Shulman 1980:306–7.

43. Hiltebeitel 1995, citing Ar. Narulla and interviews with Alis at the Arcot festival.

44. Ibid., 15.

rigid a response from his worshipers. Nothing even vaguely androgynous can maintain its equilibrium in his presence; the male parts—outside him—must be either hidden or, more likely, destroyed, converted into an isolated feminine mode. Nor can this extravagant masculinity find any sustained complementarity in marriage: The Mohinī union appears to be little more than a poignant fiction, and is, in any case, evanescent, a momentary promise on the verge of death. All too swiftly, the Alis become widows. The wish for female completion of the rudimentary male emerges here in the context of its total impossibility under these conditions of polarized identities; and the local myth of transvestite marriage embraces and expresses the stark conflict that informs this wish. Unilateral males simply cannot mate successfully with unilateral (here, sex-changed) females. The only liaison that stands a chance, however transient, is that between two asymmetrical androgynes.

The Andhaka outcome, in other words, is, finally, a dead end. Polarized males as well as females will ultimately rebound in the direction of a richer and more ambiguous sexual being. Rigid isolation of gender is, perhaps, energizing in its earlier stages—witness the liberated power of the dance, as performed by the Alis; by their deity-lover Kūttāṇṭavar; and by Bhairava-Śiva, with Andhaka on his trident—but this energy is primarily destructive. It is also profoundly connected to the lurking danger of objectification. To elucidate this point, which lies close to the heart of our story, and, at the same time, to tease out a somewhat more normative picture of gender composition, we now discuss the main *purāṇic* sequel to the Andhaka myth, which extends it, reworking its themes, by one generation.

6
Āḍi and Vīraka: Becoming a Rock

Andhaka, who is Śiva's son, has a son of his own, named Āḍi.[45] Like his father, Āḍi has an antagonistic relationship with Śiva, and interesting complications in the composition of his sexuality. And again, like Andhaka, Āḍi draws to himself the theme of sexual reversal or transformation, though in his case, the dynamics of this change are very different; he himself is capable of undergoing an extreme oscillation in gender. Equally impressive, for our purposes, are the continuities established with the dice game and the theme of congealing into frozen form. The *Matsyapurāṇa* gives a lucid, relatively early version of the story:

45. According to *Skandapurāṇa* 6.230, Andhaka also had another son, called Vṛka, who plays an active and unsettling role in the traditions of Hāṭakeśvara in Gujarat.

After their wedding, Śiva and Pārvatī began to play dice. A terrible noise upset them—the howling and ranting of Śiva's followers, dwarfs and clowns and various other misshapen, monstrous creatures. One of these, named Vīraka or Vīrabhadra ["Hero"], was adopted by Pārvatī as her son.

Then the god lay down in bed with Pārvatī and, teasing her, he said: "Next to me, you look black like a snake coiled around the sandalwood tree." Pārvatī was furious: "One always pays the price of one's own callousness and frozen sensitivity [*jāḍya*]. I worked hard to get you for my husband, and my reward is constant humiliation and disrespect. I am neither crooked nor uneven—you're the one with such qualities, which is not surprising, considering the company you keep. I'm going away to the mountain, since my life is no longer worth living."

Śiva tried to apologize: "Don't be angry, I was only kidding. You don't know yourself very well, do you? I guess one shouldn't joke with someone who gets offended so easily." But she was adamant, unwilling to be appeased, and now he became angry and said, "You really are just like your father, Himâlaya—hard, rocky, impenetrable, crooked in all your little ways, unpleasant as ice." "Look who's talking," she screamed, "you crooked, heartless male; you're all dried up like the ashes you wear on your body, shameless enough to wander naked in cemeteries, disgustingly draped in skulls. . . . What's the use of more words?" And she hurried off, intent on ridding herself of her dark skin, and leaving her beloved Vīraka to guard the door of the palace, lest, in her absence, Śiva find comfort in the arms of some other woman.

Now the demon Āḍi, the son of Andhaka, wanted to kill Śiva, so he took the form of a serpent and slithered past the vigilant Vīraka. He then assumed the seductive form of Pārvatī herself and approached Śiva, who was very happy to see his wife again, although he couldn't quite understand how she could have cooled off so quickly and come back without achieving her aim. When he noticed that the auspicious sign of the lotus was absent from the left side of "her" body, he guessed that he was about to make love to a dangerous demon in disguise; so he used his penis as a thunderbolt and killed "her" in the course of love.

But Pārvatī, off in the mountains, heard from the Wind that another woman had entered her bedroom with her husband, so she cursed her son, Vīraka, to have a mother who was harsh, rugged, corrosive, salty, tough as rock. That is how Vīraka turned into a rock himself.

Heating herself with her inner fire, Pārvatī shed her dark exterior and became golden in color, like a blazing lamp. Satisfied at last, she headed home. But when Vīraka, standing steadfast at the door, saw her approach, he did not recognize her. "Go away," he said; "a demon came here in the form of my mother Pārvatī, and I failed to stop him. Śiva had to kill him. He told me to let no one else in, and my mother gave me the same order." Pārvatī was stricken with remorse: "This is what happens when you don't think things through to the end. My son, I am your real mother. I am very sorry that I cursed you. Soon, however, you will be freed from this human condition." So Vīraka allowed her to enter, and she and Śiva made love for a thousand years.[46]

46. *Matsyapurāṇa* 154:520–158.28; cf. discussion by Courtright 1985:66–68.

This is not the end of the story. When Śiva and Pārvatī give themselves to love, the universe is once again put into crisis. But note, again, how divisive the dice game is, how it leads directly into the quarrel between the lovers, and their separation, with all the consequent violence, suffering, and danger. This time it is her turn to be hard and rocky, in line with her paternal inheritance, which Śiva uses to insult her. More precisely, it begins to look as if we have again, this time in the case of the female, the kind of inside-out progression that naturally accompanies the game of dice. The softer, inner part—a heated, reddish gold—eventually comes to the surface of Pārvatī's body, while inside she has become harsh and rigid; she curses her son (Vīraka)[47] to have a stony mother—that is, she curses herself to be frozen and unyielding. No wonder this son fails to recognize his mother when she finally returns, in her new golden exterior. The tragic culmination of the irreversible curse makes explicit the identification we have suspected all along: Being human, it seems, is precisely akin to Vīraka's unhappy state, a form of temporary petrification as the son or daughter of an equally stony mother.

The male, too, is turned inside out: Āḍi, a harsh masculine son of the hyper-male Andhaka, becomes, first, a serpent (primarily, to our surprise, a sign of female identity in India),[48] and then, through the kind of total reversal usually elicited by his father, a form of the goddess. Entering "her" with his adamantine penis, Śiva destroys this false female from inside; here the hard interior space, ultimate maleness, is enclosed by an inside-out masculinity, the male masquerading as female, enacting the inversion that displays the true composite character of both sexual identities. Śiva, as a gambler, turns his inside out, slipping outward through his inner spaces, which freeze parts of him into partial forms; Āḍi, in contrast to his father, externalizes a feminine innerness that, temporarily congealed, exposes the residual male persona inside to complete destruction. More generally, it would seem that this convoluted inside-out containment is a basic feature of all sexual being; the goddess always has the male inside her, while she is somewhere inside him; both, moreover, are in constant danger of objectification, of becoming congealed pieces of a misleading surface—as, indeed, are we. Masculine identity at its height—the erect and bony penis containing hot, liquid, flooding seed—may well be a locus of femininity,[49] just as Pārvatī's supple exterior may hold within it the icy reaches of

47. See section 3 of this chapter.

48. In an oral version of the Aravāð myth, found by Hiltebeitel (1995), the skeletal hero wonders how he will be able to fight in this reduced state; his mother Ulūpī, the Snake-Woman, sends him snakes to replace the missing flesh. In Tamil, the mound of Venus is conventionally compared to a snake. The soft, pliant, flowing serpent is, perhaps, the very opposite of the stone *liṅga* (that is, of extruded masculinity at its most objectified and concrete).

49. See Egnor 1978:69; O'Flaherty 1980:318.

an all-too-masculine, rough and crooked, Himâlayan stone. If one gender is thus effectively wrapped inside the other, largely deriving from the other, we would perhaps do better to think of gender generally as an infinite concentric regress, male within female, within male, within female—or as an endless spiral that is also a continuum and a function of the process of becoming different, of externalizing oneself into difference through time. One might then consider, for a moment, what it means in such a system to fuse two such convoluted beings in a marriage, or, contrariwise, to attempt to disentangle and finally distinguish one of these strands from its complementary and energizing counterpart, as Andhaka and Bhṛṅgin seek to do.

And one might contemplate the ironies implicit in a poem like the following, by the Telugu devotee Dhūrjaṭi, who lived in sixteenth-century Andhra, and who calls out to Śiva—the same Śiva of our myths, here identified as the lord of the ancient temple at Kāḷahasti, near the northern border of the Tamil country—in tones that suggest the profound similarities between this god's embodied, engendered mode of being and our own:

Is there sweet water
shimmering with lotus
inside a barren rock?
Can you find a Brahmin house
where Untouchables live?
Think it over—
these two examples, these woeful
guises, O Lord of Kāḷahasti—
and don't give up
on me.
Think of your own
exquisite qualities.[50]

We know something, by now, of these qualities, and what they mean to "him" and "his" universe, which also happens to be ours. We also know the answer to the two questions the Telugu poet poses for his god. It remains only to remind ourselves that this Śiva of Kāḷahasti inhabits the innermost space of this elegant stone shrine in the form of a *liṅga* of wind, a dense gust of godhood continuously revealed, day and night, by the lamps in the dark sanctum, with their flickering flames.

50. *Srīkāḷahastīśvaraśatakamu* of Dhūrjaṭi, 102.

III

Melting and Marrying

Joining body to body
is no great achievement.
The connection that matters
is heart with heart.[1]

1
Color and Heat

Congealed in form and lost in time, Śiva searches for a way back to the starting point, before the game began. The greater part of Śaiva mythology documents this search, its twists and turns, destructive dead ends, sudden shifts in levels. Of its paradigmatic character for us, his devotees—similarly lost and congealed—we need say very little. Our vision remains focused on the intra-divine process, from the vantage point of the shattered cosmos in which this god must find his way. He is still a player in the disrupted game, and thus subject to conditions of fragmentation, obscured self-knowledge, engenderment, imbalance, and isolation. He is also in movement or in process, from within this given set of internal conditions.

In this chapter, we will be concerned with the thermochromatic aspects of Śiva's process, in relation to a latent metaphysical psychology and to the sexual ontology implicit in the dice game. Separated from his female part, Śiva will reclaim the goddess in marriage in a "red," impassioned, heated mode. We can summarize the mythic sequence, which we have already encountered in various partial forms, as follows:

When Śiva's wife Satī died in the fire at her father Dakṣa's sacrifice, Śiva, overcome with grief, wandered with her corpse on his shoulder for many days. The

1. *Niraṅkuśopākhyānamu* of Rudrakavi, 4:79.

universe could not sustain this sorrow: The gods cut Satī's corpse into pieces, which fell at different places throughout the world. That is how the shrines of the goddess came into being.

But Śiva remained disconsolate. At length, he gave himself to the heated inner mode of Yogic meditation, in the highest mountains; he was desperately seeking the deepest self. But Satī was reborn as Pārvatī, the daughter of Himâlaya; and already as a young girl, she knew she wanted Śiva for her husband. Her father, the Mountain, sent her to serve the god in his meditation. Later, when she had grown to puberty, Pārvatī asked, and received, her father's permission to devote herself to *tapas* focused on the great deity she was determined to marry.

The demon Tāraka threatened the stability of the cosmos, and the gods knew that only a son born from Śiva could lead their army against him. But Śiva was lost in his inner world, utterly uninterested in any woman, hence unlikely to produce a son. Indra, king of the gods, decided to send Manmatha—Desire itself—on a suicide mission: he was to shoot his arrows of flowers at the meditating Śiva and thus make him fall in love.

Manmatha proceeded to the mountain where Śiva was performing his Yoga; Spring, with its intoxicating breezes, accompanied him in his approach. He found the god absorbed in meditation, on the point of finding the self he was seeking. Now Manmatha drew his bow and shot an arrow that struck Śiva in the heart. The god, disturbed, no longer whole, opened his eyes and saw Desire; in terrible anger, Śiva burned Manmatha to death with the fire of his third eye.

But Śiva also saw something else in this moment of destruction—the radiant Pārvatī, sitting not far away, on the Mountain, her inner being concentrated in love for Śiva. He wanted her—Manmatha, in dying, had achieved his mission—and he came at once to test her love, disguising himself as an old Brahmin. In this form, Śiva excoriated Śiva, that ugly, naked beggar who makes his home in the burning ground, who smears his body with ashes taken from burned corpses; how could a beautiful young woman choose someone like that for her husband? But Pārvatī insisted she would marry no one other than Śiva, and turned away from the beggar. At that moment, Śiva revealed himself to her in his true form, which is subject to passion; and he promised to fulfill her longing. With her father Himâlaya's consent, Pārvatī was married to the great god; and the newlyweds gave themselves over to games of love for a thousand years.[2]

We will examine the stages and essential features of this mythic moment, taking, as our base text, the outstanding classical account by Kālidāsa, the limpid narrative lyric called (somewhat misleadingly) *Kumārasambhava*, "The Birth of the Son."[3] If we pay attention to the thematic and textural singularities

2. For versions of this segment of Śaiva myth, see *Matysapurāṇa* 154; *Śivapurāṇa* 2.2.2–20 (heavily influenced by Kālidāsa's *kāvya*); and sources cited by O'Flaherty 1975: 326. See the discussion in O'Flaherty 1973.

3. Kālidāsa himself never mentions this title in the text of his poem. *Sambhava* is not so much "birth" as "becoming," an emerging into being. We accept the general view that

of Kālidāsa's poem, the hidden logic of the myth may become apparent.[4] It is important to keep in mind that Śaiva cosmology has a structure, within which not everything is possible. As in other Indian systems, this one devotes considerable energy to exploring its own limits and possible permutations. Here we can say, on the basis of what we have seen in the first two chapters, that, once the initial disruption takes place within the godhead, the resulting imbalance pushes the newly autonomized forces in certain characteristic directions, although a high degree of uncertainty marks individual moves and reconfigurations. Within the devolving cosmos, with the wholeness of the godhead itself at stake, the Andhaka outcome delineates one conspicuous boundary, a vector taken to its furthest reach.

Andhaka has shown us the male principle in near-total isolation, in a context of internal devastation. The countervailing movement is one of internal fullness aimed at reinstating or reconstituting the lost fragments of the god, including the feminine part that has torn itself away. This process unfolds through the complementary activation of three related aspects: (1) a turning inward, the internalization of those energies that had been spent in the self-externalizing drive of the divinity—here we may imagine the god as sucking into himself, by powerful attraction, everything that exists, as it were, outside him; (2) an internal heating or melting, transformative of state (sometimes described in terms of a ripening);[5] and (3) a rediscovery of the preexisting totality within, which requires the presence of a female otherness surviving in continuous conjunction with, and incipient separation from, the male. Another way to picture this is in terms of self-deobjectification, although the resulting appearance of a more fluid self also entails states of discontinuity and further ruptures in holistic being. We refer to this process, as a whole, by the familiar word *tapas*, usually mistranslated as "penance" or "austerities."

We should, then, begin by ruling out the associations that a term like "penance" suggests. Indeed, we should state categorically that asceticism, in the Western sense, hardly exists in the Hindu frame and is quite foreign to any Hindu metaphysics (despite 200 years, or more, of translations from Sanskrit that have adopted this kind of terminology). True, both Śiva and Pārvatī are said to torture their bodies—for example, by standing in cold pools during the winter; by sleeping on the ground; by wearing the harsh bark garments suited to the

---

Kālidāsa's work includes only the first eight cantos of the extant text (see, most recently, Satya Vrat Shastri 1992). Citations here refer to the edition of M. R. Kale 1967 (hereafter cited as *KS*).

4. Kālidāsa's version is, of course, illuminated by the *purāṇic* sources, especially *Matsyapurāṇa* 154.

5. Cf. *KS* 6.16.

wilderness; and so on. But these acts are, in themselves, only surface manifestations of a more general attack on the surface; they are conducive to the internalized self-heating that gives *tapas* its purpose, and to the consequent transitions among levels and higher-order integrations that the *tapasvin* 'self-heater' strives to effect. It is in this context, too, that we can speak of an erotic or seductive side to the process, and that we can begin to understand the necessary relationship between Śiva's *tapas* and his marriage.

Tapas "cooks," "melts," "dissolves" all that is hard, stony, external.[6] In doing so, it enhances and brings into play the latent wholeness internal to the *tapasvin*—always, by definition, a bisexual wholeness, which is also potentially generative of newer, perhaps more powerful forms of self.[7] *Tapas* "heats"—and therefore, as David Knipe has noted, the internal *tapas* fire can cause pain, like all other forms of heat in India.[8] But such pain is of a different order, and, as such, easily distinguished from the rigors of "asceticism" as we normally understand the word. Stated more generally, *tapas* tends to trigger an upward transition in levels of being or awareness—and this transition is naturally accompanied by the anguish inherent to growth; or, since we are dealing with the melting down of fixed structures and congealed boundaries, we could describe the process as partly analogous to the violent attack on externalities that is so often described in the myths.[9] But *tapas* is far more promising than external violence, inasmuch as it proceeds from within—the domain of holism—and directs energy primarily inward. The Vedic texts explicitly link *tapas* with this kind of internal movement, or of lively innerness. Thus the inner self (*antarâtman*) of the fivefold divinity (*puruṣa*) is precisely this fiery force of *tapas*; hence the very lifebreath (*prāṇa*) of this heated being is hot (*uṣṇatara*); when he—the divine male (*puruṣa*)—is extruded (*nirukta*), he burns.[10] Internal being tends to be heated, and any act of internalization fans the flames. At the same time, as the above text indicates, *tapas* also enables the kind of internal transformation that can drive toward active and creative externalization—for example, in sacrificial rites.[11]

Heated innerness thus has several consistent features. It is active, dynamic, and fluid; dissolving borders, it establishes a continuous connection between

6. See the rich discussion by Malamoud 1989:35–70. On *tapas* in the Vedic sources, see Shee 1980.

7. See Kaelber 1989:29–43.

8. Knipe 1975:130–32.,

9. See our discussion in chapter I, section 10.

10. *Jaiminīya Upaniṣad Brāhmaṇa* 3.32.1–5; see the discussion in Knipe 1975:121. The extrusion of divinity is linked with language, another fiery power.

11. See Malamoud 1989:47.

hitherto isolated domains or states of being;[12] it is transformative and generative, whether of the externalized cosmos or of the internalizing wholeness of divinity; in its holistic potential, it is also far more closely linked to ultimacy than is any bounded and extruded mode. *Tapas*, in short, reproduces the continuous density of divine being that we have posited as preceding the game of dice; as such, it is capable of burning away the gaping gaps that emerge out of the game. It is no wonder that the god chooses this method after the game explodes in conflict. Turning inward, he seeks to heat himself to wholeness. Still, in all our texts, this movement falls short of final success.

We have seen the god's *tapas* emerge as a theme at Elephanta: There, following the direction of circumambulation around the central *liṅga* shrine, the Andhaka panel is followed by the god as dancer, and then by his meditational, or Yogic, mode. If Andhaka is one limit to the system (and the dance serves as a climax to the Andhaka myth), then we may think of the Yogic *tapas* as a rebound movement aimed at reconstitution. Having destroyed the caricature of isolated maleness within himself, Śiva can turn back toward holism, which is also a pulling inward. Eventually, this revised direction will culminate in marriage, which will, in turn, unfold again toward fragmentation; at Elephanta, the "final" framing panel shows us Rāvaṇa driving the two divine selves, Śiva and Pārvatī, back together, in a state of temporary harmony and poise.

This description suggests a hierarchy of states, with the initial holistic being at the highest (or deepest, most encompassing) point. The first devolution outward, or downward, produces the androgyne—two genders flowing into one another, yet already sufficiently defined to suggest eventual autonomization and separation. Marriage constitutes a further descent, characterized by the reunion of distinct personae; but this erotic integration of male and female is still superior to the harsh isolation of a unilateral gender such as we see in Andhaka/Bhṛṅgin, the blind and bony male. In this sense, Śiva's marriage always marks a movement back toward wholeness, even if this movement is later inevitably halted and reversed. Thus, in this reading, *tapas* and eroticism are *not* deeply at odds; rather, *tapas* naturally moves the *tapasvin* toward erotic fusion with his or her lost otherness. *Tapas*, as a process of reconstructed wholeness, is enormously attractive to these split-off and fragmented selves; here again, the most pressing contrast is with figures such as Andhaka and Aravāð, the hypertrophied and residual males who totally polarize any kind of relations (one can approach them only as "pure" males or as self-emasculated, "pure" females).[13] *Tapas* allows, indeed constitutes the necessary ground for, the recombination of two potentially whole—that is, innately androgynous—beings,

12. *Tapas* thus naturally accompanies Yoga, an effort at "yoking" and "connecting."

13. See chapter II, section 5.

even if erotic fusion remains, perforce, on a lower plane than the fluid wholeness imagined at the deepest (most inner) core. Put somewhat differently, the process propelled by *tapas* is one of softening, turning hardness (including the resilience of differentiation and categorical distinctions) into flux, enabling all that is exterior to flow back into the interior. Eroticism fuses, closing gaps, erasing boundaries, whereas externalization congeals gaps and hardens fragmented entities. Externalization is inherently antierotic, and internalization is *always* erotic; *tapa*s turns Śiva's or Pārvatī's interiors soft, makes them capable of joining everything together. Again we see that *tapas* easily, indeed inevitably, motivates the marriage of these separated selves, whatever reversals or future devolutions remain in store.

Moreover, it is surely wrong to make this progression a linear one, and to construct the story in such a way that one stage logically informs or, indeed, determines, the next. The uneven oscillation between potentialities of wholeness and dissolution is more deeply structured into the initial intuitions about this god than is the highly selective and sequential vision of any given narrative. Nevertheless, each version does make precisely this kind of selection, producing a seemingly necessary sequence. Thus, in strictly narrative terms, the *Kumārasambhava* takes us from the moment of Pārvatī's birth as the daughter of the Mountain Himâlaya through Śiva's burning and subsequent revival of Kāma, the god of desire; then to Pārvatī's seductive *tapas* and trial by her prospective bridegroom; and finally to the wedding of the divine couple and its erotic aftermath. In the background is the gods' request from Brahmā for a general to lead them in battle against the predatory demon Tāraka; Brahmā assumes that only a son born of Śiva's seed can assume that role. Kālidāsa tells us nothing about the eventual birth of this son (Kumāra), but he describes in great detail, with subtlety and an expressivity focused on existential and ontic concerns, the earlier four stages in the process mentioned above. One way to understand his sensibility, as it moulds the inherited myth, is to note the striking chromatic progressions that he builds into his descriptions, especially the consistent interplay of whites and reds.

2
On Redness

In essence, the *Kumārasambhava* is a book of rubescence, smoldering and glowing; a book, we might almost say, *about* redness and its meanings. *Tapas* is a red heat; the goddess is primarily red, on fire, as is Śiva himself, under his covering of white ash; her love or passion for Śiva, and his for her, is *rāga*, or *anurāga* ("redness"); Kāma/Manmatha goes up in blazing red flames; an auspicious and vital redness colors the natural world, with its flowers and minerals, and the human ritual world within which the divine wedding is arranged and celebrated; finally, the work closes with one of the most famous passages in Sanskrit literature, describing a violently red sunset as seen from the mountain heights. This persistent redness is, however, consistently framed by either white or black, or a combination of the two. The combinations are themselves significant, as we will see.

Take, for example, the thematic register linked to the closing sunset. It is very striking to find that this fiery closure is already adumbrated at the very outset of the *Kumārasambhava,* in the fourth verse of the opening canto, which begins with a long description of the white and stony Himâlaya:

> That mountain bears rich mineral-beds
> streaking its peaks red like a timeless sunset—
> reflected piecemeal in tattered clouds—
> and serving the courtesans of heaven
> when they paint themselves
> in the flurries of love.

The mountain is frozen, snow-white—and vibrant with redness, that colors both the passing clouds (torn into fragments by the mountain peaks) and the bodies of the Apsaras dancers in their erotic playfulness (*vibhrama*). So the icy slopes are a site of fiery love—there is a persistent sense of the mountain as unexpectedly alive with passion. The crimson sunset is "timeless," outside the temporal constraints that bind the god. Lest this association seem wholly arbitrary, we will cite the aftermath of the overpowering sunset in Canto 8, when Śiva points out to his bride:

> The Moon has cast off his red glow
> and has become pure in all his fullness.
> Those immaculate by nature
> emerge unstained
> by the vagaries of time. (8.65)

"Vagaries" strives to convey the power of *vikriyā*—trans-form, deformation, aberration—here, a destructuring dependent on time (*kāla* again, as in the previous verse). The reddish glow of the moon, as it first rises, is a heated or impassioned state (*raktabhāva*) that eventually gives way to a pure, white wholeness, a perfect circle against the undifferentiated dark sky. Note the movement—from red to white; from heated feeling to cool radiance; from time-bound deformation to natural purity and wholeness. A similar sequence may be projected onto the godhead, whose initial wholeness has shattered into transforms (*vikriyā,* or *vikāra*), which, heated to redness, strive to recompose the wider unity out of the disjoined, devolving materials of selfhood.

Time is part of this process of congealing devolution, perhaps its diagnostic feature. The *Kumārasambhava* begins with its consequences: vertical descent along the axis symbolized by the rocky, frozen Himâlaya, closed in on itself. White here, at the outset of the poem, seems to mark stasis, and impenetrable hardness, a density without gaps or inner space.[14] And yet, as we have just seen, and as the poet goes on to insist repeatedly, this snow-white mountain is streaked with red, with traces of fiery liveliness, interaction, passion—there are bloodstains on the snow, left by lions who have attacked elephants (1.6); women of miraculous beauty write love letters with red mineral ink on white birch bark (1.7); the red lotus blossoms in pools drenched by brilliant sunlight (1.16). We could thus speak of redness painted on a white background, which, while subsuming it, also hints of a potential for unfreezing—as if the whiteness could eventually be heated into a domain of loving and relating.

Such, precisely, is the process that overtakes the god. Kālidāsa tells us—this is really the beginning of the story per se—that Śiva began to heat himself (*tapas cacāra*) by lighting a fire, which is another form of himself, because of "some desire or other" (*kenâpi kāmena*, 1.57). The indeterminacy of the description seems to suit the open-ended nature of the process—although by now we know something of that mysterious desire and its ludic origins. He is, perhaps, wanting the (female) parts of himself that he has lost. However, at this stage Śiva is, by implication (and reading the surface of the text), not yet subject to the "vagaries," or aberrational transforms, that we have just noted in relation to the term *vikriyā*, for he allows the young Pārvatī to serve him, even though she might be seen as a potential diversion or obstacle to his goal (*pratyarthibhūtā*):

> *vikārahetau sati vikriyante*
> *yeṣāṃ na cetāṃsi ta eva dhīrāḥ*
>
> Even when there is reason to transform,
> the mind of a true hero
> will *not* change form.

Here the term is *vikāra*, a synonym of *vikriyā*, from the same root. Still, we might wonder, given all that is about to happen, if the poet is not hinting at irony—at a *vikāra* that is already working on this god from inside, however controlled and impassive he might appear. The very syntax of the Sanskrit suggests this: The first half of the line tells us that "they are disturbed when

14. On the conjunction of hardness with stasis, see 6.73 (*kāṭhinyaṃ sthāvare kāye bhavatā sarvam arpitam*).

there is reason to be transformed"; the negative *na* only upsets this notion at the very end of the clause. Or perhaps Śiva is not truly captured by the category of hero; for, as we see in the following cantos, and as we know from the point of departure, he is the first to experience the vagaries of time and change.

3
The Self Disguised

Here is how it happens. Nothing ever proceeds simply or directly in the stories of Śiva, nor is the shortest distance between two points ever a straight line. Kāma/Manmatha has been sent on his desperate mission by the gods; his orders are to shoot the intoxicating flower arrows of passion at Śiva, thereby making him fall in love. Śiva, seated in the lotus position on the Himâlayan peak, is turned deeply inward, searching there, inside him, for his self. But the mountain also belongs to Pārvatī, who has grown up there, and who has patiently served this great meditating god, whom she hopes to marry. So it happens that at the very moment that Śiva "sees" or recovers his hidden self, these other two figures, Kāma and Pārvatī, converge on him from another direction, with a program of their own.

Kāma, noticing Pārvatī's presence, is reassured. His first glance at the god had so overwhelmed him that, in panic, he dropped his bow and arrows. He realizes, of course, that he has little chance of getting away alive. But so ravishing is Pārvatī's beauty that he takes heart, confident that, whatever may happen to him, his mission will be accomplished. Could anyone, even Śiva, fail to love this woman?

Initially, Desire merely watches as she approaches the threshold of the meditation site; she seems to know—at any rate, the poet knows—that this god will be her husband *(bhaviṣyataḥ patyur umā ca śambhoḥ/ samāsasāda pratihārabhūmim).* At precisely this juncture, in the close proximity of the goddess:

> He saw it,
> what they call the self,
> the deepest light
> inside him,
> saw it through Yoga
> and at once desisted. (3.58)

Śiva has reached his goal, an inward vision; his eyes are closed, as when Andhaka was born (again, with the goddess beside him). But Andhaka's birth is not a true inner movement; it is, rather, an occlusion and a blocking, or a blinding, and it entails a loss of density in the godhead, a falling into darkness and space. Here, by way of contrast, the dense weight of divinity is nearly total—the serpents who bear the earth on their hoods can barely sustain the burden of this spot where the god is sitting (59). But he is finished (*upararāma*), whole, at rest. He loosens his fixed yogic posture, releases a breath.

He is ready for love. In the midst of this vision of total concentration and perfectly centered sensation, Pārvatī's girlfriends scatter a profusion of flowers and green tendrils at the god's feet (61). The goddess herself bows to him, in a flurry of feeling and falling blossoms. He blesses her: she will have a husband who never divides his love for her with another (*ananyabhājaṃ patim āpnuhi*). These are words which can never go astray or be reversed (63). Does he know that he is blessing, or binding, himself?

Kāma knows—like a moth facing flame, he again takes up his bow. The goddess stretches out her red hand toward the blazing god (*giriśāya . . . tapasvine*)—still burning with the energy of his inner fusion—to offer him a garland of lotuses gathered from the waters of the Ganges (this garland is also a bit dried and withered from the heat of the sun; this is a moment of seemingly universal fire). Śiva moves to receive this gift, in the warmth of his love. But the Sanskrit is a little ambiguous: he might also be moving to take *her* back into himself (*pratigrahītum . . . tām upacakrame ca*). The feminine accusative *tām* certainly refers to the garland mentioned in the previous verse, even as it seems to suggest the real object of his desire, the goddess reaching out to him. As this is happening, Kāma brings together the unerring arrow called Bewildering and his bowstring. He prepares to shoot.

Kālidāsa paints this pregnant scene:

> He was a little,
> just a little,
> shaken, like the ocean
> when the moon first rises.
> He fixed his eyes, wide open,
> on Umā's face, her full red lips,
>
> and all the rest of her
> that was opening up
> in feeling, her body
> quivering like kadamba leaves
> as she stood away from him,
> at a slight angle, her face continually
> more lovely, eyes
> restless and wild. (67–68)

So much for the stillness of internal fusion. The infinitesimal disturbance (*kiṃcit-parilupta-dhairya*) the god must feel is, in fact, infinitely powerful, a wondrous movement: this innocent word *kiṃcit*—"just a little"—often means something miraculous, real beyond words.[15] By now, both Śiva and Pārvatī are staring with open eyes, directed outward; and she is poised, with great precision, in oblique relation to him (*sācī-kṛtā*), as we so often see her in the iconography. She is also opening up, revealing her emotion (*vivṛṇvatī* . . . *bhāvam*); this verb, *vivṛ*, is the signifier of space—always, in this text, an inner space or gap, where a subject can exist. Pārvatī is already, at this stage, such a subject, capable of eliciting an answering spaciousness inside the god.

He tries to regain control of himself, and he is curious as to the cause of this inner agitation or aberration (*vikṛti*, 69). Looking around, he sees Kāma, bending back his bow. But the arrow is never released; it is, in fact, utterly superfluous. Śiva has already been drawn out of his dense totality of being, in response to Pārvatī's compelling presence (and, perhaps, to the rhythm of his own ineluctable process). Desire is prowling within him, and making him angry. He opens the third eye, on his forehead, always a window to his deeper, more internal state. We have characterized this state as one of fire: flames flash out and destroy hapless Kāma/Manmatha in his transparent ambush.

This burning of Kāma is, as Wendy Doniger has argued, an erotic act by the god, and the ultimate sign of Kāma's victory over Śiva.[16] Were he impervious to desire, Śiva would have left Kāma alone; nor would he feel the need to flee the meditation zone "in order to escape the proximity of women" (*strī-saṃnikarṣaṃ parihartum icchan*, 74). At this juncture, Śiva disappears, while Pārvatī, traumatized by what she has witnessed, closes her eyes. Her father, the Mountain, gathers his distraught daughter in his arms. The first stage in the tortuous *tapas* of reunion has been achieved.

Śiva is now in love—we know it, he knows it; only Pārvatī does not yet know it. He is not quite sure of her, and wishes to test her. But there is also a deeper question, of considerable consequence. This god has, as we saw, found his self, through *tapas* and Yoga; and, under attack by Desire, he has turned back from, away from, this self, toward Pārvatī. How whole can he be in this return to the world of gaps and displacements, of external boundaries and their frustrations? Or, more obliquely—remember that the two potential lovers stand poised obliquely, vis-à-vis one another, in Kālidāsa's poignant phrase—which self does he bring into play at this moment of meeting?

15. Cf., e.g., *Uttararāmacarita* of Bhavabhūti 1.27 (*kimapi kimapi* . . . Ghanaśyāma: *anirvācyaṃ yathā tathā* "indescribable").

16. See O'Flaherty 1973.

It is a self in disguise. Kālidāsa carefully refrains from identifying "him"—there is just "some long-haired yogi or other" (*kaś-cij jaṭilaḥ*), rather free with words (*pragalbha-vāk)*, fiery in form, who seeks out Pārvatī in her meditational state (5.30). She, for her part, has gone beyond the furthest reaches of *tapas*—those who know the past call her Leafless (Aparṇā), since she refused to eat even those dry leaves that fell automatically from the trees (28). She has outdistanced, by far, those great *tapasvins* who hardened their bodies with various tortures; her body is delicate as the stalk of a lotus (29), yet she has used it harshly, exposing it to outer pain—in the interests of softening and melting her own innerness.[17] The anonymous stranger finds it hard to understand her motivation: She was born into a wealthy family, she has preternatural beauty, lacks nothing; if it is a husband that she seeks, *tapas* (see figure 27) is hardly the proper method—a precious stone is sought by others, and has no need to go searching itself (45). He wants Pārvatī to tell him her secret, asks that she not treat him as "other" (*na māṃ paraṃ sampratipattum arhasi,* 39). Indeed, in a sense, he is certainly not foreign to her, to this feminine persona intent on reclaiming her place within him. He thus knows—apparently, from his own experience no less than from the various signs she is revealing to him—precisely what she wants, although she refuses to articulate this desire in words; her sighs, heated from within, are eloquent enough; still, his mind is full of doubt (46). We suggest that this statement be taken in all its fullness, for it proceeds directly out of the god's situation of disguise; the stark division between his inside and his outside makes doubt the natural content of his consciousness. For this very reason, he needs *her* to confirm his own desire, thereby closing, at least in part, the painful disjunction in his modes. He gives voice to this doubt, in language which, like so much of what God says in the mythic texts, is pregnant with irony because of its indirect, but strangely accurate, literalism:

> *na dṛśyate prārthayitavya eva te*
> *bhaviṣyati prārthita-durlabhaḥ katham//*
>
> One cannot see, one cannot find
> the man whom you would have to seek.
> How can it be that one you want
> escapes so easily? (46)

The god knows he is invisible to her, perhaps also finally unreachable in any real future (and there is marked stress in this line on the future-tense verb

17. On Pārvatī's inner transformation as portrayed by Kālidāsa in this poem, see the incisive remarks by Tubb 1984:231.

FIGURE 27. Pārvatī, absorbed in *tapas,* is tested by Śiva in Brahmin guise. Ellora, Cave 21.

bhaviṣyati)—for his slippery character informs the entire process that both he and his bride undergo. Śiva is always slipping into the rents and spaces within him. At the same time, he—the masquerading stranger—finds it hard to see Pārvatī suffering, fading away like the moon during daytime (48). Her longed-for lover, whoever he may be (*ko' pi tavêpsito yuvā*), must be hard indeed, if he can ignore her remarkable beauty—the reddish-yellow hair falling in profusion onto her cheeks, where, once, earrings made from lotuses would dangle in play (47). How long does this have to go on?

Why, Gaurī, strain yourself
so long? I have my own
stock of *tapas*, saved up
from early exercise.
Take half for yourself, find
the husband you hunger for:
I, too, want to know him well. (50)

All these statements are all too true: Śiva is hard (*sthira*), congealed—this is the primary existential burden with which he struggles—and he indeed wants to know the husband Pārvatī is seeking, that is, himself; to this aim he is prepared to offer her half of his own inner reserves.

She cannot, or will not, answer, but one of her companions now makes the quest explicit. Pārvatī, she informs the visitor, is in love with Śiva, who is "unenticeable by beauty" (or, punning: "enticeable by formlessness" [*arūpa-hārya*], 53); the only way to win him for a husband is through *tapas*. He is exactly what the stranger has said (she repeats his phrase verbatim): *prārthita-durlabha,* "wanted and elusive" (*"How can it be that one you want / escapes so easily?"*). Pārvatī thus suffers the endless hunger of desire; she is discontented with dreams or songs or painted images of her absent lover. Who can say when the god will relent and approach her (61)?

The disguised Brahmin—"beautiful to the death" (*naiṣṭhika-sundara*)—wonders if all this is not, perhaps, a joke, now that the reality of Pārvatī's wish is no longer hidden, in the least (62). But the lovely goddess acknowledges the truth of her companion's words: Her *tapas* is indeed aimed at achieving the transition to a higher level of being, the classic rupture of existential planes (*jano 'yam uccaiḥ-pada-laṅghanôtsukaḥ*, 64). This can only mean a union with the god. And now, faced with this bold confession, the Brahmin launches a violent attack on Śiva—an attack, that is, on the unbalanced, incongruous self that he has temporarily disguised. How could Pārvatī seriously want *him*, this eery and inauspicious god, for a husband, with his ashes taken from the cremation ground; his elephant's skin still dripping blood; his utter lack of normal virtues and proper habits; his naked indigence; his ugliness, his mysterious pedigree? What could be less appropriate than a union of the delicate goddess with this repelling creature?

You stubbornly set your heart
on a great no-thing [*a-vastu-nirbandha-pare*]!
How will this hand of yours
let Śiva's hand, slimy with snakes,
tie the wedding band? (66)

Would even an enemy, or a stranger, allow the delicate bride to walk barefoot through the burning ground (Śiva's usual haunt), leaving a trail of red footprints (68)? This girl should be borne aloft, on her wedding day, by a regal elephant—not carried off on a decrepit old bull. A sight like that could only inspire hilarity and contempt (70).

And so on—until Pārvatī can stand it no longer, this torrent of insults directed at the god she loves (*by* the god she loves), and turns away.

ito gamiṣyāmy athavêti vādinī
cacāla bālā stana-bhinna-valkalā/
svarūpam āsthāya ca tāṃ kṛta-smitaḥ
samālalambe vṛṣa-rāja-ketanaḥ//

taṃ vīkṣya vepathumatī sarasâṅga-yaṣṭir
nikṣepaṇāya padam uddhṛtam udvahantī/
mārgâcala-vyatikarâkulitêva sindhuḥ
śailâdhirāja-tanayā na yayau na tasthau//

"I had best be going," she said, and moved,
the rough dress chafing at her breasts.
And Śiva, the bull-bannered, smiled
and held her back, assuming
his true form.

Now she saw him: she was shaking,
her body drenched in sweat,
one foot raised
to take a step,
but, like a flood thwarted
by a mountain in its path,
that daughter of the Mountain King
could neither flow
nor cease. (84–85)

The slowly intensifying incongruities have culminated in a moment of stasis, or of mental paralysis—the dependable trigger of transcendence—so beautifully embodied by the explicit simile of the flooding river held in check by the mountain. Pārvatī, true to her nature, is fluid; Śiva, true to his, is immovable stone. An irresistible force has encountered an indomitable resistance. Out of this state of blockage—out of the whole process of self-unfolding—the two parts of the splintered deity reconnect. Insofar as Pārvatī exemplifies a devotional stance in this context, we can say that, in this paradigmatic meeting, the devotee turns away from his god, while the latter will not let go. The moment of coalescence between psycho-ontic levels is also the moment Śiva's disguise is torn away, leaving behind the frozen surface structure; the living presence of the now visible deity holds the female in place, near to him, opening up the possibility of their mutual softening and return.

But Śiva has become present by virtue of the masquerade, which moves him through a series of stages—self-scrutiny, doubt, verbal attack on the self—in relation to the woman whose love he appears to be testing. In a deeper sense, however, the test is really his. Pārvatī is working, clearly and directly, toward the rupture of planes, a transition in internal state that is meant to produce an expansive union with the god; this is an approach toward greater holism and a kind of integration, in the direction of the androgyne. *Tapas*, as she says, is the most promising route toward this goal. Śiva, however, has left his meditation, turned away from the vision of an ultimate self and toward an oblique mode of disguise; he, too, moving outward toward the surface, is now intent on an erotic union made possible by his *tapas*. In effect, the god has slipped away from the point of greatest depth and into a partial and superficial self, a sort of nonself that hides and dissembles, both in body and in words. On this level, Śiva's presence before Pārvatī is precisely this slippage; or, in the terms used earlier, we could say that for us, who reproduce Pārvatī's perspective, the god inhabits his own elusive inner spaces. His selfhood exists, then, in the mode of vanishing—whether hyperobjectified, like Bhṛṅgin, or superficially and dubiously defined, as in the moment of disguise. Moreover, the mask Śiva assumes is clearly more reified and hardened than his "real" face, though less concretized and defined than the initial, subtle division between male and female. Masking marks, for this god, a process of increasing externalization within the general mode of separation and gender isolation, in which eroticism—the immediate issue in this passage—appears as a temporary reversal or displacement.

Another way to put this would be to predicate the existence of at least three unstable forms of divine selfhood: (1) the most exterior, which presents itself in disguise (this is the self that speaks audibly to us—but it is always in danger of further attenuation outward, in the direction of Bhṛṅgin's desiccated and empty state); (2) the "mythic" persona of incongruous attributes and actions, which the former, surface persona describes and mocks; and (3) the dense innerness out of which both the first and second forms have emerged, through the game, and toward which the god is drawn in *tapas*. There is surely some dimension in which these selves coexist in simultaneity without fully coinciding, but this is not a dimension accessible to ordinary experience, even the god's ordinary experience of his own internal world—where gaps and breakages seem to predominate. The same sense of discontinuous awareness and tenuous presence could thus be said to apply to the god's sought-after self-knowledge.

To close these gaps would be to foreclose Śiva's conscious selfhood. And it is just this that the erotic finally cannot do. Pārvatī has won her lover and is being readied for the wedding. She is, as we would expect, mostly red—with red fingers; red cosmetics and powders; a glowing complexion; red lips; feet painted red, in a blessing (7.17–19, 23)—yet this rubescent brilliance is clothed in blinding white:

Like the foamy shore of the ocean of milk
on an autumn night drenched in moon,
her splendid new silks glistened white
in the new mirror in her hand. (7.26)

As so often in Hindu texts, the mirror seems to indicate a reflexive wholeness,[18] appropriate to this moment when Pārvatī dreams of reclaiming her androgynous identity:

The women blessed her
as she bowed before them:
"Enjoy love
from your husband
that is never broken"—
but she went beyond their loving words
by assuming half his body. (7.28)

She will assume her place within him; the marriage moves her in this direction, and the red henna on her body seems to indicate a kind of further heating, a liquefaction of the bride that is meant to open her up to fusion and interpenetration. Still, as in all the other contexts of holistic being that we have seen, Pārvatī's fulfillment carries hints of incipient fragmentation:

Like a vine breaking into blossom
or night bursting with stars
or a river fluttering with birds,
her body was flush
with ornament. (7.21)

The vine, perhaps, is reddish, flowering into white; the river is white, spotted with birds always identified, by the medieval commentators, as the *cakravāka*—the golden-reddish lovers cruelly separated, by universal law, every night from

18. See Handelman 1995.

sunset until dawn. These *cakravāka* birds, loved by Sanskrit poets as models of constancy in recurrent suffering, are striking intimations of division structured into the wedding of the goddess—insistent intimations, for the poet repeats the image:

> They rubbed her body with white aloe,
> and on her skin they painted yellow leaf designs
> until she was more blinding in her brilliance
> than the white sands of the Ganges,
> where the *cakravāka*s leave their footprints. (7.15)

A profusion of gold-red footprints trace love-in-separation on the Ganges's banks, as the yellow-red designs map future boundaries onto the body of the bride. The *cakravāka* is absent even from the simile, which makes do with traces in the sand, footprints of sadness and parting. As we will see, this bird that epitomizes yearning will persistently follow the god and goddess into their lovemaking, and beyond.

4
Spaces and Gaps

Red draped in white, dotted with gold—this is the radiant promise of union. A river of white that is stained red with longing—the goddess flows unsteadily toward her groom. Both partners in this projected fusion are caught up in a fantasy of continuous being—a perfect white, or total red; in any case, the final loss of all distinctions and all exteriority—but the fantasy is repeatedly punctured as discontinuities reemerge. For the moment, the god has gone from a stony whiteness to a state of burning red flame. Marriage fans these flames, as we see in Canto 8, with its graphic depictions of the newlyweds' lovemaking (see figures 28 and 29). As if to articulate the cosmic implications of this state, so that the universe mirrors the intradivine process, the *Kumārasambhava* ends with a brilliant sunset: The whole world is awash in redness. To be more precise, this famous sunset is the penultimate moment of the text; it is followed by the inevitable darkness and moonrise—a return, as it were, to the enveloping white background with which we began. Yet within this recurrence of the frame, a residue remains from the awakened fire; something in the internal composition of the divine has been temporarily altered. We wish to focus on two principal features of this change—one relating to the issue of separation, spatial opening, and uncertainty; the other, to the balance of inner forces at the close.

FIGURE 28. The fruits of *tapas*. Śiva and Pārvatī. Kitching, Orissa [Archaeological Survey Office].

First there is sunset, golden red, shimmering, and fading—like a golden bridge built by the sun from his own reflection in the waters of the western lakes (8.44). Already, the bridge suggests the opening of a gap; and, indeed, this notion of an interspace suddenly, painfully, appearing becomes central to the entire passage. As night falls, the loving *cakravāka* birds are forced unwillingly to separate until morning (as in all other nights):

daṣṭa-tāmarasa-kesara-tyajoḥ
krandator viparivṛtta-kaṇṭhayoḥ/
nighnayoḥ sarasi cakravākayor
alpam antaram an-alpatāṃ gatam//

Moaning, they let the lotus stalks fall
from their mouths as, helpless,
they crane their necks
in backward longing
and the tiny space
opening between them
steadily becomes
less tiny. (32)

This verse is one of Kālidāsa's great miracles, a subtle and plaintive evocation of the gap or interstice (*antaram*) growing ever wider. One can feel the emp-

FIGURE 29. Detail, Śiva and Pārvatī. Kitching, Orissa.

tiness slowly, inexorably, expanding, as if from within. The poet returns again to this word:

> The lotus has closed its petals,
> yet for a moment it leaves a gap,
> a tiny space that could be home,
> alive with love,
> for the bee. (39)

Darkness is falling, the flower is folding inward—but a gap, vibrant with affection, remains precariously open.

As the sunset passes and darkness reigns, this empty space (*antaram*, *vivara*) continues to grow:

> Two moons—the icy circle,
> a ripe *priyaṅgu* fruit
> hung in the sky, and its reflection
> in the pool—mimic
> the *cakravāka* lovers, torn apart
> by empty space. (61)

Separation is the order of the night: the *cakravāka*s experience it first, and also symbolize it, demonstrating its power and their own helplessness, a paradigm for the distance inherent in reflections. Not all the exquisite beauty of the moonlight, flooding a world lost to blackness, can truly compensate for the suffering implicit in this empty gap—implicit too, it seems, in the mere existence of differentiated genders, male and female, who are subject to separation. This is a problem on all levels, from that of the dense, androgynous godhead down. Something basic and recurrent in the world, in the god, in us, is always torn apart.

It is hardly a surprise that this return to whiteness is also connected to notions of congealing and solidifying, very much as in the initial picture of the frozen mountain and frozen god:

> Pieces of moonlight, which shattered
> as they fell, like gentle flowers,
> through branches and leaves,
> lie scattered beneath the trees,
> so solid you could pick them up
> and weave them into
> your flowing hair. (8.72)

Śiva is speaking to Pārvatī, translating, into her own language, the ecstasies of the nocturnal landscape, and, at the same time, personalizing them, connecting them to her body, her needs. The world is lost in whiteness that has crystallized, become tangible and objective.[19] As if unable to contain so much light—just as the night-blooming lily is said to explode under the impact of the moonlight streaming inward (8.70)—Pārvatī now sips red wine, offered to her in a stone-red goblet by the goddess of the Gandhamādana forest, at the instigation of her lovesick, still overheated husband (8.75).

The god has married; an inner fire unites him to his red bride, abrogating the distance that has plagued them from the start of the game. A modicum of wholeness has been reconceived. But from within this state of relative integration, another internal movement of separation has already occurred. As Śiva himself informs Pārvatī (8.51), the *cakravāka* paradigm applies precisely to him as well (he is faithful, full of love—and, we must assume, driven to separation). This statement of the god's is strong and suggestive, as if he were saying: "*I* am the *cakravāka*: I am with you, but I am also divided from you by recurrent black space." Gaps consistently open up internally, in his connectedness with other beings, on various levels; the vision of holistic stasis, a total whiteness, is perforated by the dark interstices that signal disjunction, uncertainty, and devolution. The poem that begins with the frozen, white mountain that is sprinkled with intermittent redness ends in a blackness dappled with white. Blackness is wholeness seeping up from below, a state or domain entirely lacking in distinctions (57), the cosmic equivalent of the Andhaka outcome. But the blindness that signals emptiness, the discontinuous space that gapes open within being (especially divine being), is, here, sporadically illuminated by lunar residues of whiteness, as if to mark an enduring potentiality for some still unrealized level of the ruptured whole.

In fact, the poet takes a further step toward the full articulation of this oddly unbalanced and incomplete state of being. If the *Kumārasambhava* asks, from its own perspective, some of the fundamental questions posed by the dice game (and resumed throughout the Śaiva corpus)—the question of what it means to have an engendered godhead, and how we can understand the tangled interrelationships of its autonomized parts—the "answer" with which it closes eloquently recapitulates the chromatic hierarchy that emerges from this story:

tena bhaṅgi-viṣamôttara-cchadaṃ
madhya-piṇḍita-visūtra-mekhalam/
nirmale 'pi śayanaṃ niśâtyaye
nôjjhitaṃ caraṇa-rāga-lāñchitam//

19. See Mallinātha ad 8.74: *gaṇḍa-sthala-pratimbimba-saṅkramaṇa-mūrcchitā candrikā* . . . (on the moonlight congealed in reflection on Pārvatī's cheeks).

Though dawn came
in all its purity,
the god refused to leave his bed,
with her belt, broken, all bunched up,
lying forgotten in the middle,
and the rumpled sheets stained red
by her painted feet. (8.89)

The Sanskrit ends with the red stains (*caraṇa-rāga-lāñchitam*), and the transition in state is now clear. The goddess seems to be missing from this vignette, but her signs are everywhere. Dawn is luminous and pure (*nirmala*), like the immaculate character (*nirmala-prakṛti*) of those unaffected by deformative time, as we recall from an earlier verse:

Those immaculate by nature
emerge unstained
by the vagaries of time.[20]

Helical but continuous, a line leads from the timeless sunset of the opening verses of the text *through* this general conclusion—by now a little ironic, given all we have seen of the divine process—and then directly to the rumpled bed with its red sheets:

That mountain bears rich mineral beds
streaking its peaks red like a timeless sunset—
reflected piecemeal in tattered clouds—
and serving the courtesans of heaven
when they paint themselves
in the flurries of love. (1.4)

Now, at this moment of impending closure, Kālidāsa returns to the hierarchical interplay of white and red, no-time and time. We take leave of Śiva as he lingers in bed at dawn, his attention absorbed not in the distant meditative reaches of his self, but in the blood-red stains from Pārvatī's feet. His own state is no less uneven (*viṣama*) than the rumpled sheets, no more continuous or orderly than the torn belt left forlornly in the middle. Moreover, as the commentator suggests, the indications (imprinted in the bedding) are that Pārvatī has had the upper hand—that she has taken the male role (*puruṣāyitam*) in love, being active, aggressive, aware.[21] If one had to guess, one would surely say,

20. 8.65; see section 2 of this chapter.

21. Mallinātha ad 8.89.

on the basis of this verse alone, that the god remains entirely under the sway of his love. But there is no real need to guess:

> Since day and night he hungered
> for the sweetness of her mouth,
> the constant taste of joy,
> whenever anybody came to see him
> he would make himself unseeable,
> forewarned by Vijayā at the door. (8.90)

Now we know why Śiva is invisible to us, and, indeed, to anyone who needs him: He is entirely and exclusively absorbed in the process of reabsorbing his female self. Can he see himself in this process, as, he has said earlier, he yearns to do?

> One cannot see, one cannot find
> the man whom you would have to seek.
> How can it be that one you want
> escapes so easily?

Transparent to himself, or opaque, as the case may be, Śiva slips ever deeper into the gap. Moreover, there is no conceivable limit to his quest:

> *sama-divasa-niśītham saṅginas tatra śambhoḥ*
> *śatam agamad ṛtūnāṃ sârdham ekā niśêva/*
> *na sa surata-sukhebhyaś chinna-tṛṣṇo babhūva*
> *jvalana iva samudrântargatas taj-jalaughaiḥ//*
>
> Midnight or morning,
> it was all the same
> to Śiva in his obsession:
> One hundred and fifty seasons
> passed like a single night.
> His thirst for loving remains alive,
> ceaseless and compelling,
> as the flame at the heart of the ocean
> will never be quenched
> by its infinite waves. (8.91)

This is Kālidāsa's final word on this god. Hardly an image of balance or containment, it seems more a statement about devolving time—for, in the end, as we know, the submarine fire will exhaust the ocean, and will then burst forth to destroy the world.[22] Within this devolution, however, normal temporal distinctions have become irrelevant; so intent is the god on loving that days and nights, years and hours, are no longer differentiated in his awareness. The red-hot time of passionate connection is, in this sense, remarkably close to the non-time of unbroken wholeness. Still, liquid feeding, unending coitus—none of this provides a solution to Śiva's thirst, to the continuous drive toward reinternalizing a cosmos ejected, objectified, and lost in the game of dice. Joy feeds the thirst without sating it, and the god's reunion with Pārvatī remains fissiparous and dynamic, failing to achieve anything like the original androgynous completion. This is what happens, it seems, when Śiva plays dice with himself, with his partner, with the universe, with us—as play he must.

22. See O'Flaherty 1971; on this verse, O'Flaherty 1973:287–89

IV

Conclusion

The most superfluous question is nevertheless: "Why?"[1]

1
Fullness

So why does he do it? Why does this god keep slipping into the game of dice, knowing, as he seems to, that he will almost certainly lose, and that other destructive consequences will flow from this defeat? This "superfluous" question is never directly addressed in the texts we have cited; and we might well wonder if it makes sense to speak, in this context, of a divine intentionality or desire (although there is definitely room to speak of "agency," in complementary and contrasting modes). Still, we have been concerned all along with uncovering a kind of logic that animates the stories, a logic embedded, perhaps, in largely implicit or intuitive perceptions that inform the telling and texture alike; and there is reason, at least, to speculate about the conceptual forces that animate and drive this logic into the narrative patterns that we have examined. We are thus concerned with a level that is both deeper and more concealed than any philosophical teleology or rationalized theology (such as one might find in Śaiva Siddhānta, for example). On this level, four major vectors appear to coincide.

The first is tautological: Śiva plays because he is a player; his innerness is infused with play (*līlâtman*).[2] In a manner that defies simple definition, this godhead is continuously moved from within, in the direction of playing with itself, without purpose or goal. Such play always appears to entail both a diminishment in his being—Śiva shrinks into the emerging framework of the dice

1. Tandori 1983:21.

2. See chapter I, section 8, n. 130.

game, or into his own emptinesses—and forms of excess, spilling over, self-extrusion; in effect, these two processes are really one. Play turns this godhead inside out. Even when this direction is reversed, and the externalized fragments are reinternalized (as when Andhaka is reabsorbed in Śiva, or the goddess drawn back into his body through *tapas*), convex, objectified remnants tend to survive outside; first among them is the *liṅga*, the sign of the god's presence, a dense and ultimate extrusion. The *liṅga*, so the *purāṇas* tell us, was torn violently from Śiva's body and then fixed in place in our disastrously externalized domain.[3] The play intrinsic to this godhead moves dependably into various forms of constrictive trauma. Still, the playful impulse is always, in every context, irresistible; what is inside simply must *play itself out*.

Second, part of this process emerges from the feminine component of the god, the *śakti* energy that activates the whole and, in some sense, seduces this deity into the game. As Pārvatī tells us in the *Kedārakhaṇḍa*:

> I just wanted to play with him, for fun, for the sake of the game, in order to play with the causes of his emerging into activity.

There is something fundamental to the feminine, as such, that produces this result, that energizes the holistic godhead in the direction of play, and that then triumphs over the defined and split-off male component within the game. It would seem that femininity implies, for our Śaiva poets, an innerness moving outward.

> If the goddess wins, that means externalization; if Śiva wins, that means non-externalization.[4]

Maleness, an excess of externalized constituents—like Bhṛṅgin, a bag of hard, dry bones thinly linked by empty spaces—naturally seeks to reinternalize, sucking the missing parts back toward and into its hungry self; but the female, for her part, is less caught up in the negative consequences of play—above all, its tendency to fragment. Is this because the part, autonomous and largely self-contained in its partiality, is less in need of the unfractured whole? Pārvatī's movement is, in general, far less desperate than Śiva's; nor is she delimited or deceived by masquerading surfaces and crooked words. In the stories cited, feminine interiority expands, achieves autonomy, and enriches itself at the expense of a male godhead rather helplessly trapped in play. (One needs, how-

3. See Shulman 1986.

4. *Skandapurāṇa* 4.88.5–12.

ever, to look closely at stories told from the vantage point of the goddess—and, even more, at stories told by women to other women.)

Third, there is something else at stake—the modes and forms of god's self-knowledge. The dense, divine being may be characterized by omniscience, by definition. But omniscience may not count as knowledge at all. As the tricky, fluid Unfettered says to Śiva:

> You are famous for your omniscience, but that may be just like the wood apple eaten by the elephant. You may lack an inside altogether; what you have is only an attractive surface. . . . This omniscience of yours is inappropriate. Throw it away.[5]

What we might think of as real knowledge, in which self contends with other, *always* requires a dimension of occlusion and limitation. It is in this sense that the dice game may be said to liberate parts of the divine self from their undefined, holistic simultaneity in order to bring them within range of some other form of the god's consciousness; he will know these parts as belonging, in whatever fragmentary fashion, to himself. Such knowledge lacks attributes of fullness and, perhaps, of coherence—and the parts that have broken loose in the game tend to be either threatening (like Andhaka) or saturated with the experiences of separation and anxiety—but the godhead needs and strives to achieve precisely this partially occluded awareness. As Abhinavagupta tells us, "If Śiva were to remain in his unitary mode and form, he would lose both his godliness and his claims on consciousness."[6] We know ourselves only in a context of not knowing, out of which fullness can be posited; and in the purposeless world of intrinsic playfulness—perhaps *only* in such a world—critical forms of self-awareness become unexpectedly accessible.

Fourth, we have to bear in mind, always, that it is the divine whole that enters into play: Unimaginable fullness, without gaps or intervals, begins to loosen its total connectivity; gaps and boundaries open up, crystallize, congeal; pieces are lost, temporarily at least, to the outside—as the god becomes lost in the externalizing spaces of his own self. In some sense, it appears, to our surprise, that this divinity must suffer from a hidden horror of holism. Unruptured completion is somehow intolerable in this system; it is always restlessly taking itself apart, spilling over in an excess of plenitude, playing itself into fractured forms. As Kālidāsa says in one of his most famous verses:

5. *Niraṅkuśôpākhyānamu* of Rudrakavi, cited in chapter II, section 12.

6. *Tantrâloka* of Abhinavagupta 3.100:
asthāsyad eka-rūpeṇa vapuṣā ced mahêśvaraḥ/
mahêśvaratvaṃ saṃvitvam atyakṣyat. . . .

ramyāṇi vīkṣya madhurāṃś ca niśamya śabdān
paryutsukī-bhavati yat sukhito 'pi jantuḥ/

Any creature,
however happy,
seeing beauty,
hearing sweet sounds,
is always overcome with longing,

Aesthetic delight is marked by yearning, by hunger and a mysterious restlessness—all apparently features of fullness, or of sensual and existential satiety. Kālidāsa's hero offers an explanation for this empirical observation:

tac cetasā smarati nūnam abodha-pūrvam
bhāva-sthirāṇi jananântara-sauhṛdāni//

for memory then brings to mind
what was unrecognized before—
loves left over from other lives,
still dense with feeling.[7]

But this explanation is seemingly far less compelling, even for the Sanskrit poet, than the primary observation of the perils and ambivalences of fullness.[8] There is, then, a real question as to whether Śiva, who seems so intent on restoring the lost wholeness, really wants, or only wants, this always elusive state.

And do *we*? Do our needs and wishes coincide with his? There seems to be a countervailing tension built into the complementary perspectives on this process (our vision, and that of the god). Think, again, of the chromatic sequencing we have observed: Śiva goes from the red-hot density of total being to various cooler, icy-white states—in the course of play—and then, through *tapas*, to another fiery red mode of reinternalization, primarily erotic in tenor. His pattern, in linear reduction, is thus red-white-red. But we know from studies of rituals in South India, beginning with a pioneering essay by Brenda Beck,[9] that a pervasive pattern involves the movement from a white (inactive) border to a heated red state of active divine presence, and then back to an encompassing, cooling, protective whiteness. The moment of the

7. *Abhijñānaśākuntala* 5.2.

8. See Shulman (in press). We wish to thank V. Narayana Rao for noting this articulation of the linkage between fullness and longing.

9. Beck 1969.

encounter with the heated god or goddess is thus bounded on both sides by colder states: white-red-white. This makes good sense: One doesn't really want to keep a heated deity around; one wants contact, always temporary (and transformative), and then a reversion to bounded selfhood. The heated god or goddess is thus deposited in the river or the tank at the end of the ritual cycle. Put differently, if *we* exist only in the gaps and spaces of the divinity, then we will have an existential investment in cooling and congealing the god, in stabilizing those gaps. Śiva, from his vantage point, seems eager to burn away the inner discontinuities, melting white into a continuous red and thereby consuming all residually external beings like ourselves. The two interests, ours and the god's, appear to clash.

Is there also a level at which they intersect? The two chromatic sequences outlined above also speak to another central question: Which is the greater anxiety, that attendant on *having* a self, or that involved in *losing* a self? We tend, from the lower end of the devolutionary spiral, to focus on the latter danger; self-extinction is our final nightmare. We would like to survive in the cracks and crevices of god, though not without moments of intense contact with him: *white-red-white*. But the dense ultimacy of divine existence may be more fearful of the former eventuality, that of sustaining a tentative and partial selfhood. Hence, Śiva acts to burn away Andhaka, his dark, aberrant self-realization as crystallized, embodied space: *red-white-red*. Yet Andhaka may also, in his own right, long for this conclusion, just as the god may well seek to leave behind him, or outside him, the extruded detritus of self scattered in our world, our bodies, his shrines. In the metapsychology of the dice game, an ambivalent selfhood, expanding through self-diminution, vanishing through violent reabsorption, is also perpetually at stake.

2
Hunger

Let us formulate these perceptions in a somewhat different mode, relying again on an ancient cosmogonic text to provide focus and an expressive idiom. Śiva's cosmos is constituted as a hierarchical encompassment, in which organization is transformational, continuous, and paradoxical, and in which shifts are those between fragmentation and holism, descent and ascent, exteriority and interiority, expansion and density. Such movements raise epistemological issues for the study of cosmology, including those intimated above: Do god and human beings differ on the desirable character of the cosmos? What is the nature of the god's awareness in relation to the process of self-externalization in play?

Cosmic fullness may be identified with the self's lack of self-conciousness and desire:

> Then there was neither death nor no-death,
> no sign of night or of day.
> The One breathed, breathless,
> through its own impulsion,
> and there was no Other of any kind.[10]

Here, the cosmic self is so densely packed with the utterly homogeneous holism of no-time and no-space that there is no place for otherness. The self reverberates softly within itself through breathing/nonbreathing, moving in liquid rhythm to its own unconscious existence. Complete within itself, and completely without self-division, the self has no intentionality and, so, no motive to change.[11] On this level, the worlds of cosmos, including that of human order, have no existence. Division and change happen after the playful twitch of *līlā*. The Self apparently cannot know whether this motiveless twitch will or will not occur, or when.

But other myths of cosmogenesis point toward the god's desire for fullness, thereby implying an ontological disinterest in other, lower orders of beings, even though the self will fill itself only through otherness. Can holism itself be a kind of hunger? Consider this Vedic story of the birth of Rudra, "the Howler," a precursor to Śiva:

> There was nothing here in the beginning. This was covered with Death, with hunger—for hunger is Death. He made a mind for himself, thinking, "Let me have a self." He was luminous with light, and from this radiation (< √ *arc*), water was born. . . . For light [*arka*] is water. The foam that was on the water solidified and became the earth. He exhausted himself upon that [earth]; out of him, exhausted and heated, the brilliant flux of fire emerged. He divided himself into three parts—sun, and wind [and fire], which are the threefold breaths of life. . . .[12]
>
> He felt desire for a second self. With his mind, he united with Speech [*vāc*]—that is, Death united with hunger. The seed of that union became the year, for

10. *Ṛg Veda* 10.129.2. See chapter I, section 7.

11. It is unclear when this is a condition of unconsciousness or of nonconsciousness. The former may allow for states of dreaming, or imagining, and is thus already a movement toward consciousness. Nonconsciousness seems to preclude this and, so, is more distant from a state of awareness.

12. There follows a description of the god as a horse, swelling into the cardinal points of space, and firmly set in water.

> prior to that there was no year. He carried him for a year and brought him out. No sooner was the child born than he opened his mouth to swallow him, and the child screamed "*bhāṇ*"—and that scream became Speech. He thought: If I kill him, I will have but little food. With that Speech, with that Self, he brought forth all this—the Ṛc, Yajus, and Sāman, the meters and sacrifices, human beings and animals. And everything that he brought forth, he began to devour.[13]

Like the twitch of *līlā* in the Cosmic Self, the creation of this cosmos is paradoxical. Here the Self, who does not yet know himself, thinks his mind into being in order to have a self that is conscious of itself. Cause and effect are created simultaneously, such that each precedes the other in this nonlinear, recursive world. The thought of self (which implies self-consciousness) before the existence of self, without which there is no thought of self-awareness, is undoubtedly paradoxical. Although there is no mention here of playfulness, this cosmic creation is as pervaded by the processuality of paradox as that triggered by the twitch of *līlā*.

This self has no fullness and feels its absence. Death hungers. Death is hunger. Death is nothing. Death is emptiness. Yet Death has intention. His nothingness and hunger are linked to his intentionality, seeking fullness and completion. (By contrast, when the Self attains self-awareness through the twitch of *līlā*, the fullness of the cosmos is linked to nonintention. The Self seeks nothing, and coming into self-consciousness is an act of play.) Death wants something that he feels lacking. His hunger, his nothingness, already point him beyond himself, before he even has a self, in order to fill and thus fulfill his holism. From the outset, Death already contains the fracture of absence that will open his interiority to the creation of otherness and exteriority. This is the flaw in Death's holism. Perhaps, Death feels desire; indeed, *aśanāyā* ("hunger"), his partner, is a feminine noun. But what should Death—nothingness—desire? His first self-division, into the basic elements—fire, sun, wind—gives him life. Alive now, self-conscious, Death feels his own nothingness, his emptiness, and desires his second self. Death's hunger for selfhood turns out to be the desire for life (his threefold division). Coming alive, he desires otherness (his second self), with which to fill himself. Death, the apparent absence of being, nothingness, descends, inside out, into life, further fragmenting his holism.

Epistemically, in this myth, the Self kills himself—kills Death—in order to give birth to the Other, to something other than his own self. Death continues to destroy his totality by entering into union with Speech (again, a feminine noun: Speech is identified here with hunger, the hunger of the self). Death then

13. *Śatapatha Brāhmaṇa* 10.6.1–5. See the discussion in Shulman 1993:128.

carries within himself the seed of this union with himself. The seed is his offspring, the year. The year is time. Within his self, Death gestates the endless divisions of time that will spill out of him into an infinity of fragmentations, the continuum of the descending godhead. He will fall into the holes within his own being, the intervals of time and the loci of space, where he has created the human and other levels of the cosmos as refractions of his own being. This myth is thus a pivot in the epistemic question of whether god and human beings differ in their respective interests. Death is also the destroyer of time, of human existence. Death may also be understood, then, as the highest, most abstract encompassment of the cosmos, nullifying all differentiation within himself. Death is the destroyer of all otherness and, therefore, of his own conscious selfhood. Through Death, the cosmos becomes homogeneous and whole, erasing humanity. From the perspective of the Self as Death, why should it desire life? In another sense, though, this myth is rigged, since Death is equated with hunger: Perhaps this is the human vision of death?

Death gives birth to the child, time. Death externalizes the fragmentation of periodicity. Time screams through an exhalation, further externalizing the otherness of Death toward life. (The child is Rudra—the Howler, the Screamer.) The text cited above tells us that this scream becomes Speech. Speech, then, is also externalized, becoming integral to the otherness of Death. Speech falls into, and survives in, the holes within the god, communicating between the god and his descending levels of otherness. All speech requires interpretation[14]—speech, therefore, is also full of holes, of the ambiguities of multiple meanings, of the otherness that constitutes its being—just as it precariously joins self and other. Moreover, speech (though not, of course, *all* speech) is achieved through exhalation—so the continuous practice of speech in this cosmology is that of externalization and descent. Grammar and the production of words and their connections—through exhalation beyond the self—are also the lineal hardening of speech outside its relatively greater fluidity and its recursiveness as thought within the mind. In phenomenological terms, the exhalation of speech is, of course, that of audible sound, which travels between people, between self and other, thus bringing distance and space into being.[15]

Death, on giving birth to life, is tempted immediately to swallow his offspring, assuaging his own hunger and reinternalizing his son. Yet as Death comes alive through the creation of his own otherness, of holes within his cosmic being, his hunger (also, one may add, his sensuousness) increases. His son, and the level of cosmic fragmentation and descent that the son signifies, are

14. This is in Langer's (1953) sense of speech as discursive symbolism.

15. See Straus 1966.

no longer sufficient to fill the holes in Death's cosmic being, thereby satiating his selfhood. Therefore, Death externalizes and tears open more and more holes within himself. These descending levels of otherness are increasingly finite and solid, forms of increasing thingness, rather than nothingness. He devours them ceaselessly, trying to fill, and fulfill, himself. This is the world that human beings know—the hole, within our own being, into which we, too, inevitably fall.

This myth of Death's desires highlights the inherent conflict of wills between god and human beings. Death wants life in order to nullify it and, thus, to fill himself. Death cannot succeed. Seeking life in order to devour it, he kills it. Killing life, he empties it. Therefore, he devours emptiness, and is doomed endlessly to seek life in order to fulfill himself as death. So long as death is imagined as hungry, he cannot escape the paradox of his being. But Śiva is not Death.

The materials we have discussed clearly suggest that although the interests of Śiva and human beings overlap, they also diverge quite radically. From Śiva's perspective as the cosmic encompassment, the evolution of the cosmos is the devolution of his integrity of being—his toppling into the holes that open within his being, where humans and others come into existence, and where he, too, becomes other than he is at the innermost and uppermost levels of the cosmic continuum. The further out and the lower he goes, the closer he comes to us, and the more like us he becomes—fragmented, solid, open to the seduction and control of others. This state undoubtedly has its pleasures for him, but he also often seeks to return to the ideal condition of cosmic homogeneity and holism, where the differentiation of his being is erased. From the human perspective, god's fragmentation and devolution create the phenomenal and existential worlds in which one lives, throughout one's life, as fully and ably as one can. Except for mystics, the reality of life is usually immediate, rather than immanent. The existence of humanity is endangered if Śiva returns to the homogeneous holism of the cosmos, since then the human world would cease to exist. Therefore, the human quest includes an intention to keep god, and the cosmos, in an imbalanced condition that inhibits or restricts god's return to ultimate innerness. For humanity, this task is difficult to accomplish, since Śiva is a holographic god.

3
Signs

Ordinary English usage prefers the sequence "part and whole" to that of "whole and part." Given the linear thrust of language, precedence in sequencing for two coordinate terms has cultural significance. "Part and whole" suggests that the part is privileged, and that the whole is formed through, and given meaning by, the organization of its parts. "Whole and part" signifies the converse, privileging the whole and implying that it encompasses, forms, and gives meaning to its parts. The difference between these two expressions is not just a semantic quibble. Indian, and especially Śaiva, cosmology gives precedence, power, and meaning to the integrity of the whole in organizing its parts, as we have indicated throughout this book—hence our interest in the holographic metaphor described below.

Holography is a relatively new form of photography, with curious resonances in the organization of certain cosmologies.[16] A holography is produced when a single laser light is split into two. One beam is bounced off the object that is being photographed, while the second is made to collide (through the use of mirrors) with the reflected light of the first. The pattern that results is recorded on holographic film. This pattern looks as if it is composed of meaningless, irregular ripples and whorls that pass through one another, but when a laser beam is shone through the film, a three-dimensional image of the original object appears. This image retains its integrity of form from all angles of vision, in keeping with the shape that should appear from each angle.

For our purposes, there are two fascinating properties of the holographic image. One is the relation between the whole and part. Unlike a photograph, all the information of the hologram is contained and reproduced in any part of it. Any part of the holographic film, when cut away from the whole, will reproduce the totality of the three-dimensional image when a laser beam is directed on that part.[17] Information in the holograph is distributed nonlocally—the whole is in every part.[18] Put otherwise, information is embedded in the holograph so densely and recursively that everything is connected simultaneously to everything else. Moreover, this information is actually embedded within embedments (that are embedded within other embedments, and so on). In some sense, deep innerness and dense recursivity emerge from the same reality in holography. The structuring of the holograph (like those of some quantum and "chaotic" phenomena) is characterized by self similarity.[19] David Bohm, the quantum physicist who has taken up the holographic analogy, theorized that "at the subquantum level . . . location ceased to exist. All points in

16. The idea of holographic organization is also used, for example, to conceptualize certain properties of the brain (such as memory; see Pribram 1977), and of the quantum world (Bohm 1981).

17. Keepin 1994; Bohm 1981: 143–47.

18. Talbot 1992:48.

19. See Grössing 1993:80.

space became equal to all other points in space, and it was meaningless to speak of anything as being separate from anything else."[20]

We referred above to Śiva as a holographic god. This metaphor became relevant to us only at the time of writing this conclusion, and we have not used it in formulating our interpretation of Śiva's cosmos—yet the two bear tantalizing resemblances in certain crucial respects. Myths of Śiva are replete with themes relating to the fragmentation of the god's holism, and to the regeneration of the cosmos from its fragment or fragments. The whole, shattered, is reconstituted from its part. One exemplary fragment is Śiva's sign, the *liṅga*: Here, the part is the whole, just as the whole is contained in every one of its parts, however much these have been torn. In terms of linear thought and mechanistic metaphors, this formulation is paradoxical, fantastic, and impossible. Yet its possibility exists in the conception of extreme density of no-space and no-time where everything is connected to everything else, which characterizes the innerness of Śiva and, therefore, of his cosmos. In this regard, there is no logical, or logistical, difficulty in Śiva's regaining the homogeneity of cosmic holism following fragmentation. And this poses the potential problem of the extinction of the human level of existence.

The second property of holographic thinking that bears on our discussion of Śiva's cosmos is that of processuality—specifically, the changes that the process itself undergoes, from deeper energy to momentary surface matter, (whose course may be turbulent and unpredictable), and then back into energy again. We consider David Bohm once again: "The ultimate nature of physical reality is not as a collection of separate objects (as it appears to us), but, rather, it is an undivided whole that is in perpetual dynamic flux, . . . a constant state of flow and change."[21] He called this flow "holomovement" and argued that "every portion of the flow contains the entire flow."[22] The holomovement, writes Bohm, "is undefinable and immeasurable."[23] The hidden, deep order of the flow (in Bohm's terms, the implicate, "enfolded" order) is composed of energy waves; while matter, surface appearance (the explicate, "unfolded" order), is constituted as unfolded surface manifestations of enfolded order that is continuously enfolded back into the greater, encompassing, implicate domain. Thingness, one may say, is enfolded by no-thingness, and is a descending transformation of the latter.

20. Talbot 1992:41; see Bohm 1981. And cf. Bohm's dialogues with Krishnamurti (Krishnamurti and Bohm 1981).

21. Keepin 1994:11.

22. Ibid., 12; Bohm 1981:172.

23. Bohm 1981:151.

Thus, for example, energy that unfolds may be perceived momentarily and locally as an electron particle, as matter, which, during the next moment, is enfolded again into the implicate order of energy waves, and is replaced by another such unfolding. A series of continuing, adjacent unfoldings and enfoldings constitutes the appearance of the continuous motion of a particle, or, for that matter, of the existence of the entire physical universe. These two orders, the implicate and the explicate, interpenetrate in all regions of space/time, "and each region enfolds all of existence, that is, everything is enfolded into everything."[24]

When Śiva's cosmos is thought of in terms of such holomovement flows, it becomes enormously flexible—tearable, contractible, stretchable, expandable, densely fluid, always flowing, its dimensionality open-ended. The greater encompassment extends and descends into levels and realms where perceptions of separateness and emptiness open up, and where a hardening form and matter take (explicate) shape. The interpenetrating enfolding of the cosmos within the cosmos suggests that the greater encompassment, Śiva himself (ultimately implicate), can appear suddenly, anywhere, anytime, as he moves from flowing fold to flowing fold without descending the hierarchical cosmic order, level by level. This, of course, is precisely how Śiva behaves in his unpredictable appearances, disguises, and tricks. Paradoxes of existence abound, but there are no impossibilities of being. A hole in the cosmos is merely a part of the whole. A tear is sealed as it rends.

Both Śiva and the cosmos are tremendously resilient. And yet the dice game, a model of cosmos that mediates and radically alters the relationship of the whole to the part, threatens this resilience. To continue for a moment with the quantum analogy, the dice game makes a part of the cosmos "local," forcing it to lose its nonlocality.[25] The dice game creates parts that do not contain the whole. The part becomes a reduction, from which the whole cannot be totally reconstituted. Therefore, the cosmic level of human beings is less endangered. But in this way, chaos enters the cosmos, and thus the viability of the whole cosmos (including the human level) is indeed threatened, even if only for relatively brief periods. Perhaps this tells us why Śiva, with his face etched in rage, destroys Andhaka with such utter fury.

The dice game is the major source of chaos in Śiva's cosmos. This notion resonates to some extent in the chaos theory of nonlinear systems—this theory deals with unexpected perturbations of a deterministic system that cannot be predicted from its previous or initial states.[26] Following the appearance of such

24. Keepin 1994:13–14.

25. Grössing 1993:76.

26. See Gleick 1987.

unexpected turbulence, the system will eventually return to an ordered state, something like that which preceded the disturbance. One cannot therefore know what a nonlinear system (deterministic or not) will do next, for it generates instability and, perhaps, randomness.[27] Tiny indeterminacies generate huge variations. The system has been stretched. New possibilities, new information, become integral to the system; yet it retains a deep, ordered structure that informs both perturbations and instabilities. Through time, chaos reveals its underlying, deeply embedded structure of order, and the chaotic system becomes ordered once again—though whether it is exactly the same system or not is open to argument.[28] Moreover, this deeply embedded order, regardless of the depth one pursues, continually evinces that which Hayles calls "hazy regions," that are not resolvable into either order or chaos.[29] Openings to chaos are not reducible to order.

Chaos theory postulates the inability to fully predict the operations of nonlinear systems, since the uncertainty of turbulence is generated from expectations implicit in the system, and not from any unusual conditions. In Śiva's cosmos, the dice game is a generative source of relatively short-term turbulence, during which explorations of identity and of the nature of the cosmos occur. One of the intriguing aspects of this turbulence is the often sudden speed of its onset and the ferocity of its consequences—thus, the androgyne is torn apart; thus, the slicing rapidity of throws of the dice; thus, the shocking appearance of Andhaka, of blackness from within blackness. Deleuze and Guattari comment that "chaos is defined not so much by its disorder as by the infinite speed with which every form taking shape within it vanishes. It is a void that is not a nothingness but a virtual . . . drawing out all possible forms. . . . Chaos is an infinite speed of birth and disappearance."[30] Just as the model of the dice game reduces Śiva, so the chaotic consequences of the game also open him to other realities—virtualities—into which he is plunged and within which he plays out the sudden onsets of virtually becoming Other that are enfolded within his being and that are his keys to the emotions and knowledge of self.

But the game frequently is initiated only by a more exterior and lower cosmic being than Śiva himself. The game mediates between god's perspective and that of human beings, but its impulsion usually seems to come from below, more from the direction of the human level. More often than not, the game

27. Gleick 1987:251.

28. Kellert 1993:73.

29. Hayles 1991:235; see also Kosko 1993:63.

30. Deleuze and Guattari 1994:118.

is virtually imposed on Śiva.[31] The game itself—its rules—takes shape during the playing. The game contracts and fragments Śiva's being, breaking down (but also opening up) the more direct, holographic relationship between the cosmic whole and cosmic part. Śiva's way back to holism is made more lengthy and problematic; indeed, he never fully achieves this condition, since something will always occur to subvert it. Deeply loved by human beings for what he has become, Śiva is a profoundly embattled god. When he moves toward holism, something will happen to undermine this process. It is this aspect that is almost deterministic. *When* it will happen is unpredictable, but that something destructive will emerge from the subversion of holism is certain. The nature of the threat, and exactly how Śiva will deal with it, are not determined; nor can we, or he, know when and how this turbulence will occur again.

4
Selves

Somewhat stubbornly, perhaps, we have resisted discussing at length the inevitable question raised by the dice—the question of what we call chance. Even now, at the end of our book, we will resist formulating the question in a dichotomous mode: Is the game Śiva plays one of skill or of chance? There are excellent reasons to renounce this formulation. Where Wittgenstein has argued that any true question must be capable of being answered,[32] we would be tempted to invert the order: Most answers preexist in, or are predetermined by, the question's frame. The choice we are so often offered in analyses of the Indian games of dice nearly always distorts the very nature of those games in their cosmological settings. There is, it is true, a component of calculated skill in Śiva's dicing—although the primary skill seems to lie in the tricky fluidity the successful player brings to the rule-bounded domain of the game. There is also deep uncertainty. Nothing, however, suggests that this uncertainty is of a random order.[33] On the contrary, it emerges from a process that has striking regularities in pattern and course.

31. Interestingly, Hayles (1991:173) argues that "chaotic unpredictability and nonlinear thinking . . . have tended to be culturally encoded as feminine. Indeed, chaos itself [in the West] has often been depicted as female." As noted, in Śiva's world it often is Pārvatī who inveigles him into the game.

32. See the discussion by Narayana Rao 1996.

33. Without becoming overly involved in issues of chance, there are instructive contrasts in the construction of chance universes and their disorders if one compares, for example, Luke Rinehart's fabulist novel, *The Dice Man* (1972), to Borges's fable, "The Library of Babel" (1970). Rinehart's protagonist takes all decisions solely on the basis of

We know that Śiva will lose the game; in some sense, he knows it, too. There are ritual contexts which attempt to reverse or control that outcome; the game is thus highly sensitive to context. There are also currents we might define as "mystical," which insist that the discontinuities in the godhead that are so central to this game can be restored to wholeness through deep acts of consciousness (indeed, these discontinuities may well be classed as illusory in an ultimate perspective). Here, as is usual in India, myth reveals itself as the realistic genre par excellence, in its own self-definition. Once the dice are thrown, there will be gaps in being, in experience, in awareness. Their forms are infinitely variable, yet in certain ways recurrent: the male will set himself off from the female; androgynous fusion is ruled out; knowledge lives and breathes through blockage and occlusion; all the coordinates of our inner worlds—time, space, name, identity—reflect the drive to objectify and thereby delimit and destroy. Parts of the god, parts of ourselves, keep going dead and dry. Reconstituted holism is finally impossible. Like withered Bhṛṅgin, we are the spectral witnesses of this unending game.

In this world of ongoing playfulness, uncertainty has a structure, and gaps have meaning. Chance and probability are not issues in this kind of ludic self-creation. The question, one fraught with uncertainty, is, rather: What will come forth from this interplay of wins and losses? The descent of the higher being, the loser, is intimately connected to the ascent of the lower being, the winner. The players are locked together in the generation of consequence, and god is not exempt from interdependence. The winner moves into the center; the loser, to the periphery. As the loser is diminished in knowledge and power, these qualities of the winner grow more full.

---

rolls of the dice of chance, of randomness (whose existence, of course, may not be possible to prove—cf. Kosko 1993:44–51). He and his agency survive by elaborating and living through all these outcomes—in other words, by the continuing attribution of meaning (and nonmeaning) to chance and to its chances that grow ever more elaborate (and structured). Conversely, Borges's protagonists endlessly search for meaning in the library of infinity in which they find themselves existing, a cosmos without meaning. Thus, writes Borges: "A blasphemous sect suggested that the searchers should cease and that all men should juggle letters and symbols until they constructed, by an improbable gift of chance, these canonical books [that contained the meaning of the library]. . . . The sect disappeared, but in my childhood I have seen old men who . . . would hide in the latrines with some metal discs in a forbidden dice cup and feebly mimic the divine disorder" (1970:83). The contrast is that of creating cosmos through chance and shaping its randomness into meaning, and existing by chance in a cosmos of randomness that offers no possibility of meaning. In certain senses, Rinehart and Borges complement one another, but both are utterly unlike Śiva's world.

These ludic models force the cosmos into directions that subvert its natural order of hierarchy. Moreover, they drive the players toward the generation of forms that accentuate the asymmetrical absence of those very qualities not permitted entry into the game, but that are essential for the fullness of self and cosmos. Thus, blind Andhaka is created from Śiva's absence of vision. Forms like Andhaka and Bhṛṅgin are the involution of parts of the self elaborated to the limits of their imbalanced extremes. The consequences of these involuted asymmetries for the cosmic self, for the cosmos, are destructive. Śiva and Pārvatī are forced to recognize, to struggle with and to overcome these imbalanced exaggerations of themselves. The ludic contest becomes the deadly one of self versus other, where the other is part of self. At stake are the coherence and viability of encompassing self-identity, and, therefore, the cosmos itself. Critical knowledge of selfhood is attained through the struggle with qualities of self that are made to spiral out of control.

Were the game to proceed to its conclusion, the scattered tokens of self—themselves riddled with holes in modern sets of *chaupar*—would be successfully reassembled and reunited, for one of the players, in the empty inner core marked on the board. We might then think of this inner space as more heated than the rest of the squares, heated perhaps to the point of the total connectedness of fluid flame. Occasionally, when the human trickster plays with god, this point is reached, and this always means god's defeat. But when Śiva plays with his wife, the game inevitably implodes. Disorderly dispersion, rather than a reunion, is the result—regular, even predictable, but uncertain in its configuration and its further development. That we can speak of it all is yet another consequence of this repeated disruption.

Implosion is the quality of innerness trapped in the game; both players are trying to attain it, and, thereby, to encompass the other within self. It never works, neither for Śiva, nor for his female persona. It is this innermost quality of dense encompassment that is taken apart, diminished, and explored through the game of dice. The game itself is a shift toward the surface—hence a kind of disguise. As such, the godhead may well fail to penetrate its full meaning; but Bhṛṅgin, macabre witness,

screams out loud,
his mind aflame
because of everything
his master lost—

no alms, no ornaments,
no qualities to call his own.

All bone himself, Bhṛṅgin's mind, at least, can melt in flame; and his cry must also have something of that fiery innerness that offers hope. Sound conjoined with awareness, so the *Nirukta* intimates, is a kind of burning, somehow akin to the bursting forth of fire latent in wood[34]—thus truly a mode of connecting, or reconnecting, from within. Thus, like the newborn Rudra's cry of *bhāṇ* that both expresses and fills the utter emptiness gaping open in the face of Death, now inside out, alive, and self-possessed,

this endless scream
might just redeem
the world.

34. The *Nirukta* (1.18) states the matter negatively: What is uttered without understanding fails to ignite, like dry wood in the absence of (external) fire.

References

Texts in Sanskrit, Tamil, and Telugu

Abhijñānaśākuntala of Kālidāsa. 1957. Edited by M. R. Kale. Bombay: Booksellers' Publishing Company.

Aruṇâcalapurāṇam of Ĕllappanāyiðār. 1920. Madras: A. Iraṅkacāmi Mutaliyār and Sons.

Aṣṭādaśa upaniṣadah. 1958. Poona: no publisher cited.

Haravijaya of Ratnâkara [n.d.] Varanasi: Caukhambha Samskṛta Saṃsthāna [Kāśī Saṃskṛta Granthamālā 223].

Harivaṃśa. 1971. Poona: Bhandarkar Oriental Research Institute.

Jaiminīya Upaniṣad Brāhmaṇa. 1967. Tirupati: Kendriya Sanskrit Vidyāpīṭha Series, 5–6.

Kāñcīmāhātmya. 1906. Edited by P. B. Ananthachariar. Kāñcipuram: Śāstramuktâvali.

Kāñcippurāṇam of Civañāðayoki. 1937. Edited by C. Aruṇai Vaṭivelu Mutaliyār. Kāñcipuram: S. Kāḷappa Mutaliyār.

Kantapurāṇam of Kacciyappacivâcāriyar. 1983. Tiruppaðantāl: Śrīkāci maṭam.

Karpūracaritabhāṇa of Vatsarāja. 1989. Edited by S. S. Janaki. Madras: Kuppuswamy Sastri Institute.

Kathāsaritsāgara of Somadeva. 1977. Delhi: Motilal Banarsidas.

Kumārasambhava of Kālidāsa. 1967. Edited by M. R. Kale. Delhi: Motilal Banarsidass.

Kumārasambhava of Nannĕcoḍa. 1978. Edited by Nelaṭūri Veṅkaṭaramaṇayya. Hyderabad: Andhra Pradesh Sahitya Akademi.

Kūrmapurāṇa. 1972. Edited by Anand Swarup Gupta. Varanasi: All-India Kashiraj Trust.

Liṅgapurāṇa. 1885. Calcutta: Nūtana Vālmīki Press.

Mahābhāṣya of Patañjali. 1880. Edited by F. Kielhorn. Bombay: Government Central Book Depot.

Mataṉakāmarājaṉ katai. 1975. Madras: Ār. Ji. Pati and Sons.

Matsyapurāṇa. 1907. Poona: Ānandâśrama Sanskrit Series 54.

Niraṅkuśôpākhyānamu of Kandukūri Rudrakavi. 1976. Edited by Repūru Anantapadmanābha Rāvu. Kaḍapa: Ākāśavāṇi.

Nirukta of Yāska. 1927. Edited and translated by Lakshman Sarup. Lahore: University of the Punjab.

Padmapurāṇa. 1893. Poona: Ānandâśrama Sanskrit Series 131.

Padmapurāṇa, svargakhaṇḍa. 1972. Edited by Asoke Chatterjee Sastri. Varanasi: All-India Kashiraj Trust.

Pāratavĕṇpā of Peruntevaṉār. 1973. Edited by Irā. Ilaṉ̃kumarað. Madras: South Indian Saiva Siddhanta Works Publishing Society.

Pĕriya Purāṇam of Cekkiỳār. 3rd printing, 1975. Edited by C. K. Cuppiramaṇiya Mutaliyār. Coimbatore: [ovait tamiỳccaṉ̃kam.

Priyadarśikā of Śrīharṣa. 1948. Edited by P. V. Ramanujaswami. Madras: V. Ramaswamy Sastrulu and Sons.

Rāmāyaṇa of Vālmīki. 1958. Madras: N. Ramaratnam.

Ṛg Veda. 1957. Surat: Svādhyāya Maṇḍala.

Saduktikarṇâmṛta of Śrīdharadāsa. Edited by Sures Chandra Banerjea. 1965. Calcutta: K. L. Mukhopadhyay.

Śatapatha Brāhamaṇa. of the White Yajur Veda. 1903–1910. Calcutta: Bibliotheca Indica.

Śivapurāṇa. 1953. Bombay: Śrī Veṉ̃kaṭeśvara Steam Press.

Skandapurāṇa. 1867. Bombay: Śrī Veṉ̃kaṭeśvara Steam Press.

Śrīkāḷahastīśvaraśatakamu of Dhūrjaṭi. 1966. Edited by Niḍadavolu Veṉ̃kaṭa Rao. Hyderabad: Andhra Pradesh Sahitya Akademi.

Subhāṣitaratnakoṣa. of Vidyâkara. 1957. Edited by D. D. Kosambi and V. V. Gokhale. Harvard Oriental Series 42. Cambridge, Mass.: Harvard University Press.

Tantrâloka of Abhinavagupta. 1987. Edited by R. C. Dwiwedi and Navjivan Rastogi. Delhi: Motilal Banarsidass.

Tevāram of Appar (Tirunāvvukk'aracu nāyaðār). 1961. Tarumapuram: Tarumaiyātīðam.

Tiruccĕṅkoṭṭumāṉmiyam of A. Muttucāmikkoðār. 1938. Tiruccĕṉ̃koṭu.

Tirukkovalūrppurāṇam. 1901. Edited by Veṉ̃kaṭâcala Uṭaiyār Saundararāja Uṭaiyār. Kumpakonam: Lart Rippeð Yantiraccālai.

Upatecakāṇṭam of Ñāðavarotayar. Edited by V. S. Cĕṉ̃kalvarāya Piḷḷai. 1950. Madras: Government Oriental Manuscripts Series IV.

Uttararāmacarita of Bhavabhūti, with commentary by Ghanaśyāma. 1971. Edited by P. V. Kane. Delhi: Motilal Banarsidass.

Vāmanapurāṇa. 1967. Edited by Anand Swarup Gupta. Varanasi: All-India Kashiraj Trust.

Varāhapurāṇa. 1981. Edited by Anand Swarup Gupta. Varanasi: All-India Kashiraj Trust.

Vedāntasūtra of Bādarāyaṇa, with Śaṅkara's commentary. Bombay: Nirnaya Sagara, 1934.

Villiputtūrār pāratam. 1971. Edited, with commentary, by Vai. Mu. Kopālakiruṣṇamācāriyar. Madras: Vai. Mu. Kopālakiruṣṇamācāriyar Kampĕði.

Viṣṇu-māyā-nāṭakamu of Cintalapūḍi Yĕllanāryuḍu. Pithapuram: Śrī Vidvajjanamanorañjini Press, 1937.

Other Sources

Arnold, Peter (ed.). 1985. *The Book of Games*. New York: Exeter Books.

Bateson, Gregory. 1972. "A Theory of Play and Fantasy." In *Steps to an Ecology of Mind*. New York: Ballantine, 177–93.

Bateson, Gregory. 1980. *Mind and Nature: A Necessary Unity*. New York: Bantam.

Beck, Brenda E. F. 1969. "Colour and Heat in South Indian Ritual." *Man* 4:553–72.

Beck, Brenda E. F. 1982. *The Three Twins: The Telling of a South Indian Folk Epic*. Bloomington: Indiana University Press.

Beck, Brenda E. F. 1993. *Elder Brothers Story. Aṇṇaṉmār katai*. Madras: Institute of Asian Studies.

Becker. A. L. 1989. "Aridharma: Framing an Old Javanese Tale." In A. L. Becker (ed.), *Writing on the Tongue*. Ann Arbor: University of Michigan Press, 281–320.

Berkson, Carmel (with Wendy Doniger O'Flaherty and George Michell). 1983. *Elephanta, the Cave of Shiva*. Princeton: Princeton University Press.

Biardeau, Madeleine. 1971–72. "Brahmanes et potiers." *Annuaire de l'école pratique des hautes études* 79:31–55.

Black, Max. 1962. *Models and Metaphors: Studies in Language and Philosophy*. Ithaca, N.Y.: Cornell University Press.

Bloomfield, Maurice. 1897; reprinted, 1964. *Hymns of the Atharva-Veda*. Sacred Books of the East 42. Delhi: Motilal Banarsidass.

Bohm, David. 1981. *Wholeness and the Implicate Order*. London: Routledge and Kegan Paul.

Borges, Jorge Luis. 1970. *Labyrinths*. London: Penguin Books.

Brown, W. Norman. 1972. "The Indian Games of Pachisi, Chaupar, and Chausar." In Rosane Rocher (ed.), *India and Indology*. Delhi: Motilal Banarsidass, 297–302.

Buckley, A. D. 1983. "Playful Rebellion: Social Control and the Framing of Experience in an Ulster Community." *Man* (n.s.) 18:383–95.

Burrow, T. 1980. "Sanskrit MĀ—'To Make, Produce, Create.'" *Bulletin of the School of Oriental and African Studies* 43:311–28.

Cardona, George. 1991. "A Path Still Taken: Some Early Indian Arguments Concerning Time." *Journal of the American Oriental Society* 111:445–64.

Claus, Peter J. 1986. "Playing *Cenne*: The Meanings of a Folk Game." In S. H. Blackburn and A. K. Ramanujan (eds.), *Another Harmony: New Essays on the Folklore of India*. Berkeley: University of California Press, 265–93.

Colie, Rosalie L. 1966. *Paradoxia Epidemica: The Renaissance Tradition of Paradox*. Princeton: Princeton University Press.

Collins, Charles Dillard. 1988. *The Iconography and Ritual of Śiva at Elephanta.* Albany: State University of New York Press.

Concise English Dictionary. 1982. Ware, Hartfordshire: Omega Books.

Crooke, William. 1894. *The Popular Religion and Folklore of Northern India*. Allahabad: Government Press.

Courtright, Paul B. 1985. *Gaṇeśa, Lord of Obstacles, Lord of Beginnings.* New York: Oxford University Press.

Daniels, Valentine. 1984. *Fluid Signs: Being a Person the Tamil Way*. Berkeley: University of California Press.

Das, Veena. 1985. "Paradigms of Body Symbolism: An Analysis of Selected Themes in Hindu Culture." In R. Burghart and A. Cantlie (eds.), *Indian Religion.* London: Centre of South Asian Studies, School of Oriental and African Studies, 180–207.

de Vreese, K. 1948. "The Game of Dice in Ancient India." In *Orientalia Neerlandica*. Leiden: The Netherlands Oriental Society, 349–62.

Deleuze, Gilles and Felix Guattari. 1994. *What Is Philosophy*? London: Verso.

Deshpande, Madhav. 1992. *The Meaning of Nouns: Semantic Theory in Classical and Medieval India.* Nāmārtha-nirṇaya *of Kaundabhaṭṭa*. Studies of Classical India 13. Dordrecht: Kluwer Academic Publishers.

Dessigane, R., Pattabiramin, P. Z., and Filliozat, J. 1960. *La legende des jeux de Çiva à Madurai.* Pondichéry: Institut Français d'Indologie.

Detienne, M., and Vernant, J-P. 1978. *Cunning Intelligence in Greek Culture and Society*. Hassocks, Sussex: Harvester Press.

Dimock, Edward C. 1976. "Religious Biography in India: The Nectar of the Acts of Caitanya." In F. E. Reynolds and D. Kapps (eds.), *The Biographical Process: Studies in the History and Psychology of Religion*. The Hague: Mouton, 109–117.

Dimock, Edward C. 1989. "Līlā." *History of Religions* 29: 159–73.

Donaldson, Thomas E. 1987. *Hindu Temple Art of Orissa*. Leiden: E. J. Brill.

Doniger, Wendy. 1993. "The Scrapbook of Undeserved Salvation: The *Kedāra*

Khaṇḍa of the *Skanda Purāṇa*." In Wendy Doniger (ed.), *Purāṇa Perennis: Reciprocity and Transformation in Hindu and Jaina Texts*. Albany: State University of New York Press, 59–81.

Doniger, Wendy. In press. *The Bed Trick: An Encyclopedia of Sexual Masquerades*.

Doniger, Wendy. See O'Flaherty, Wendy Doniger.

Dorai Rangaswamy, M. A. 1958. *The Religion and Philosophy of Tēvāram*. Madras: University of Madras.

Dumont, Louis. 1970. *Homo Hierarchicus*. London: Paladin.

Egnor, Margaret Trawick. 1978. "The Sacred Spell and Other Conceptions of Life in Tamil Culture." Ph.D. dissertation, Department of Anthropology, University of Chicago.

Eliade, Mircea. 1964. *Shamanism: Archaic Techniques of Ecstacy*. New York: Pantheon.

Falk, Harry. 1986. *Bruderschaft und Würfelspiel: Untersuchungen zur Entwicklungsgeschichte des Vedischen Opfers*. Freiburg: Hedwig Falk.

Fink, Eugen. 1968. "The Oasis of Happiness: Toward an Ontology of Play." *Yale French Studies* 41:19–30.

Flueckiger, Joyce Burkhalter. 1987. "Brave Daughters, Bound Kings: A Tradition of Disguise and Reversal in Central India." Paper read at the annual meeting of the Association of Asian Studies, Boston.

Flueckiger, Joyce Burkhalter. 1996. *Gender and Genre in the Folklore of Middle India*. Ithaca, N.Y.: Cornell University Press.

Gadamer, H.J. 1988. *Truth and Method*. New York: Crossroad Press.

Geertz, Clifford. 1973. *The Interpretation of Cultures*. New York: Basic Books.

Gleick, James. 1987. *Chaos: The Making of a New Science*. London: Cardinal Books.

Goffman, Erving. 1974. *Frame Analysis*. New York: Harper and Row.

Gopinatha Rao, T. A. 1914–1916. *Elements of Hindu Iconography*. Madras: Law Printing House.

Grierson, George A. 1904. "Guessing the Number of Vibhītaka Seeds." *Journal of the Royal Asiatic Society*, 355–57.

Grössing, Gerhard. 1993. "Atomism at the End of the Twentieth Century." *Diogenes* 163:71–88.

Hacking, Ian. 1975. *The Emergence of Probability*. Cambridge: Cambridge University Press.

Handelman, Don. 1981. The Ritual-Clown: Attributes and Affinities." *Anthropos* 76: 321–70.

Handelman, Don. 1987. "Myths of Murugan: Asymmetry and Hierarchy in a South Indian Puranic Cosmology." *History of Religions* 27:133–70.

Handelman, Don. 1990. *Models and Mirrors: Towards an Anthropology of Public Events*. Cambridge: Cambridge University Press.

Handelman, Don. 1991. "Symbolic Types, the Body, and Circus." *Semiotica* 85:205–25.

Handelman, Don. 1995. "The Guises of the Goddess and the Transformation of the Male: Gangamma's Visit to Tirupati and the Continuum of Gender." In D. Shulman (ed.), *Syllables of Sky: Studies in South Indian Civilization in Honor of Velcheru Narayana Rao*. Delhi: Oxford University Press, 281–335.

Hawley, J. S. 1981. *At Play with Krishna: Pilgrimage Dramas from Brindavan*. Princeton: Princeton University Press.

Hayles, N. Katherine. 1991. *Chaos Bound: Orderly Disorder in Contemporary Literature and Science*. Ithaca, N.Y.: Cornell University Press.

Heesterman, Jan. 1957. *The Ancient Indian Royal Consecration: The Rājasūya Described According to the Yajus Texts and Annotated*. 'S-Gravenhage, The Netherlands: Mouton.

Heesterman, Jan. 1993. *The Broken World of Sacrifice: An Essay in Ancient Indian Ritual*. Chicago: University of Chicago Press.

Hein, N. 1987. "Līlā." In *Encyclopedia of Religion,* Mircea Eliade (Gen. Ed.). New York: Macmillan, 8:550–54.

Hiltebeitel, Alf. 1976. *The Ritual of Battle*. Ithaca, N.Y.: Cornell University Press.

Hiltebeitel, Alf. 1987. "Gambling." In *Encyclopedia of Religion*, Mircea Eliade (Gen. Ed.). New York: Macmillan, 5: 468–74.

Hiltebeitel, Alf. 1995. "Dying before the Mahābhārata War: Body-Building for Aravāð." *Journal of Asian Studies* 54:447–73.

Hofstadter, Douglas R. 1980. *Gödel, Escher, Bach: An Eternal Golden Braid*. New York: Vintage.

Holy, L., and Stuchlik, M. (eds.). 1981. *The Structure of Folk Models*. New York: Academic Press.

Hughes, P., and Brecht, G. 1984. *Vicious Circles and Infinity: An Anthology of Paradoxes*. Harmondsworth, Eng.: Penguin.

Huizinga, J. 1970. *Homo Ludens: A Study of the Play Element in Culture*. London: Paladin.

Ions, Veronica. 1970. *Myths and Legends of India*. London: Hamlyn.

Kaelber, Walter O. 1989. *Tapta-Mārga: Asceticism and Initiation in Vedic India*. Albany: State University of New York Press.

Kapferer, Bruce. 1983. *A Celebration of Demons: Exorcism and the Aesthetics of Healing in Sri Lanka*. Bloomington: Indiana University Press.

Kapferer, Bruce. 1988a. *Legends of People, Myths of State: Violence, Intolerance, and Political Culture in Sri Lanka and Australia*. Washington, D.C.: Smithsonian Institution Press.

Kapferer, Bruce. 1988b. "The Cosmology of Gambling." Unpublished manuscript.

Keepin, William. 1994. "David Bohm: A Life of Dialogue between Science and Spirit." *Neotic Sciences Review* Spring:10–16.

Keith, A. B. 1908. "The Game of Dice." *Journal of the Royal Asiatic Society*, 824–28.

Kellert, Stephen H. 1993. *In the Wake of Chaos: Unpredictable Order in Dynamical Systems*. Chicago: University of Chicago Press.

Kent, Jody. See Tatz, Mark.

Kinsley, David R. 1975. *The Sword and the Flute: Kālī and Kṛṣṇa, Dark Visions of the Terrible and the Sublime in Hindu Mythology*. Berkeley: University of California Press.

Knipe, David. 1975. *In the Image of Fire: Vedic Experiences of Heat*. Delhi: Motilal Banarsidass.

Kosko, Bart. 1994. *Fuzzy Thinking*. London: Flamingo.

Kramrisch, Stella. 1981a. *The Presence of Śiva*. Princeton: Princeton University Press.

Kramrisch, Stella. 1981b. *Manifestations of Śiva*. Philadelphia: Philadelphia Museum of Art.

Krishna Sastri, H. 1974. *South-Indian Images of Gods and Goddesses*. Delhi: Bharatiya Publishing House.

Krishnamurti, J., and David Bohm. 1981. *Truth and Actuality*. London: Victor Gollancz.

Kulke, Hermann. 1970. *Cidambaramāhātmya*. Wiesbaden: Otto Harrassowitz.

Langer, Susanne K. 1953. *Feeling and Form*. London: Routledge and Kegan Paul.

Lannoy, Richard. 1971. *The Speaking Tree: A Study of Indian Culture and Society*. London: Oxford University Press.

Lincoln, Bruce. 1986. *Myth, Cosmos, and Society: Indo-European Themes of Creation and Destruction*. Cambridge: Harvard University Press.

Lüders, Heinrich. 1907. "Das Würfelspiel im alten Indien." *Abhandlungen der Königliche Gesellschaft der Wissenschaftlichen zu Göttingen*, Phil.-Hist. Kl., N.F. IX, 2:3–74.

Mahalingam, T. V. 1972. *Mackenzie Manuscripts*. Vol. 1. *Tamil and Malayalam*. Madras: University of Madras.

Malamoud, Charles. 1989. *Cuire le monde. Rite et pensée dans l'Inde ancienne*. Paris: Editions La Decouverte.

Marriott, McKim. 1989. "Constructing an Indian Ethnosociology," *Contributions to Indian Sociology* (n.s.) 23:1–39.

Masthanaiah, B. 1978. *The Temples of Mukhalingam*. New Delhi: Cosmo Publications.

Miller, Jeanine. 1985. *The Vision of Cosmic Order in the Vedas*. London: Routledge and Kegan Paul.

Muniswamy Chetty, P. M. [n.d.] *Tirumala-Tirupathi. Sri Venkatesvara's Story and Mahatmyam.* Tirupati: Chukkala Singaiah Chetty.

Narayana Rao, Velcheru; Shulman, David; and Subrahmanyam, Sanjay. 1992. *Symbols of Substance: Court and State in Nāyaka Period Tamil Nadu.* Delhi: Oxford University Press.

Narayana Rao, Velcheru. 1996. "Telugu Riddles and Enigmas." In Galit Hasan-Rokem and David Shulman (eds.), *Untying the Knot: On Riddles and Other Enigmatic Modes.* New York: Oxford University Press, 191–207.

Norbeck, Edward. 1971. "Man at Play." *Play, A Natural History Magazine Supplement* December: 48–53.

O'Flaherty, Wendy Doniger. 1971. "The Submarine Mare in the Mythology of Śiva." *Journal of the Royal Asiatic Society*:9–27.

O'Flaherty, Wendy Doniger. 1973. *Asceticism and Eroticism in the Mythology of Śiva.* London: Oxford University Press.

O'Flaherty, Wendy Doniger. 1975. *Hindu Myths.* Harmondsworth, Eng.: Penguin.

O'Flaherty, Wendy Doniger. 1980. *Women, Androgynes, and Other Mythical Beasts.* Chicago: University of Chicago Press.

O'Flaherty, Wendy Doniger. 1984. *Dreams, Illusions, and Other Realities.* Chicago: University of Chicago Press.

Östor, Akos. 1980. *The Play of the Gods: Locality, Ideology, Structure, and Time in the Festivals of a Bengali Town.* Chicago: University of Chicago Press.

Panduranga Bhatta, C. 1985. *Dice-Play in Sanskrit Literature.* New Delhi: Amarprakashan.

Parry, Jonathan. 1985. "The Aghori Ascetics of Benares." In R. Burghart and A. Cantlie (eds.), *Indian Religion.* London: Centre of South Asian Studies, School of Oriental and African Studies, 51–78.

Patkar, M. M. 1963. "The Role of Gambling in Ancient Indian Society and Some Sanskrit Words Pertaining to the Game." *Vishveshvaranand Indological Journal* 1:141–53.

Pribram, Karl. 1977. *Languages of the Brain.* Monterey, Calif.: Wadsworth Publishing.

Putnam, S. (ed. and trans.). 1955. *The Portable Rabelais.* New York: Viking.

Ramanujan, A. K. 1973. *Speaking of Śiva.* Harmondsworth, Eng.: Penguin Books.

Ramanujan, A. K. *A Flowering Tree,* in press.

Rinehart, Luke. 1972. *The Dice Man.* London: Panther.

Rocher, Ludo. 1986. *The Purāṇas.* (*A History of Indian Literature* II.3). Wiesbaden: Otto Harrassowitz.

Roghair, Gene H. 1982. *The Epic of Palnāḍu: A Study and Translation of Palnāṭi Vīrula Katha.* Oxford: Clarendon Press.

Ryle, Gilbert. 1975. *The Concept of Mind* (13th ed.). London: Hutchinson.

Satya Vrat Shastri. 1992. "The Kumārasambhava—Its Genuine Portion." *Journal of Oriental Research Madras* 56:303–05.

Schechner, Richard. 1988. "Playing." *Play and Culture* 1:3–19.

Shee, Monika. 1980. Tapas *und* Tapasvin *in den erzählenden Partien des Mahābhārata*. Reinbek: Verlag für Orientalistische Fachpublikationen.

Shimkhada, Deepak. 1983. "A Preliminary Study of the Game of Karma in India, Nepal, and Tibet." *Artibus Asiae* 44:308–22.

Shulman, David. 1980. *Tamil Temple Myths*. Princeton: Princeton University Press.

Shulman, David. 1985. *The King and the Clown in South Indian Myth and Poetry*. Princeton: Princeton University Press.

Shulman, David. 1986. " Terror of Symbols and Symbols of Terror: Some Notes on the Myth of Śiva as Sthāṇu." *History of Religions* 26:101–24.

Shulman, David. 1989. "Outcaste, Guardian, and Trickster: Notes on the Myth of Kāttavarāyað." In Alf Hiltebeitel (ed.), *Criminal Gods and Demon Devotees*. Albany: State University of New York Press, 35–67.

Shulman, David. 1990. *Songs of the Harsh Devotee: The Tevāram of Cuntaramūrttināyaṉār*. Philadelphia: Department of South Asian Regional Studies, University of Pennsylvania.

Shulman, David. 1992. "Devana and Daiva." In A. W. Van den Hoek, D. H. A. Kolff, and M. S. Oort (eds.), *Ritual, State, and History in South Asia: Essays in Honour of J. C. Heesterman*. Leiden: E. J. Brill, 350–65.

Shulman, David. 1993. *The Hungry God: Hindu Tales of Filicide and Devotion*. Chicago: University of Chicago Press.

Shulman, David. 1994. "On Being Human in the Sanskrit Epic: The Riddle of Nala." *Journal of Indian Philosophy* 22:1–29.

Shulman, David. 1995. "First Man, Forest Mother: Telugu Humanism in the Age of Kṛṣṇadevarāya." In D. Shulman (ed.), *Syllables of Sky: Studies in South Indian Civilization in Honor of Velcheru Narayana Rao*. Delhi: Oxford University Press, 133–61.

Shulman, David. "The Prospects of Memory," in press.

Sivaramamurti, C. 1974. *Nataraja in Art, Thought and Literature*. New Delhi.

Slaate, H.A. 1968. *The Pertinence of Paradox*. New York.

Smith, Brian K. 1989. *Reflections on Resemblance, Ritual, and Religion*. New York: Oxford University Press.

Smith, David. 1985. *Ratnākara's* Haravijaya*: An Introduction to the Sanskrit Court Epic*. Delhi: Oxford University Press.

Soar, Michaela. 1988. "The Tirtha at Ellora." In Ratan Parimoo, Deepak Kannal, and Shivaji Panikkar (eds.), *Ellora Caves: Sculpture and Architecture*. New Delhi: Book and Books, 80–103.

Straus, Erwin W. 1966. *Phenomenological Psychology*. London: Tavistock.

Syrkin, A. 1965. "Chornoye solntze." *Kratkiye soobshcheniya instituta narodov azii* 80:20–32.

Talbot, Michael. 1992. *The Holographic Universe*. New York: Harper Collins.

Tandori, Dezso. 1983. *Birds and Other Relations*. Translated by Bruce Berlind. Princeton: Princeton University Press.

Tatz, Mark, and Jody Kent. 1977. *Rebirth: The Tibetan Game of Karma*. New York: Anchor Books.

Temple, Richard Carnac. 1883. *The Legends of the Panjab*. Bombay: Education Society's Press.

Thibaut, G. (trans.). 1962. *The Vedânta Sūtras of Bādarāyaṇa, with the Commentary by Śaṅkara*. New York: Dover.

Thieme, Paul. 1962. "Chess and Backgammon (Tric-Trac) in Sanskrit Literature." In E. Bender (ed.), *Indological Studies in Honor of W. Norman Brown*. New Haven, Conn.: American Oriental Society, 204–16.

Trawick, Margaret. 1990. *Notes on Love in a Tamil Family*. Berkeley: University of California Press.

Trawick, Margaret. See Egnor, Margaret Trawick.

Tubb, Gary. 1984. "Heroine as Hero: Pārvatī in the *Kumārasambhava* and the *Pārvatīpariṇaya*." *Journal of the American Oriental Society* 104:219–36.

Turner, Victor. 1974. "Liminal to Liminoid in Play, Flow, and Ritual: An Essay in Comparative Symbology." *Rice University Studies* 60 (3):53–92.

van Buitenen, J. A. B. 1972. "On the Structure of the Sabhāparvan of the Mahābhārata." In J. Ensink and P. Gaeffke (eds.), *India Maior: Congratulatory Volume Presented to J. Gonda*. Leiden: Brill, 68–84.

van Buitenen, J. A. B. (trans.). 1973. *The Mahābhārata: The Book of the Beginning*. Chicago and London: University of Chicago Press.

Vasumati, E. [n.d.] *Telugu Literature in the Qutub Shahi Period*. Hyderabad: Abul Kalam Azad Oriental Research Institute.

von Wright, Georg Henrik. 1971. *Explanation and Understanding*. London: Routledge and Kegan Paul.

White, David G. 1989. "Dogs Die." *History of Religions* 28:283–303.

Whitehead, A. N., and B. Russell. 1927. *Principia Mathematica*. Cambridge, Eng.: Cambridge University Press.

Winnicott, D.W. 1971. *Playing and Reality*. London: Tavistock.

Yusa, M. 1987. "Paradox and Riddles." In *Encyclopedia of Religion*, Mircea Eliade (Gen. Ed.). New York: Macmillan. 11:189–95.

Zerubavel, Eviatar. 1991. *The Fine Line: Making Distinctions in Everyday Life*. Chicago: University of Chicago Press.

Zimmer, H. 1984. *Artistic Form and Yoga in the Sacred Images of India*. Princeton: Princeton University Press.

Index